世遗之城：泉州

QUANZHOU: A WORLD HERITAGE CITY

丝路扬帆——宋元泉州的商品制造

Sailing on the Maritime Silk Road: Commodity Production in Song-Yuan Quanzhou

中共泉州市委宣传部　编

海峡出版发行集团 | 福建人民出版社
THE STRAITS PUBLISHING & DISTRIBUTING GROUP | FUJIAN PEOPLE'S PUBLISHING HOUSE

目 录

Contents

引　言

泉州海外贸易始于南朝，隋唐五代得到发展，兴盛于宋元，衰落于元末明初。唐代时，已出现“市井十洲人”和“船到城添外国人”的繁荣景象；五代时，泉州社会经济发展，海外贸易繁荣，“海上泉州时代”开启。唐末五代时，中国历史上出现中原人口第二次南迁的高潮，泉州历经唐、五代海外贸易的发展，其特殊经济地位引起人口聚迁。泉州“八山一水一分田”，地少人多的矛盾已经出现，以农业为主的经济发展模式受到“泉地斥卤”和“桑蚕不登于筐茧，田亩不足于耕耘”的阻碍。

Introduction

Overseas trade in Quanzhou began in the Southern Dynasties (420—589) and developed during the Sui, Tang, and Five Dynasties (581—960), reaching its peak during the Song and Yuan dynasties (960—1368) before declining in the late Yuan and early Ming dynasties. During the Tang Dynasty (618—907), a prosperous scene of "ten regions of people in the market" and "foreigners thronging into the city when the ships arrive" had already emerged. During the Five Dynasties (907—960), the society and economy of Quanzhou developed rapidly, and overseas trade became prosperous, marking the beginning of the "Maritime Quanzhou Era." At the end of the Tang Dynasty and during Five Dynasties, China experienced the second wave of migration. Many people from the Central Plains moved to the south. And Quanzhou, having undergone the development of overseas trade during the Tang and Five Dynasties, attracted a large population with its special economic status. The contradiction between the scarcity of land and high population density in Quanzhou, with 80 percent of its area covered by mountains, 10 percent by water, and 10 percent by farmland, had already emerged. The traditional development model which relied heavily on agriculture but was hindered by saline soil, silkworm baskets never being full and farmland being insufficient for plowing and harrowing, had already faced challenges.

泉州沿海漫长曲折的海岸线。（陈英杰 摄）
The long and winding coastline of Quanzhou. (Photo by Chen Yingjie)

北宋谢履《泉南歌》写道："泉州人稠山谷瘠，虽欲就耕无处辟。"北宋时，泉州人多地少的矛盾依旧突出，占城稻首先在泉州地区引种并广泛推广，虽然缓解了粮食紧缺的问题，但传统农业并不能保障基本生活。泉州人面临着在经济上进行重新选择的机遇和压力。

泉州处于东南沿海的边陲，沿着漫长的海岸线分布着"三湾十二港"的天然港口群。在唐五代海外贸易传统优势的基础上，利用好这一地理条件，有利于进一步发展海外贸易，以缓解人口压力并促进经济繁荣，因此，调整产业结构和经济发展模式成为官方和民间的共识。

During the Northern Song Dynasty (960—1127), Xie Lyu wrote *Quannan Song*, in which he stated that "Quanzhou is densely populated, and the mountains and valleys are barren. Even if people want to farm, they have no land to cultivate." The contradiction between Quanzhou's large population and limited land resources continued to be prominent during the Northern Song Dynasty. Champa (in present-day Vietnam) Rice was introduced to Quanzhou, and then widely promoted, which alleviated the problem of food scarcity. However, it's hard for people in Quanzhou to depend on traditional agriculture for their livelihood. They were faced with pressure, also regarded as an opportunity, to reform the economy.

Quanzhou is located on the southeastern coastal border. The natural harbor group of "Three Bays and Twelve Harbors" shapes a long coastline. Based on its traditional advantage in terms of foreign trade during the Tang Dynasty and Five Dynasties, the benefits of the geographical conditions were utilized to further develop foreign trade. This not only helped to alleviate population pressure but also promoted economic development in Quanzhou. Hence adjusting its industrial structure and economic development model became a consensus between the government and people.

以传统农业为主的经济发展模式逐渐转型为以农业为辅助，手工业、商业为主体，外贸为核心的港口经济结构，手工业蓬勃发展，官营手工业作坊和私营手工业作坊并存，产品甚饶足并过洋，海外贸易规模不断扩大。泉州人走向海洋，问生涯于波涛万顷之中，由此拉开了泉州作为海上丝绸之路重要港城的命运大幕。

在经济重心南移和北人南迁的大背景下，北宋时于泉州设市舶司，南宋初年南外宗正司迁入泉州。税收优惠和招商补官等政策精准扶持，港口、航标、桥梁、道路等水陆交通设施不断完善，再加上皇族、地方官员、本地商人以及外来番商等多元社群不断推动，异军突起的泉州，成为宋元中国的世界海洋商贸中心。

The economic development model, which relied mainly on traditional agriculture, was gradually transformed into a port economic structure that featured handcraft industry and commerce as the main body, supplemented by agriculture, and centered on foreign trade. The handcraft industry flourished. Official workshops and private workshops coexisted. Their products were so abundant that many of them were shipped overseas, which increased the scale of overseas trade. Quanzhou people turned to the sea, earning their livelihood among the waves, thus ushering Quanzhou onto the journey of growing into an important port city on the Maritime Silk Road.

Against the backdrop of the economic center moving south and the migration of people from the north to the south, Shi Bo Si (Maritime Trade Office) was established during the Northern Song Dynasty, and the Southern Clan Office moved to Quanzhou during the early Southern Song Dynasty. Targeted policies such as tax incentives, official post designation according to one's contribution to overseas trade, as well as the continuous improvement of river, sea and land transport facilities, including ports, navigation marks, bridges, and roads, were implemented. In addition, its multi-cultural communities, including the royal family, local officials, local merchants, as well as foreign merchants, continued to push for progress. The rising Quanzhou became Emporium of the World in Song-Yuan China.

谢履在《泉南歌》中写道：“州南有海浩无穷，每岁造舟通异域”，南宋吴自牧也有《梦粱录》“若欲船泛外国买卖，则是泉州便可出洋”之言。泉州依托发达的造船技术，主动走出去发展海外贸易，把泉州乃至周边州府的地域特产和传统手工业作坊产品作为贸易品“梯行万国”运往海外销售，把商品卖给世界；返航时沿途采购一些国家和地区的物产，诸如珠宝、香料等，运回泉州并在国内销售。南宋李邴《咏宋代泉州海外交通贸易》中“苍官影里三州路，涨海声中万国商”（见宋本《方舆胜览》）是宋代泉州海外交通贸易盛况的生动写照；元末高僧宗泐的“缠头赤脚半蕃商，大舶高樯多海宝”反映元代时来泉的番商、番货越来越多，泉州吸引了世界各国番商运来各自国家的特产到泉州销售。这便是宋元泉州海外贸易“走出去”和“引进来”的繁荣盛况。

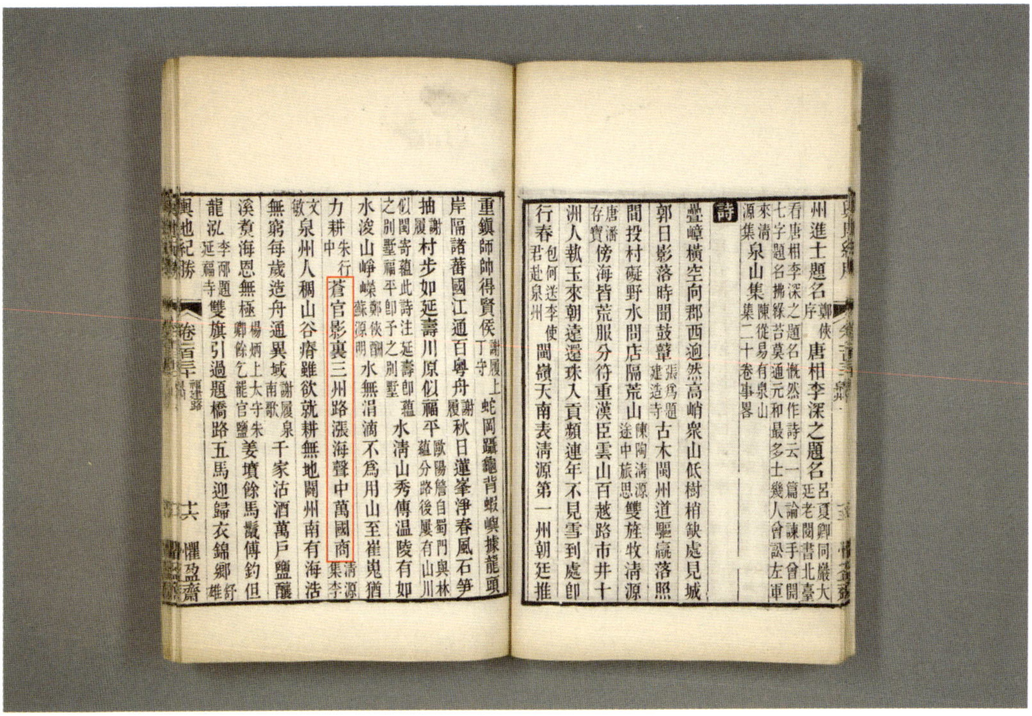

《舆地纪胜》中关于宋代泉州海外交通贸易盛况的记载 。（林瀚 供图）
A record of the prosperous scene of overseas communications and trade in Quanzhou during the Song Dynasty in *The National Gazetteer of Sights*. (Courtesy of Lin Han)

Xie Lyu wrote in his *Quannan Song* that the south coast of the city met endless sea, and that every year people built ships to trade with foreign countries. Wu Zimu of the Southern Song Dynasty (1127—1279) also mentioned in his *Record of a Dream of Sorghum* that if one wanted to engage in foreign trade by ship, then Quanzhou would be a convenient port for setting sail. Quanzhou relied on its advanced shipbuilding technology to actively develop overseas trade. People transported local specialties and traditional handcrafts from Quanzhou and surrounding prefectural cities as trade goods overseas and sold them to the rest of the world. When returning, they would purchase products from other countries or regions, like jewelry, spices and other items, brought them back to Quanzhou and sold them at home. In Li Bing's poem, *Quanzhou Overseas Communications and Trade During the Song Dynasty*, the stanza "In the shade of pines and cypresses is the road of Quanzhou to Fuzhou and Zhangzhou; / Amidst the sound of rising tides, merchants from all nations thronged to Quanzhou" (in *The National Gazetteer of Southern Song Dynasty*) vividly depicts the prosperous scene of overseas communications and trade in Quanzhou during the Song Dynasty (960—1279). Zongle, an eminent monk in the late Yuan Dynasty, wrote, "Half of the foreign merchants who came here were barefoot and turbaned. The large ships had tall masts and carried many sea treasures." This reflects the vast increase of foreign merchants and goods in Quanzhou during the Yuan Dynasty (1271—1368). Quanzhou attracted foreign merchants from all over the world to sell their specialties. The above-mentioned scenes show how prosperous Quanzhou's overseas trade was during the Song and Yuan dynasties, where goods were both exported and imported.

宋元泉州以“刺桐港”之名驰誉世界，东面通高丽、日本，南面通东南亚、南亚诸国，西面通西亚的波斯、阿拉伯诸国，甚至到达地中海沿岸国家，或南下非洲东岸诸国。人们把这些海上贸易往来的各条航线通称为海上丝绸之路。由于陶瓷也经由这条海上交通路线销往各国，西方的香料通过这条路线输入中国，一些学者也称这条海上交通路线为“陶瓷之路”或“香瓷之路”。宋元泉州既“卖世界”也“买世界”，对外通商的国家和地区从南宋时的58个增至元代时的99个。这近百个国家和地区分布在阿拉伯半岛、印度半岛、马来群岛、中南半岛和东亚地区，甚至远及非洲东北沿岸。参与贸易活动的有泉州商人、外地商人和外国番商，外国番商包括阿拉伯商人、波斯商人和印度商人等。泉州销往世界的商品有瓷器、纺织品、铜铁制品、茶、盐、酒、糖等，以瓷器、丝绸、铜铁制品为大宗。泉州“买世界”的商品主要有来自大食、渤泥、三佛齐、阇婆、真腊、占城等地的香料，和来自锡兰、三佛齐、南毗、麻逸、苏禄等地的珠宝。

During the Song and Yuan dynasties, Quanzhou was renowned worldwide for its Zayton Port ("Zayton" is another name for ancient Quanzhou). In the eastward direction, it connected with Goryeo and Japan; in the southward direction, it built links with various countries in the Southeast Asia and South Asia; the ships sailed further west to Persia and Arab countries in West Asia, and even to the countries along the Mediterranean coast, or southward to the countries along the east coast of Africa. Those sea trade routes were commonly referred to as the Maritime Silk Road. Due to the fact that ceramics were transported through this sea trade route to various countries, and spices from western countries were imported to China through this route, some scholars have also referred to this maritime trade route as the "Porcelain Road" or the "Spices and Porcelain Road." Quanzhou not only sold its products to the rest of the world, but also bought products from the rest of the world. The number of countries and regions with which Quanzhou established trade links increased from 58 during the Southern Song Dynasty to 99 during the Yuan Dynasty. These countries and regions were distributed in the Arabian Peninsula, the Indian Peninsula, the Malay Archipelago, the Indochina Peninsula, and East Asia, and even as far as the northeast coast of Africa. Those who engaged in trade were Quanzhou merchants, out-of-towners, and foreign traders. Among foreign traders, Arab merchants, Persian merchants, and Indian merchants actively involved themselves. Goods sold by Quanzhou to the rest of the world included porcelain, textiles, copper and iron products, tea, salt, liquor, sugar and so on, among which porcelain, silk, and copper and iron products were the most commonly traded. Quanzhou's imports mostly included spices from places such as Dayi (the country of the Arabs), Borneo (on Kalimantan Island), Srivijaya (an ancient country on Sunda Islands), Java, Chenla (in present-day Cambodia), and Champa, as well as jewelry from places such as Xilan (present-day Sri Lanka), Srivijaya, Namburi (in present-day Kozhikode in India), Mait (an ancient country in the Philippines), and Saltanah Sulu (an ancient country with Sulu Archipelago as its ruling center).

在 10—14 世纪长达 400 年的宋元泉州海外贸易中，进出口货物的数量无法统计，有多少远洋商船进出泉州港无法统计，在海上丝绸之路上有多少因风暴、触礁而沉没海底的商船也无法统计。宋代有 3 艘有代表性的泉州造水密隔舱福船满载陶瓷铜铁等外销商品驶离泉州，扬帆海外。它们分别是泉州湾宋代海船、“南海 I 号”沉船和“华光礁 I 号”沉船。“南海 I 号”沉船和“华光礁 I 号”沉船都曾是满载着包括泉州陶瓷在内的中国商品出洋去的，而泉州湾宋代海船是满载东南亚香料回航的，有来有往，构成了宋元泉州“买世界”和“卖世界”的缩影。宋元泉州制造在七八百年后的今天依然惊艳世界。

As for the 400-year overseas trade of Song and Yuan dynasties, the quantity of imported and exported goods cannot be accurately determined. The number of foreign merchant ships entering and leaving Quanzhou Port cannot be counted, and neither can the number of merchant ships sinking to the bottom of the sea due to storms or crashing into reefs along the Maritime Silk Road. In the Song Dynasty, three typical Quanzhou-made *Fu-Chuan* (literally meaning "Fortune Vessel") with watertight bulkheads, fully loaded with ceramics, copper and iron products, and other export goods, sailed from Quanzhou to foreign countries. They were Song Dynasty Oceangoing Ship in Quanzhou Bay, the "Nanhai No. 1" Shipwreck, and the "Huaguang Reef No. 1" Shipwreck. Both the "Nanhai No. 1" Shipwreck and the "Huaguang Reef No. 1" Shipwreck were loaded with Chinese goods, including Quanzhou ceramics. The ships sailed overseas. The Song Dynasty Oceangoing Ship in Quanzhou Bay undertook its return voyage, loaded with Southeast Asian spices. The scene of coming and going forms a microcosm of Quanzhou "buying products from the rest of the world" and "selling products to the rest of the world" during Song and Yuan dynasties. Today, Quanzhou's manufacturing prowess in Song-Yuan period continues to impress the world.

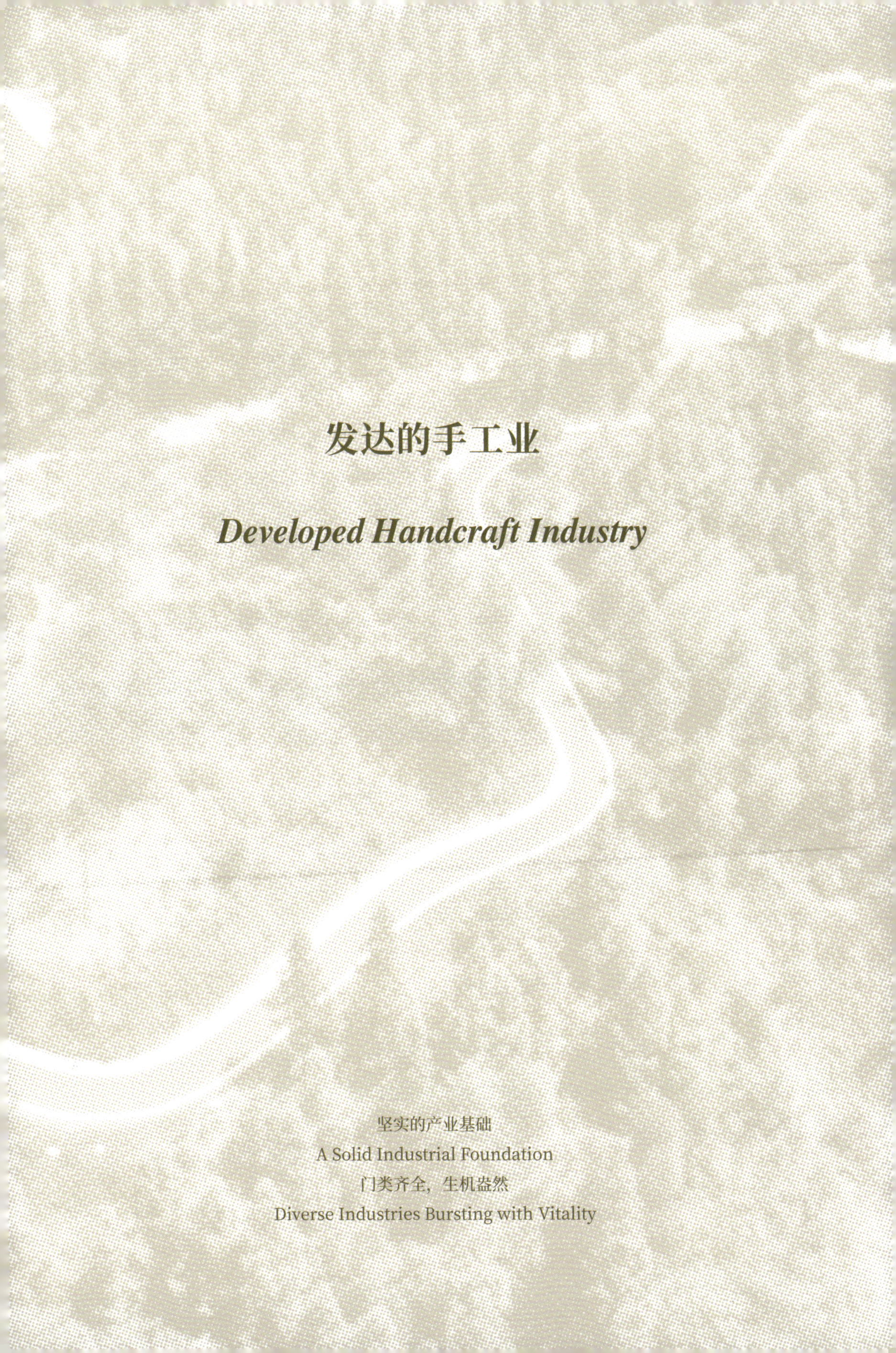

发达的手工业

Developed Handcraft Industry

坚实的产业基础

A Solid Industrial Foundation

门类齐全，生机盎然

Diverse Industries Bursting with Vitality

泉州湾宋代海船复原模型。（成冬冬 摄）
A model reconstructing the Song Dynasty Oceangoing Ship in Quanzhou Bay. (Photo by Cheng Dongdong)

《蓝蓝泉州湾》是泉州广为传唱的市歌，“蓝蓝泉州湾、青青戴云山，海上丝路从这里铺向世界……”开篇点明泉州背山面海的山海格局，一方水土养一方人，泉州成为闻名世界的古代海上丝绸之路的重要起点城市。古代泉州在宋元时期进入鼎盛发展阶段，不到 400 年便经历了四次飞跃：第一次在北宋中期，赶上并超过明州，仅次于广州；第二次在南宋初年，赶上广州，与广州并驾齐驱；第三次在南宋末年，超过广州，成为全国最大的贸易港；第四次在元初，成为东方第一大港。

泉州成为宋元中国的世界海洋商贸中心，不仅得益于泉州发达的海外交通，也得益于泉州发达的手工业。据记载，当时泉州的外销产品，有丝织品、瓷器、金银器皿、赤铜、铁鼎、铁针、漆器、胭脂、草席、凉伞等，其中以丝绸、瓷器、铜铁制品为大宗。

The Blue Quanzhou Bay is a popular theme song of Quanzhou. It begins with the lyrics "The blue Quanzhou Bay, the green Mount Daiyun, the Maritime Silk Road starts from here and extends to the world..." The opening line highlights the geographical features of Quanzhou: being backed by mountains and facing the sea. The unique features of a local environment always give special characteristics to its inhabitants. Quanzhou became an important starting point city of the ancient Maritime Silk Road which was renowned worldwide. During the Song and Yuan dynasties, ancient Quanzhou entered a period of rapid development, experiencing four leaps within less than 400 years. In the mid-Northern Song Dynasty, Quanzhou caught up with and surpassed Mingzhou (present-day Ningbo), ranking second only after Guangzhou. In the early Southern Song Dynasty, Quanzhou caught up with Guangzhou, and the two cities were evenly matched. In the late Southern Song Dynasty, Quanzhou surpassed Guangzhou, growing into the largest trading port in China. In the early Yuan Dynasty, Quanzhou became the largest port in the East.

Quanzhou became Emporium of the World in Song-Yuan China, thanks to both its developed overseas transportation and its thriving handcraft industry. It was recorded that Quanzhou's export products at that time included silk, porcelain, gold and silver utensils, red copper, iron cauldrons, iron needles, lacquerware, rouge, grass mats, parasols, and other items, among which silk, porcelain, and copper and iron products were the most popular.

坚实的产业基础

戴云山主峰位于泉州境内，山地外侧与河流两岸广泛分布着高低起伏的丘陵；而东部沿海地区地势较为平坦，河海交互沉积，在晋江下游形成了大小不一的冲积平原。由此形成泉州地区从戴云山脉，再到沿海丘陵、平原和海湾的倾斜状分布的地形。

晋江发源于戴云山脉，由东溪、西溪向东南汇流而成，支流密布，从山地丘陵地带流经平原，至东南海湾入海。山区至东部海滨地区河流航道发达，水路交通通畅便捷。产自河流中上游地区的瓷器、铜铁制品、茶叶、纺织品等手工业产品可顺流而下，到达泉州滨海港口；晋江和洛阳江入海口附近，由于长期河流冲刷、海水侵蚀，形成了曲折的海岸线，岛屿港湾众多，出现了“三湾十二港”的泉州港口群，从这些港口出发，循海路，北可达朝鲜半岛、日本等地，向南则可到东南亚各地，直至南亚、西亚、非洲等地。发达、便利的河流运输和海上交通，为宋元泉州产品的销售提供了可靠的交通运输保障，是泉州手工业发展的重要条件之一。

A Solid Industrial Foundation

The main peak of Daiyun mountain range is in Quanzhou. There are widely distributed undulating hills outside the mountainous areas and along both sides of the rivers. The eastern coastal area is relatively flat, with the deposition of river and marine sediments, forming alluvial plains in various sizes in the lower reaches of Jinjiang River. As a result, Quanzhou was shaped into a sloping area, stretching from the Daiyun mountain range to coastal hills, plains, and bays.

Originating from Daiyun mountain range, the Jinjiang River, formed by the convergence of Dongxi Stream and Xixi Stream, flows from the mountainous and hilly areas to the plains, meeting the sea at the southeast coast, with densely distributed tributaries. The waterway traffic from the mountains to the eastern coastal areas is well developed and convenient, allowing the handmade products such as porcelain, copper and iron products, tea, and textiles from the regions in upper and middle reaches of the river to be carried downstream to Quanzhou Port. Near the estuary of Jinjiang River and Luoyang River, river and seawater erosion over a long period of time created a winding coastline. There were numerous bays and islands around, forming the Quanzhou port group of "Three Bays and Twelve Harbors." Departing from these ports and traveling along the sea routes, one can reach the Korean Peninsula, Japan, and other places in the north, various destinations in Southeast Asia in the south, and as far as South Asia, West Asia, Africa, and other regions. The advanced and convenient river transportation and maritime traffic provided solid support for the sale of products made in Song-Yuan Quanzhou, which constituted one of the important conditions for the development of Quanzhou's handcraft industry.

云雾缭绕的戴云山，宛若仙境。（张九强 摄）
Daiyun mountain range shrouded in mist, resembling a fairyland. (Photo by Zhang Jiuqiang)

山区丘陵地带林木密集，为制瓷、冶铁、制盐等手工业发展提供了必需的燃料资源，也为造船业发展提供了优质木材。这些地区还蕴藏着极为丰富的矿产资源，如德化、永春、同安（时属泉州，今属厦门）、晋江、南安、惠安等地都有储量丰富的各种风化残余型高岭土矿藏，其他的陶瓷原料如长石、石英类原料等分布也很广且储量大，德化、永春、安溪的山区除了瓷土矿外，还有丰富的铁矿资源。泉州的这些矿产多分布于山岭、溪流之间，古代窑场、铁场环于其间，制瓷、冶铁原料一般是就近取用的，避免了长距离运输，相对方便，大大推动了宋元泉州制瓷、冶铁的发展和繁荣。

泉州东部沿海海岸线曲折，海域面积广阔，晋江、惠安、南安、同安四县临海，且地处台湾山脉雨影区内，年降水量较小，而日照时间长、夏季气温高，海水的盐浓度高。就气候、海水条件而言，十分有利于制盐业的发展。山海交融的复杂地势锁住了充沛的水汽，有利于茶树生长，孕育茶叶的一方沃土；湿热气候宜于麻、葛、蕉、纻等经济作物的生长。

泉州德化茂密的山林。（陈小阳 摄）
Dense mountains and forests in Dehua, Quanzhou. (Photo by Chen Xiaoyang)

The mountainous and hilly areas of Quanzhou are densely forested, providing essential fuel resources for the development of handcraft industries such as porcelain making, iron smelting, and salt making, as well as high-quality timber for shipbuilding. These areas are also extremely rich in mineral resources such as residual kaolin deposits in Dehua, Yongchun, Tong'an (then a part of Quanzhou, now a part of Xiamen), Jinjiang, Nan'an, Hui'an, etc. Other raw materials for porcelain making such as feldspar, quartz, etc. are also widely distributed, the reserves of which were large. In addition to kaolin deposits, the mountainous areas of Dehua, Yongchun, and Anxi also boast abundant iron ore. These minerals in Quanzhou are mostly found in mountains and streams. Ancient kilns and ironworks were built nearby, with easy access to raw materials for porcelain making and iron smelting. Long-distance transportation was avoided, which greatly facilitated the development of porcelain making and iron smelting in Song-Yuan Quanzhou.

Quanzhou boasts a winding coastline and faces wide sea. Jinjiang, Hui'an, Nan'an, and Tong'an are all located on the coast and within the rain shadow area of mountain ranges in Taiwan. They receive relatively less rainfall annually, with long sunshine hours and high temperatures in summer, resulting in high salinity of the seawater. The climate and seawater conditions were very conducive to the development of the salt industry. Mountainous areas, combined with long stretch of coast, help to retain abundant water vapor, which is conducive to the growth of tea trees, nurturing fertile soil for tea production. The humid and hot climate is also suitable for the growth of cash crops such as hemp, kudzu, abaca, and ramie.

唐五代以来，人口增长压力与泉州地区土地贫瘠现实状况的矛盾日益突出，不利于发展农业经济。泉州利用“州南有海浩无穷”的区位优势，通过“每岁造舟通异域”发展海外贸易，为发展地方经济谋求出路。宋代，泉州开始调整经济结构，形成以农业为辅助，手工业、商业为主体，外贸为核心的港口经济结构。多种经济作物大量种植，棉花、甘蔗、水果的产量大增，以此为原料的传统手工业如纺织业迅速发展，食品加工业如制糖业、果品蜜饯业、酿酒业应运而生，形成了新的手工业布局，扩大了经营范围与生产规模，这是宋元泉州手工业发展的一大特色。大量农业人口转移到手工业部门，既缓解了土地压力，又推动农渔工商各业趋于均衡发展。

Since the Tang Dynasty and Five Dynasties, the contradiction between population growth pressure and the reality of barren land in Quanzhou had become increasingly prominent, which was unfavorable for the development of agricultural economy. Quanzhou used its location advantage of "the south coast of the city meeting endless sea" and developed overseas trade through "building ships every year to reach foreign countries" to seek a way out for local economic development. During the Song Dynasty, Quanzhou began to adjust its economic structure, forming a port economy structure with handcraft industry and commerce as its main body, supplemented by agriculture, and foreign trade as its core. Various cash crops were planted on a large scale, and the output of cotton, sugarcane, and fruits increased significantly. Traditional handcraft industries such as textiles based on those raw materials developed rapidly, and food processing industries such as sugar manufacturing, fruit preserves making, and brewing also emerged, which had formed a new layout of handcraft industry and expanded the business scope and production scale, characteristic of the development of handcraft industry in Quanzhou during the Song and Yuan dynasties. A large agricultural population transferred to the handcraft sector, which not only eased the pressure on land but also promoted the balanced development of agriculture, fishery, industry, and commerce.

唐末和两宋之际，曾有两次北方人口大迁徙的高潮，大量黄河流域人民迁入江南各省，包括泉州在内的福建也吸收大量中原人口。人口南迁是宋代泉州人口骤增的主要原因之一。这些中原人中，不乏各类身怀绝技的工匠，他们带来了先进的生产技术和生产工具，应是促进宋元泉州手工业技术水平迅速提高的主要原因之一。

泉州地形复杂，山地丘陵绵延，生态环境多样，原料丰富，山溪河流密布，沿海港湾发达。这样的自然地理环境为制瓷、冶铁、制盐、造船等提供了丰富的原料和便利的交通运输，加上劳动力资源优势以及早期积累的成熟的传统工艺，促进了泉州手工业发展繁荣，源源不断地生产深受海上丝绸之路沿线国家和地区人民喜爱的“宋元泉州造”产品。

In the late Tang Dynasty and the years between the end of Northern Song Dynasty and the start of Southern Song Dynasty, there were two great waves of migration from northern China to southern China. A large number of people from the Yellow River Basin moved to provinces in the south. Fujian, including Quanzhou, also absorbed a large number of people from the Central Plains. The southward migration was one of the main reasons for the rapid increase in Quanzhou's population during the Song Dynasty. Among those people, there were many skilled artisans who brought advanced production techniques and tools, which should be one of the main reasons for the rapid improvement of the technical level of handcraft industry in Quanzhou during the Song and Yuan dynasties.

The complex terrain of the Quanzhou, with its rolling mountains and hills, ecological diversity, abundant raw materials, and numerous rivers and coastal ports, provided rich resources and convenient transportation for the development of various industries such as porcelain making, iron smelting, salt production, and shipbuilding. Coupled with the advantages of adequate labor resources and mature traditional craftsmanship accumulated in the early stages, Quanzhou's handcraft industry grew and flourished, continuously producing export products which were highly welcomed by people from countries and regions along the Maritime Silk Road, known as goods "made in Quanzhou during the Song and Yuan dynasties."

门类齐全，生机盎然

宋元时期泉州海外贸易的繁荣，与当地各种制造业的高度发达是分不开的。在众多出口商品中，当地所产商品占的比重最大。遗憾的是，有关手工业作坊的资料实在缺乏。宋元时期到过泉州的外国旅行家曾在游记中记下他们所目睹的泉州陶瓷、丝绸、造船等手工作坊及手工业水平状况等，我们可以通过这些记述去探寻、去感受。

1271 年，意大利的犹太商人雅各 · 德安科纳抵达刺桐，在此逗留长达 5 个月，写下游记《光明之城》。他曾描述泉州“各处都有巨大的作坊，在那里，数以百计的男女在一起工作，生产金属制品、瓷花瓶、丝绸、纸张等物品。这些作坊中，有的甚至有 1,000 人，这真是一个奇迹”。看到制作精美的瓷碗时，他这样说道：“虽然它们只是碗，却像玻璃酒壶一样精致。这些是世界上最精美的瓷器……” 他还提到以刺桐为名的缎子，即著名的刺桐缎。雅各在泉州还购买了土糖、藏红花、生姜、桂皮、樟脑、靛青、明矾、宝石、珍珠及“写在纸上的著作和小册子”等。

Diverse Industries Bursting with Vitality

The prosperity of overseas trade in Quanzhou during the Song and Yuan dynasties could not have been achieved without the highly developed local manufacturing industry. Among the numerous export goods, the locally produced products accounted for the largest share. Unfortunately, data on handcraft workshops during this period are rather scarce. Foreign travelers who visited Quanzhou during the Song and Yuan dynasties recorded their firsthand observations of Quanzhou's workshops making ceramics, silk, ships and other items as well as the level of handcraft industry in their travel notes. We can explore those details through their accounts.

In 1271, the Italian Jewish merchant Jacob D'Ancona arrived in Zayton, and stayed here for five months. He wrote the travelogue *The City of Light*. In Jacob's description, in Quanzhou there were workshops everywhere, where hundreds of men and women worked together to produce metal products, porcelain vases, silk, paper, and other items. There were even 1,000 people in some of these workshops, which was truly a marvel. When he saw the beautiful porcelain bowls, he said that although they were just bowls, they were as delicate as glass decanters and were the most exquisite porcelain works in the world. He also mentioned the famous Zayton Satin, whose name was derived from where it was produced. Jacob also purchased country sugar, saffron, ginger, cassia, camphor, indigo, alum, gemstones, pearls, and writings and booklets printed on paper in Quanzhou.

德化屈斗宫窑址出土的白瓷弦纹折腹碗。（成冬冬 摄）
A white porcelain bowl with angled belly and string pattern excavated from the Site of Qudougong Kiln in Dehua. (Photo by Cheng Dongdong)

德化屈斗宫窑址出土的白瓷菊瓣纹高足杯。（成冬冬 摄）
A white porcelain stem cup with chrysanthemum petal pattern excavated from the Site of Qudougong Kiln in Dehua. (Photo by Cheng Dongdong)

意大利旅行家、商人马可·波罗曾经来到泉州，这里也是他在中国游历的最后一站。《马可·波罗游记》中提到泉州德化陶瓷物美价廉："刺桐城附近有一别城，名称迪云州。制造碗及磁（瓷）器，既多且美。除此港外，他港皆不制此物，购价甚贱。"

泉州还是摩洛哥旅行家伊本·白图泰中国之行的首站。在其著作《伊本·白图泰游记》中，他盛赞了泉州的丝绸、瓷器和船舶。丝绸价格不贵，"一件布衣，可换绸衣多件"。介绍泉州瓷器时，他说："瓷器价格在中国，如陶器在我国一样或更为价廉。这种瓷器运销印度等地区，直至我国马格里布。这是瓷器种类中最美好的。"谈及泉州造船，他写道："中国船只共分三类：大的称作艟克，复数是朱努克；中者为艚；小者为舸舸姆……此种巨船只在中国的刺桐城（今泉州）建造，或在隋尼凯兰即隋尼隋尼（今广州）建造。"

Marco Polo, an Italian traveler and merchant, once came to Quanzhou, which was also his last stop in China. In *The Travels of Marco Polo*, he mentioned that Dehua ceramics in Quanzhou were beautiful and cheap. By his account, there was a small city near Zayton, called Tiunguy (Diyunzhou), where bowls and porcelain were produced in large quantities and were of excellent quality. No other ports produced these items, and they were purchased at a very low price.

Quanzhou was the first stop of the Moroccan traveler Ibn Battuta's trip to China. In his *Travels*, he praised the silk, porcelain, and ships produced in Quanzhou. The silk was inexpensive. One could exchange a cloth coat for several silk coats. When introducing Quanzhou porcelain, he said that the price of porcelain in China was low, just as or even lower than the price of pottery in his country, and that the porcelain products were sold to India and other regions, all the way to Maghreb in his country. He regarded them as the most beautiful ones among all types of porcelain. When talking about shipbuilding in Quanzhou, he described, "Chinese ships are divided into three categories: the large one is called Junk, with 'Junks' as its plural, the middle one is called Zaw, and the small one is called Kakam ... These ships are all built in Quanzhou and Guangzhou."

泉州海外交通史博物馆内的渔村造船场景再现。（段燕飞 摄）

Reconstruction of the scene of building a ship at a fishing village inside Quanzhou Maritime Museum. (Photo by Duan Yanfei)

陶瓷业。制瓷技术是古代中国的一项伟大发明。自 7 世纪起，瓷器就在东西方商贸往来和文化、技术交流中扮演着重要的角色。10 世纪始，瓷器已是中外贸易中最大宗的商品之一，风靡世界。宋元时期，泉州陶瓷生产遍及泉州城郊和山区腹地，窑场密布，目前已发现的宋元时期窑址有 150 余处，德化窑、永春窑、安溪窑、南安窑、磁灶窑、东门窑和同安窑等窑口凭借资源优势，以海外市场为导向，生产各具特色的产品。其中，磁灶窑、德化窑两大窑系的产业规模最大、产品品种最多，均在宋元时期达到其窑业生产的顶峰。外销瓷器以青瓷为主，白瓷青白瓷次之，主要产品有碗、碟、杯、壶、瓶、罐、钵、盘、盏、洗、盒、军持等，有粗瓷和细瓷之分，满足了海内外市场不同层次的消费需求，产品远销亚洲、非洲 50 多个国家和地区。据元代周达观《真腊风土记》记载，在真腊人喜爱的中国产品的排名中，泉州和龙泉的青瓷器列入瓷器首选。

磁灶窑青釉小口罐。（成冬冬 摄）
A celadon-glazed small-mouthed jar from Cizao Kilns. (Photo by Cheng Dongdong)

About ceramics industry. The technology for making porcelain ware is a great invention of ancient China. Since the 7th century, porcelain ware has played an important role in commercial, cultural and technological exchanges between East and West. Since the 10th century, porcelain ware had become one of the most traded commodities in overseas trade, and it was popular worldwide. During the Song and Yuan dynasties, ceramics production in Quanzhou spread throughout the suburbs and mountainous areas, and kilns were densely distributed, with more than 150 kiln sites from the Song and Yuan dynasties having been discovered up to now. With its advantage in terms of resources, kilns such as Dehua Kilns, Yongchun Kilns, Anxi Kilns, Nan'an Kilns, Cizao Kilns, Dongmen Kilns, and Tong'an Kilns produced a variety of ceramics with unique features, oriented toward overseas markets. Among them, Cizao Kilns and Dehua Kilns had the largest industrial scale and the richest product variety, reaching their production peak in the Song and Yuan dynasties. Celadon was the major export porcelain, with white porcelain as well as bluish-white porcelain coming second. The main products were bowls, dishes, cups, pots, bottles, jars, plates, basins, boxes, and kendis (a kind of washing bottle), classified into coarse porcelain and fine porcelain to meet different consumer demands in domestic and foreign markets. The products were exported to more than 50 countries and regions in Asia and Africa. According to *A Record of Cambodia: The Land and Its People* by Zhou Daguan of Yuan Dynasty, in the ranking list of Chinese products favored by people in Chenla, celadon produced in Quanzhou and Longquan ranked first.

泉州最早的陶瓷生产，始于夏商时期的永春苦寨坑窑、德化与永春交界处的辽田尖窑生产的原始青瓷，南朝有晋江磁灶的溪口山窑，唐代有南安园内窑，唐五代有德化墓林窑、磁灶溪墘山窑以及同安杏林窑等，但沿海地区窑业与内陆地区窑业存在较大差异，它们的陶瓷生产技术的体系与来源可能不同。此后，泉州窑业持续发展，但也存在时空发展不平衡的现象，产品基本上可满足当地人们的生活需求。宋元时期，以磁灶窑（金交椅山窑）和德化窑（尾林—内坂窑、屈斗宫窑）为代表的泉州窑业进入发展黄金期，产品精美，蜚声海内外。

The earliest ceramic production in Quanzhou can be traced back to Xia and Shang dynasties (c. 2070 B.C.—1046 B.C.) when proto-celadon was made in Kuzhaikeng Kilns in Yongchun and Liaotianjian Kilns on the border between Dehua and Yongchun. There were Xikoushan Kilns in Cizao, Jinjiang during Southern Dynasties, Yuannei Kilns in Nan'an during Tang Dynasty, Mulin Kilns in Dehua, Xiqianshan Kilns in Cizao, and Xinglin Kilns in Tong'an during Tang and Five Dynasties period. However, there are significant differences between coastal and inland kilns in terms of ceramic production technology systems and sources. Subsequently, kiln industry in Quanzhou continued to develop, but there was also a phenomenon of unbalanced development between places as well as in different times, and the products could basically meet the living needs of local people. Song-Yuan period witnessed a golden age of kiln industry in Quanzhou, with Cizao Kilns (Jinjiaoyishan Kilns) and Dehua Kilns (Weilin-Neiban Kilns and Qudougong Kiln) as typical examples. The products were exquisite, well known at home and abroad.

从生产技术上看，泉州窑业不仅积极借鉴国内南北名窑，还在实践中不断进行技术创新，扩大产能。在制坯环节，除了手制以外，还批量采用模制工艺，以提高生产效率；施化妆土和多种色釉来装饰产品，以弥补本地原料的天然缺陷，一改往日“青瓷一统天下”的局面，白瓷、青白瓷、黑釉瓷、低温的绿釉和黄绿釉瓷等品种如雨后春笋般涌现，刻划花、釉下彩绘等装饰工艺倍添雅韵，泉州陶瓷产品在海外市场更具竞争力；德化窑还注重窑炉技术革新，实现了从龙窑到分室龙窑的演变，并从平焰式火焰烧制，发展成半倒焰式火焰烧制，延长了火焰在窑室内的路程，均衡了窑温，提高了热效应，相对节约了燃料，降低了废品率。

From the perspective of production technology, Quanzhou kilns not only actively drew on the experience of famous kilns in northern and southern China, but also continuously innovated and expanded production capacity in practice. In the process of making the greenware, besides handcrafting, molding technique was also adopted extensively to improve production efficiency. Decoration techniques such as applying engobe and multi-color glaze were used to compensate for the natural defects of local materials, which had changed the situation where celadon dominated the market and brought forth a variety of products such as white porcelain, bluish-white porcelain, black-glazed porcelain, green-glazed as well as yellow-and-green glazed porcelain fired at low temperatures, etc. Other techniques such as carving and incising decoration and underglaze painting add elegance and charm to Quanzhou ceramics, making them more competitive in overseas markets. Dehua Kilns also focused their attention on technological innovation of kilns, achieving the evolution from loong-shaped kilns to multi-chambered loong-shaped kilns, and from flat flame firing to half inverted flame firing. In doing so, the distance of the flame going around the kiln was extended. The temperature in the kiln was balanced. The thermal effect was improved. More fuel was saved, and the waste rate was lowered.

在生产组织上，泉州古窑址出土的窑具上刻有多种姓氏，据此推断窑场可能采用由多个窑主或窑工合作烧窑、联合经营的生产方式，通过在窑具上署名以明确制作者、所有者。从这些生产技术、生产管理方面的创新，足见当地窑业敏锐的市场意识和快速的市场反应。

泉州瓷窑的经营者不仅响应当地市场需求，大量生产日用普通器皿和精神文化用器，还善于利用靠近港口的地理优势搜集海外市场信息，针对外贸需求进行定制生产。磁灶窑主要生产低档陶瓷产品，古人称“粗瓷”，面向海外低端市场；德化窑主要生产中、高档陶瓷产品，古人称“细瓷”，面向海外高端市场。二者共存互补，满足了海内外市场不同层次的消费需求。磁灶窑的军持、龙瓮，德化窑的军持、粉盒、小瓶等，均有明显的异域文化特征，是泉州瓷窑典型的外销瓷。《萍洲可谈》记载了海舶装运陶瓷的方式：“舶船深阔各数十丈，商人分占贮货，人得数尺许，下以贮物，夜卧其上。货多陶器，大小相套，无少隙地。”这便是当时泉州作为世界贸易中心强大陶瓷产业能力和贸易输出能力的写照。

宋德化窑刻窑工姓氏瓷。（成冬冬　摄）
Porcelain carved with the kiln worker's surname from Dehua Kilns in the Song Dynasty. (Photo by Cheng Dongdong)

In terms of production organization, the kiln facilities unearthed from the ancient kiln sites in Quanzhou bear various surnames, indicating that the kiln field might have adopted a production pattern under which multiple kiln owners or workers cooperated with each other and jointly managed. Through marking names on the kiln facilities, the producers and owners identified themselves. These technological and management innovations demonstrate the keen market awareness and rapid market response of the local kiln industry.

The operators of kilns in Quanzhou not only responded to local market demand by producing a large number of daily utensils and cultural artifacts, but also utilized the geographical advantage of being located near the port to collect overseas market information and customize products, thus meeting foreign trade needs. Cizao Kilns mainly produced low-end ceramics, also known as "coarse porcelain," targeting the low-end overseas market, while Dehua Kilns mainly produced medium- and high-end ceramics, also known as "fine porcelain," targeting the high-end overseas market. The kilns complemented each other and met the different consumption needs from domestic and foreign markets. Products like kendis and urns with loong pattern of Cizao Kilns, kendis, powder boxes, and small bottles of Dehua Kilns have distinct exotic features, making themselves typical export ceramics of Quanzhou kilns. *Pingzhou Table Talk* recorded how ceramics were loaded onto the ship: "The ship was dozens of *zhang* (a Chinese unit of length. One *zhang* equals about 3.33 meters) in width and depth, and the merchants occupied their own storage. Each one got an area about a few feet wide. People piled their goods and slept on them at night. With a lot of pottery, smaller ones were putting into bigger ones to fill every gap." This is a portrayal of Quanzhou's flourishing ceramic industry and enormous export capability as a world trade center at that time.

矿冶业。矿冶业在泉州算得上是传统手工业，历史悠久。早在五代时，安溪置县于小溪场，一个重要原因便是这里“冶有银铁”，而原址位于泉州城西龙头山的铁炉寺，就是五代南唐“晋江王”留从效的炼铁遗址，此时的泉州已有“陶瓷、铜铁泛于蕃国”的海上贸易。宋元时期，海上贸易兴盛，矿冶业也繁荣发展。当时农业生产结构调整，占城稻等粮食作物、棉花等经济作物从海外引种，加上兴修水利、开发山海等活动，对铁制农具的需求大大增加；在手工业方面，造船业繁荣发展；在商业方面，应商品流通的需要，钱币铸造不断增加。也就是说，农业、手工业、商业的发展都扩大了对铁、铜的需求。铁制农具在国内市场行销，销往两浙地区和广东产粮区，满足当地农业生产所需，是泉州换取粮食的重要交换品；铁、铜制品还作为出口商品销往东南亚各国。

铁炉寺曾是留从效铸冶之所。（吴箬云 摄）
The Iron Forge Temple was where Liu Congxiao once smelted iron. (Photo by Wu Nayun)

About mining and smelting. Mining and smelting are considered traditional handcraft industries in Quanzhou, with a long history. As early as Five Dynasties period, Anxi County was established in Xiaoxi Field. One important reason was that silver and iron smelting developed here. The Iron Forge Temple formerly located on Longtou Hill in the west of Quanzhou was where Liu Congxiao, the "Jinjiang King" of the Southern Tang in the Five Dynasties period, once smelted iron. At that time, Quanzhou had already had its ceramics, copper, and iron products widely traded with foreign countries. During the Song and Yuan dynasties, the maritime trade flourished, and mining and smelting also prospered. At that time, there was an adjustment to the agricultural production structure, and grain crops such as Champa Rice and cash crops like cotton were introduced from abroad, along with the development of water conservancy and mountain-sea development activities, which greatly increased the demand for iron agricultural tools. In terms of handcraft industry, shipbuilding thrived, and as for commerce, coin minting continued to increase to meet the need of commodity circulation. In other words, the development of agriculture, handcraft industry, and commerce increased the demand for iron and copper. Iron agricultural tools were sold in the domestic market such as Liangzhe area (roughly the modern provinces of Zhejiang and southern Jiangsu, as well as the modern metropolitan Shanghai) and Guangdong grain-producing areas, meeting the need of local agricultural production. They served as important commodities to exchange for grain. Iron and copper products were also exported to various countries in Southeast Asia.

宋代泉州冶铁场有永春的倚洋，安溪的青阳，德化的赤水、五华四处，其中尤以青阳为著。其遗址范围很大，铁渣堆积高达数米。曾炉寺西南也遗有宋人冶炼留下的铁渣堆积，面积达六亩左右，冶铁规模那时已很宏大。冶银主要集中在安溪的龙崇银场，北宋熙宁年间开始采炼，其规模也很可观。据记载，北宋治平年间，泉州还设有铜冶。

宋元泉州矿冶业的采炼技术已有很大提高，在采矿上，利用热胀冷缩原理的“烧爆法”之效率倍于人工开掘；在炼制上，炼银的“灰吹法”、炼铜的“胆水浸铜法”都应用于实践，促进了产业发展。

In the Song Dynasty, iron production sites in Quanzhou included Yiyang in Yongchun, Qingyang in Anxi, and Chishui and Wuhua in Dehua, among which Qingyang was particularly famous. The site is very large and the iron slag heap is several meters high. In the southwest of Zenglu Temple, there is also an iron slag heap left by Song people, covering an area of about six *mu* (a Chinese unit of land area. One *mu* equals about 0.16 acres). The scale of iron smelting was quite large at that time. The silver smelting was mainly concentrated in Longchong silver field in Anxi, and the mining and refining work began in the Xining period (1068—1077) of the Northern Song Dynasty. The scale was also impressive. According to historical records, during the Zhiping period (1064—1067) of the Northern Song Dynasty, copper smelting was also developed in Quanzhou.

During the Song and Yuan dynasties, the mining and smelting technology in Quanzhou had greatly improved. In terms of mining, utilizing the principle of substances expanding on heating and contracting on cooling, the "ore cracking method" was more efficient than manual excavation; and as for smelting, the method of cupellation for refining silver and the method of dipping iron plates into copper sulphate solution for refining copper were both applied in practice, promoting the development of the industry.

从经营方式看，冶场有“公冶”“私冶”之分，即官营与私营两种形式。安溪青阳下草埔冶铁遗址可谓青阳冶铁遗址群的核心区，很可能属于宋代官办铁场；离下草埔冶铁遗址不远的尚卿福林银场遗址是一处宋时官办银场。政府只对官营冶铁作坊收税，而私营的冶炼作坊，产品除政府按官价收购的部分，其余可进入流通领域自由买卖，且不需缴税。公私并存，“私冶”自由发展，对于宋元泉州矿冶业产品商品化尤为有利，这一政策也大大推动宋元泉州矿冶业的发展。

矿冶业的发展，为铸钱、铁制农具制造、铜铁类生活用品制造、造船等手工行业提供了丰富的原料。

Regarding business models, the smelting workshops included state-owned ones and private ones, run by official bodies and individuals respectively. Xiacaopu Iron Production Site of Qingyang Village in Anxi can be regarded as the core area of the iron smelting sites in Qingyang, and it is likely that it was state-owned during the Song Dynasty. Fulin Silver Smelting Site in Shangqing, not far from Xiacaopu Iron Production Site, was also operated by the government. Only state-owned iron smelteries were taxed, while private smelteries could freely trade their products without having to pay taxes, except for the portion purchased by the government at fixed prices. The coexistence of public and private ownership, with vigorous development of private smelteries, had been particularly beneficial for the commercialization of mining and smelting products in Quanzhou during the Song and Yuan dynasties, and this policy had greatly promoted the development of the mining and smelting industry in Quanzhou during that period.

The development of the mining and smelting industry provided abundant raw materials for coin minting, production of iron agricultural tools as well as copper and iron daily necessities, shipbuilding and other handcraft industries.

宋元泉州“金银铜铁，海舶飞运”，有时一次就载运价值十数万缗铜钱的金银铜铁制品销往海外（其中当有泉州产品），让海外的人们共同享用中国“宝货”。铜铁类生活用品，造船涉及的大量锚、钉，主要供应东南亚市场。在元代汪大渊《岛夷志略》的记载中，铜、铁等金属制品行销 55 个国家和地区，其中，铁制品销往 48 个国家和地区，它们在《岛夷志略》中有的直接被称为“铁”“铁器”“铁块”“铁条”，或有更详细的名称如“铁线”“铁锅”“铁鼎”等。“南海 I 号”沉船的发现为铁制品外销运输包装的方式提供了实证：铁器坯件由竹篾绑缚成捆，两捆用竹篾绑缚为一组，铁器坯件捆、组之间还垫衬了草席、竹席等编织物，整齐码放在船上；铁锅则成组相摞，倒扣在船上，铁锅之间也常见竹篾、竹席等填充物。

During the Song and Yuan dynasties, Quanzhou was known for shipping gold, silver, copper, and iron products overseas, and sometimes the products, with an equivalent worth of more than a hundred thousand strings of copper coins, were transported abroad all at once. Goods produced in Quanzhou were among them. Chinese "treasures" were, therefore, available to people in foreign countries. Copper and iron daily necessities and components of ships like anchors and nails were mainly supplied to the Southeast Asian market. According to *A Brief Account of Island Inhabitants* by Wang Dayuan of the Yuan Dynasty, metal products such as copper and iron products were sold to 55 countries and regions. Iron products were sold to 48 countries and regions. They were directly referred to as "iron," "ironware," "iron block," "iron bar," or more detailedly as "iron wire," "iron pot," "iron cauldron," and so on. The discovery of "Nanhai No. 1" Shipwreck provides evidence of how iron products were packaged for export: iron blanks were bound with bamboo strips into bundles, and two bundles were bound together as a group with bamboo strips. Woven materials such as straw mats and bamboo mats were laid between different bundles as well as different groups as cushions. All of them were neatly arranged on the ship. Iron pots were stacked in groups and placed upside down; bamboo strips and bamboo mats were also commonly seen between the iron pots as fillers.

安溪青阳下草埔冶铁遗址展示馆，沉淀着古老的冶铁记忆。（中新图片 供图）
The Exhibition Hall of Xiacaopu Iron Production Site of Qingyang Village in Anxi preserves the old memories of iron smelting. (Courtesy of CNSphoto.com)

南宋乾道年间，三佛齐向朝廷请求到州郡铸造铜瓦三万片，市舶司接到圣旨，令泉、广二州守臣监造，后因违禁未果，亦可见当时泉州铸造业规模之巨。

宋元时期泉州铜铁产量的确切数字虽无从得知，但从其矿冶、铸造的行业规模与外销情况看，产量当大大超过同时期国内许多地区，对泉州经济的发展无疑具有举足轻重的意义。

During the Qiandao period (1165—1173) of the Southern Song Dynasty, Srivijaya requested the court's permission to cast 30,000 copper tiles in the county. The Maritime Trade Office received the imperial decree, and required the officials in Quanzhou and Guangzhou to supervise the casting. However, the project failed due to violation of ban. That also demonstrates the enormous scale of the casting industry in Quanzhou at the time.

Although the exact figures for Quanzhou's copper and iron output during the Song and Yuan dynasties are unknown, the output was undoubtedly far greater than that of many other regions in China at the time, and played a pivotal role in the development of Quanzhou's economy, judging by the scale of the industry as well as its export sales.

纺织业。木棉布作为新型服饰材料在国内外都极受欢迎。宋时，木棉布已是“南北走百价”；元代，东南亚市场上已大量出现木棉布。丰富的资源与紧俏的市场需求，推动了泉州棉纺织业生产规模的扩大，以至于很大部分原料要依赖商人从海南等地转卖。

泉州纺织业多元发展，根据原材料的不同可以分为丝织业、麻纺织业和棉纺织业等。宋以前，泉州纺织业以麻、葛、蕉、纻纺织为主，不仅生产规模小，生产技术也相对落后，质量居下等；宋元时期，泉州纺织业在技术与规模上有了很大的改观。

About textiles. Kapok cloth became a popular textile material at home and abroad. During the Song Dynasty, Kapok cloth produced here had become such a greatly preferred choice in the north that its price in the north became much higher than that in the south. During the Yuan Dynasty, it became popular in Southeast Asian market. The rich resources and high market demand gave impetus to the increase in production scale of the cotton textiles in Quanzhou, so much so that a significant portion of raw materials had to be purchased from Hainan and other regions through merchants.

Quanzhou's textiles developed pluralistically, divided into silk, hemp, and cotton textiles according to raw materials. Before the Song Dynasty, Quanzhou's textiles mainly focused on hemp, kudzu, abaca, and ramie, and textiles were produced on a small scale, using relatively backward production techniques, the quality of which was inferior. However, during the Song and Yuan dynasties, Quanzhou's textiles achieved significant progress in both technology and scale.

在丝织业方面，历史上由于闽南民间种桑不得法，土地少种桑，桑园少。唐朝时，泉州大量种植桑树和养蚕，为丝织业的发展提供了充足的原料。泉州开元寺就曾是唐人黄守恭的桑园，有“桑园七里”，寺内西侧至今尚有一株老桑树，势若龙蟠，传说由唐人栽下，可见当时植桑养蚕之盛。五代时期安溪农耕和养蚕并行，养蚕业成为当时重要的农业经济。泉州城内更是一派“千家罗绮管弦鸣”的热闹景象，“泉绢”成为当时远销国外的著名产品。

宋代，种桑养蚕受到政府的重视和鼓励，劝农广植农桑，如果有人砍伐桑树当柴火，则要治罪。东石邱侍郎，不仅经营纺织，也让人在榕树、杨树旁大量种植桑树。当时，泉州丝织业已达到与盛产丝绸的四川、江浙齐名，正如苏颂诗中所云“绮罗不减蜀吴春”。丝织品税是政府重要的税收来源。

In terms of silk weaving, in the past, people in southern Fujian failed to find an appropriate way to grow mulberry trees, so there were only a few mulberry fields. In the Tang Dynasty, people in Quanzhou planted a lot of mulberry trees and raised silkworms, providing adequate raw materials for the development of the silk industry. Kaiyuan Temple in Quanzhou was originally a mulberry garden owned by Huang Shougong in the Tang Dynasty, and the garden extended seven *li* (a Chinese unit of distance. One *li* equals 500 meters). To this day, there is an old mulberry tree in the west of the temple, with a strong aura like that of a coiling loong. It is said that the tree was planted by someone living in the Tang Dynasty, indicating the flourishing of mulberry cultivation and sericulture at that time. During the Five Dynasties, sericulture grew in parallel with farming in Anxi. Sericulture became an important part of agricultural economy at that time. In the city of Quanzhou, there was a lively scene of "A thousand families weaving colorful silk fabric while the music played." The "Quan silk" became a famous product exported abroad at that time.

During the Song Dynasty, cultivation of mulberry trees and silkworms breeding received great attention and encouragement from the government. People were encouraged to take part in sericulture extensively, and anyone who cut down mulberry trees for firewood would be punished. An assistant minister surnamed Qiu in Dongshi not only engaged in textile production, but also encouraged people to plant mulberry trees alongside banyan and poplar trees. At that time, the silk industry in Quanzhou had reached the same level as Sichuan, Jiangsu and Zhejiang which were noted for their silk products, as described in Su Song's poem: "The beauty of fabrics is no less than the spring scenery of Shu area and Wu area." The tax on silk products was an important source of government revenue.

开元寺内的千年古桑。（陈英杰 摄）
The old mulberry tree in Kaiyuan Temple is about a thousand years old. (Photo by Chen Yingjie)

1975年，福州北郊的黄昇墓出土三百余件服饰及布匹，有罗、绫、绮、绢、纱、绉、锦等，是研究宋代丝织工艺的珍贵资料。随葬的两件绫织物有墨书题记，一作“宗正纺染金丝绢官记”，另一作“□□□司”。黄昇系黄朴之女，赵师恕之孙赵与骏之妻。黄朴曾担任泉州知州兼市舶司提举。赵师恕是宗室成员，曾知南外宗正事。他们执掌泉州海外贸易大权。

黄昇墓出土的丝织品，既有江浙等地的产品，也有福建本地官私手工业作坊的产品。我们有理由推测，南外宗正司迁入泉州后，在泉州设立官营织造厂，给泉州丝织业带来先进的技术；唐末五代至宋末，中原人将先进的生产技术和生产工具带到泉州。这些出土文物，从某种程度上体现了南宋泉州的“栽桑、养蚕、缫丝、织绸”工艺体系已有极大发展。泉人素有“百工技艺，敏而善仿”的传统，据清代《西山杂志》记载，南宋绍兴年间，东石的邱侍郎家经营丝织业，把缫丝纺纱机从手摇式巧妙改良为“两人穿踏”式，提高了生产效率，人们纷纷推广。

In 1975, over 300 pieces of clothing and fabrics were unearthed from the tomb of Huang Sheng, located in the northern suburbs of Fuzhou. These included fabrics such as *luo, ling, qi, juan, sha, zhou,* and *jin,* all of which are precious materials for the study of silk weaving technology during the Song Dynasty. There were two pieces of silk fabrics with ink writing which read "dyed silk owned by Southern Clan Office" and "(?) Office" respectively. Huang Sheng is the daughter of Huang Pu and the wife of Zhao Yujun who is the grandson of Zhao Shishu. Huang Pu once served as Prefect of Quanzhou and Superintendent of Maritime Trade Office. Zhao Shishu was a member of the imperial family, and once administered the affairs of the Southern Clan Office. Both of them were in charge of overseas trade in Quanzhou.

The silk fabrics excavated from Huang Sheng's tomb included products from Jiangsu and Zhejiang, as well as locally made products from state-owned and private workshops in Fujian. It is reasonable to speculate that members of Southern Clan Office established state-owned weaving workshops after they relocated to Quanzhou and thus they brought advanced technology to Quanzhou's silk industry. From the late Tang Dynasty and the Five Dynasties to the end of the Song Dynasty, people from the Central Plains brought advanced production technology and tools to Quanzhou.These unearthed cultural relics, to some extent, reflect that the technological system covering mulberry planting, sericulture, silk reeling, and silk weaving during the Southern Song Dynasty had been greatly developed. People in Quanzhou had always been known for "being dexterous and quite capable of learning a hundred crafts." According to *Xishan Miscellaneous Records* of the Qing Dynasty (1644—1911), during the Shaoxing period (1131—1162) of the Southern Song Dynasty, the assistant minister surnamed Qiu in Dongshi, undertook silk weaving. He improved the silk reeling and spinning machine by changing the hand crank design into the foot-treadle design, which greatly increased production efficiency. The machine was, therefore, widely used.

南宋地理学家赵汝适在《诸蕃志》中记述了泉州丝织品已远销今日之日本、朝鲜、越南、柬埔寨、印度、斯里兰卡、菲律宾、印度尼西亚、马来西亚、坦桑尼亚等国。据日本古代典籍记载，1105 年，泉州商人李充前往日本贸易，所带货物中就有三种精美的丝织品，分别是象眼（一种高级丝织品）、生绢和白绫。元代地理学家汪大渊在《岛夷志略》中提到，当时中国出口的商品中，丝织品就有 30 多种，它们经由泉州港等港口销往越南、柬埔寨、泰国、缅甸、印度等 70 多个国家和地区。值得一提的是，宋元泉州织造的刺桐缎，不仅是外销商品，还是王室馈赠友好国家的珍贵礼品。元朝皇帝送给印度国王的五百匹丝绸中，刺桐缎就有一百匹。

In his book *Records of Foreign Countries*, Zhao Rukuo, a geographer of the Southern Song Dynasty, wrote that Quanzhou silk products had been exported to present-day Japan, DPRK, Vietnam, Cambodia, India, Sri Lanka, the Philippines, Indonesia, Malaysia, Tanzania and other countries. According to an ancient Japanese classic, in 1105, Li Chong, a merchant in Quanzhou, went to Japan for trade, and among the goods he brought were three kinds of exquisite silk fabrics, namely *xiang yan* (a premium silk product), *sheng juan* and *bai ling*. Wang Dayuan, a geographer of the Yuan Dynasty, mentioned in *A Brief Account of Island Inhabitants* that there were more than 30 kinds of silk fabrics among the goods exported from China at that time, and that they were sold to more than 70 countries and regions including Vietnam, Cambodia, Thailand, Myanmar, and India through ports such as Quanzhou Port. It is worth noting that Quanzhou's Zayton Satin (a type of silk fabric known for its delicate design), produced during Song and Yuan dynasties, was not only an export commodity but also a precious gift given by the royal members to countries with which China had built friendly relations. Among the 500 pieces of silk sent by the Yuan emperor to the king of India, there were 100 pieces of Zayton Satin.

在棉纺织业方面，泉州山海兼备的自然条件与湿热的气候宜于麻、葛、蕉等植物的生长，在泉州的经营热潮中，所属各县都大力开垦山地，种植麻纻作物以供纺织所需。惠安的北镇布、永春的白纻布都十分著名，安溪以女工为主生产“冬棉夏葛”，南安蕉布与建州花练也是名产。

木棉作为利润甚高的经济作物，在平原地区广为种植，棉纺织专业户大量涌现，随处可见“玉腕竹弓弹吉贝（即木棉）”的景象，木棉布逐渐取代麻类纤维成为主要衣料。安海陈氏家族广种木棉，以所产木棉花与人交易棉纱，雇人织布，所织之布雅而有致，运销交趾，交趾人称其布为“陈氏之布”。

As for the cotton textiles, the adjacence to both mountains and the sea, along with the humid, hot climate, provided favorable conditions for the growth of plants such as hemp, kudzu, and abaca. During the period when trade was flourishing in Quanzhou, all counties made an effort to reclaim lands and plant hemp and ramie for textile production. Hui'an's Beizhen cloth and Yongchun's white ramie cloth were very famous, while Anxi mainly produced cotton cloth in winter and kudzu cloth in summer, with female workers as the mainstay. Nan'an's abaca cloth and Jianzhou's *hua lian* were also renowned products.

As a highly profitable cash crop, cotton was widely planted in plains. Many households specializing in cotton textile production emerged, and the sight of "moving jade-like wrists to fluff the cotton using bamboo bows" was common. Cotton fabrics gradually replaced hemp fibers as the main clothing material. The Chen Family of Anhai cultivated cotton extensively, traded their cotton for yarn, and hired workers to weave fabrics. Their products were elegant and beautiful, and were sold to Jiaozhi (present-day northern Vietnam). Jiaozhi people called it "Chen Family cloth."

制茶业。我国茶叶栽种历史悠久，相传在 4,000 年前人们就利用茶叶治病。泉州在晋朝已有种茶的历史记载。南安莲花峰有“莲花茶襟”“太元丙子”的题刻（太元丙子即东晋太元元年），这是福建最早有关茶的题刻。唐以来，泉州种茶已相当普遍，陆羽曾在《茶经》中提到，对于包括泉州在内的十一个地方所产的茶叶还不太清楚，每每得到一些品尝一下，觉得味道非常好。唐末诗人韩偓流寓南安，他在《信笔》一诗中提到“乡俗摘茶歌”，说明那时采茶已成为乡俗。五代安溪饮茶之风盛行，人们将茶叶作为馈赠友人的珍品。宋朝，泉州种茶更为普遍，蔡襄曾在《茶录》中提到，泉州七县皆种茶，以晋江清源洞及南安一片瓦寺产者品质尤佳。

About tea industry. China has a long history of tea cultivation, and according to legend, tea was used for medicinal purposes 4,000 years ago. There are historical records of tea cultivation in Quanzhou during the Jin Dynasty. The Lotus Peak in Nan'an has an inscription which reads "vast expanses of tea gardens around the Lotus Peak" and "Tai Yuan Bing Zi" (referring to the year of 376, the first year of Taiyuan period of the Eastern Jin). It is the earliest tea-related inscription in Fujian. Since the Tang Dynasty, tea cultivation in Quanzhou had become quite common. In his *The Classic of Tea*, Lu Yu noted that the quality of tea produced in 11 regions including Quanzhou was not well-documented, and that he found the tea pretty tasty when he got some. Han Wo, a poet who had once lived in Nan'an, mentioned folk songs of tea picking in his poem *Writing Freely*, indicating that tea picking had become a local custom. During the Five Dynasties, the trend of drinking tea in Anxi was prevailing, and people regarded tea as precious gifts for friends. In the Song Dynasty, tea cultivation in Quanzhou became more common. According to Cai Xiang's *The Record of Tea*, all seven counties in Quanzhou grew tea, with the best products found in Qingyuan Cave in Jinjiang and Yipianwa Temple in Nan'an.

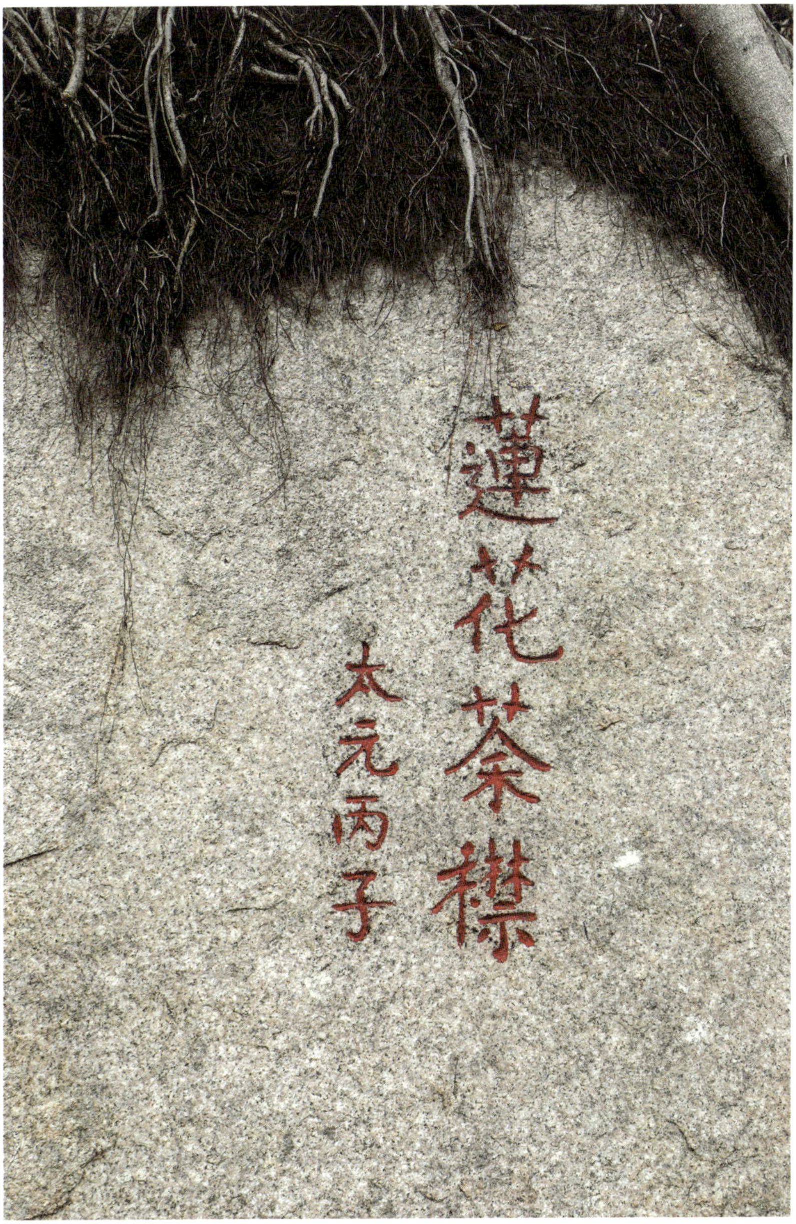

南安莲花峰“莲花茶襟”“太元丙子”题刻。（成冬冬 摄）
An inscription which reads "vast expanses of tea gardens around the Lotus Peak" and "Tai Yuan Bing Zi" on the Lotus Peak in Nan'an. (Photo by Cheng Dongdong)

饮茶品茶是宋元时期官方祭典九日山祈风之后不可缺少的活动。九日山部分摩崖石刻记述了宋代的茶事活动。九日山的《重建三贤祠记》记录了南宋淳祐十二年（1252）夏重建三贤祠完工后官员及士绅在石佛岩喝茶之事，石刻上的“啜茗”二字至今仍清晰可见。在九日山西峰蔡襄题字石刻的上方，有一方石刻记载了南宋宝祐六年（1258）三月的一次饮茶活动。莲花峰也有几处宋代茶事石刻，例如泉州郡守高惠连于北宋大中祥符四年（1011）所题“岩缝茶香”和宋宗室赵师耕于南宋淳祐七年（1247）所题“斗茶而归”。岩缝茶因生长于石缝中而得名，最早的记载见于北宋。南宋以后，当地僧人精心焙制，遂成历史名茶。“斗茶而归”石刻见于莲花峰东面，反映了宋时泉州斗茶风的盛行。

Drinking tea and appreciating tea during the Song and Yuan dynasties became an indispensable activity after the Jiuri Mountain Wind-Praying ritual ceremonies held by officials. Some of the cliff inscriptions in Jiuri Mountain documented the tea-related activities during the Song Dynasty. The *Reconstruction of Three Masters Memorial Temple* inscribed on Jiuri Mountain recorded the tea drinking activity of officials and gentry at Stone Buddha Rock after the completion of the reconstruction of Three Masters Memorial Temple in the summer of 1252. The two characters "Chuo Ming" meaning "sipping tea" inscribed on the cliff are still clearly visible today. Above the stone inscription by Cai Xiang on the west peak of Jiuri Mountain, there is a stone inscription recording a tea drinking activity in March in the lunar calendar in 1258. There are also several stone inscriptions about tea-related activities during the Song Dynasty at Lotus Peak, such as "Fragrance of Rock Seam Tea" by Gao Huilian, a governor of Quanzhou, in 1011, and "Return after Tea Brewing Contest" by Zhao Shigeng, an imperial family member, in 1247. The Rock Seam Tea got its name because it grew in rock crevices, the earliest record of which was found in the literature of the Northern Song Dynasty. After the Southern Song Dynasty, local monks carefully roasted it, and thus it became a famous variety of tea in history. The stone inscription of "Return after Tea Brewing Contest" is on the east side of Lotus Peak, reflecting the prevailing trend of tea contests in Quanzhou during the Song Dynasty.

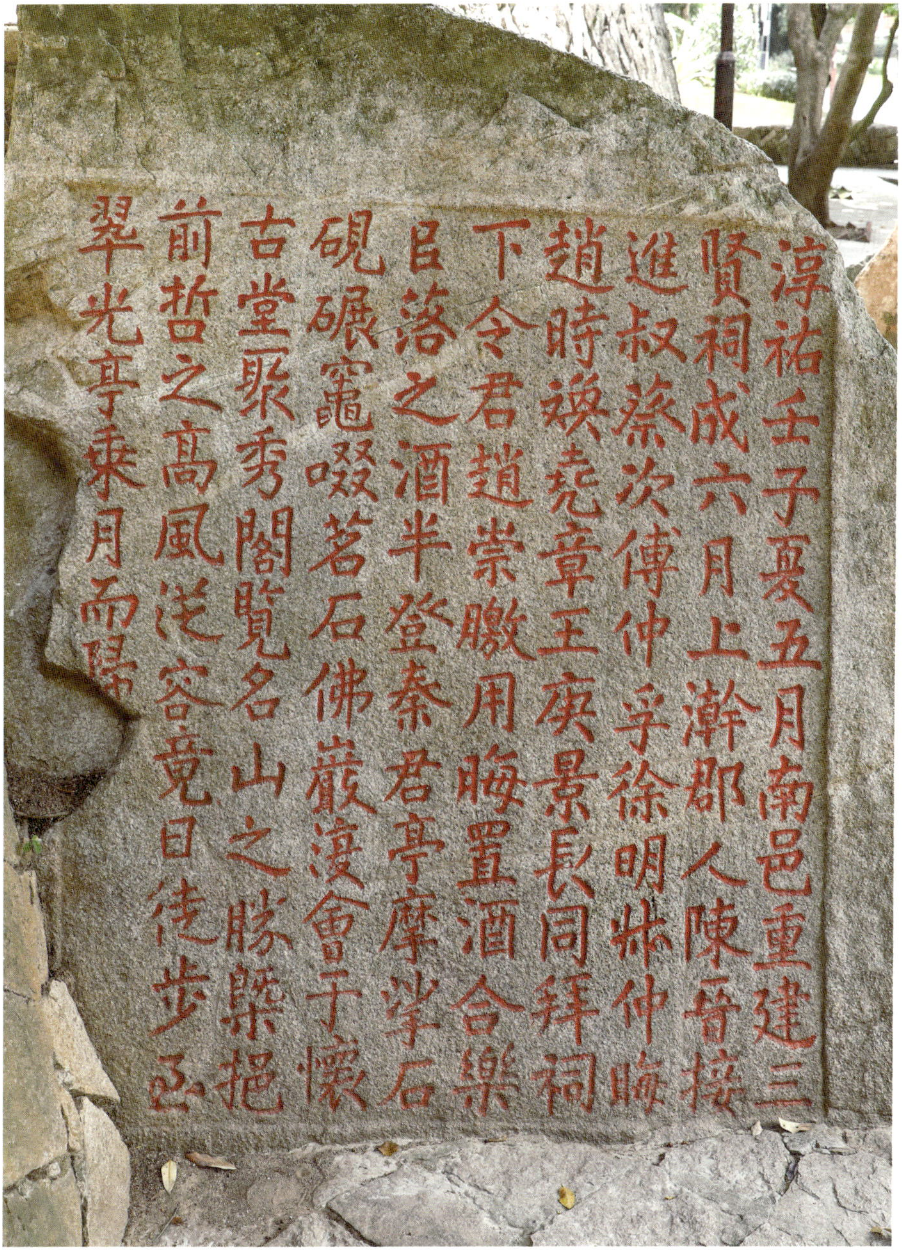

九日山的《重建三贤祠记》石刻。（成冬冬 摄）
The stone inscription of *Reconstruction of Three Masters Memorial Temple* on Jiuri Mountain. (Photo by Cheng Dongdong)

自唐至宋，制茶一般是把炙烤后的茶叶，用手或水碾碾碎，再罗细成茶末，最后压成团饼茶。当时，团状、饼状的紧压茶通常被称为“片茶”，散状的茶叶通常被称为“草茶”或“散茶”。到元代，散茶明显超过团饼茶，成为主要的生产茶类。据《王祯农书》记载，当时的茶叶有“茗茶”“末茶”“腊茶”三种。“茗茶”就是有的史书中提到的芽茶或叶茶，“末茶”是把散茶碾成碎末的产品，而“腊茶”则是“腊面茶”的简称，就是团饼茶。“腊茶”在元代“惟充贡茶，民间罕之”。

宋代外销茶叶主要是“茗茶”。据记载，泉州、广州置市舶司，招徕番商，买卖货物，其中丝绸、陶瓷、茗茶、酒，都是番商最乐意采购的中国产品。当时，安溪的茶叶销往 58 个国家和地区，遍及东南亚、西亚和北非；元代，大批宋朝遗民移居东南亚，也为茶叶外销提供了有利条件。

蔡襄在《茶录》中曾这样写道：“茶有真香，而入贡者微以龙脑和膏，欲助其香。”这是我国以香料辅佐茶香的首次记载。龙脑在宋朝时是泉州从海外经常进口的香料。蔡襄在了解泉州各县制茶技术时，发现这一人工掺入香料的工艺，于是特地记录下来。

雅各 · 德安科纳在《光明之城》中描述了他在刺桐城的一次饮茶体验：“在城里的市场上，可以看到很多好的东西，如大米、形形色色的水果、香草等。还有一种用灌木的小叶子做成的饮料，那种东西在他们中间很受重视，不过尝起来却很苦。”

From the Tang Dynasty to the Song Dynasty, tea production generally involved baking the tea leaves, grinding them into small pieces by hand or by water-powered roller, getting fine tea powder through sifting, and pressing them into compressed tea cakes. At that time, tightly compressed tea in the form of cakes or bricks was usually called *pian cha*, while loose tea leaves were typically referred to as *cao cha* or *san cha*. By the Yuan Dynasty, loose tea leaves had overtaken compressed tea cakes as the main tea products. According to *Wang Zhen's Book on Agriculture*, there were three types of tea at the time, namely *ming cha*, *mo cha*, and *la cha*. *Ming cha* is leaf tea or bud tea mentioned in some historical records, while *mo cha* is fine tea powder obtained from grinding loose tea. *La cha,* also known as *la mian cha*, refers to compressed tea. During the Yuan Dynasty, *la cha* was only produced for the court and was rarely seen among folk.

Leaf tea, or *ming cha*, was the main type of tea exported during the Song Dynasty. It was recorded that Quanzhou and Guangzhou set up maritime trade offices to attract foreign merchants and conduct maritime trade, and that silk, ceramics, leaf tea, and liquor were the most popular Chinese products among foreign merchants. At that time, Anxi's tea products were exported to 58 countries and regions in Southeast Asia, West Asia, and North Africa. In the Yuan Dynasty, a large number of Song people moved to Southeast Asia, providing favorable conditions for tea export.

Cai Xiang mentioned in *The Record of Tea* that tea had a true fragrance, and that a small amount of borneol would be added to those for the court to enhance the aroma. This is the first recorded instance of spices being used to give more pleasant smell to tea. Borneol was a frequently imported spice in Quanzhou during the Song Dynasty. As Cai Xiang broadened his knowledge about the tea production techniques in various counties of Quanzhou, he saw the technique of adding spices to the tea in use and recorded it.

Jacob D'Ancona described his experience of drinking tea in *The City of Light*: in the markets of the city, one could find many good things, such as rice, all kinds of fruits, and herb, and that there was also a drink made from small leaves of bush, which was highly valued among people in Quanzhou but it tasted very bitter.

制盐业。据记载，当时晋江有盐亭161个，惠安129个，同安则有安仁、上马栏、下马栏、庄板4个盐场，其中以惠安盐场所产“色洁白盐味淡”的盐最佳。泉州制盐业遍及濒海之区，是以其民“恃鱼盐为命”。南宋建炎二年（1128），东南岁榷福建沿海四州2,656万石，其中泉州所产之盐当为量不小。

泉州海盐制作，有煎、晒两种。大体都是取卤做原料，或柴火煎熬，或风吹日晒，水分蒸发后便能得到盐。煎盐法是刮滨海咸土淋卤，卤水通过芦管流入池中储存，测试卤水浓度是否达标（测试方法很有趣，例如，可以将桃仁或鸭蛋投入卤池，看它们是否浮起，浮起即表明卤水浓度已达标），达标后即可取卤燃薪熬盐，大锅一天可煎盐二百斤，小锅可煎盐百斤。晒盐法是先将海水引入蒸发池，日晒蒸发水分，直到卤水检测达标，再将卤水倒入结晶池继续日晒，逐渐析出食盐。相比煎盐法，晒盐法不仅简便，产量还高。宋元时期泉州海盐制作普遍以晒盐法为主，既可量产又能减少成本，山区丰富的木材资源还为盐具的制作提供了原材料。

沐浴在朝霞中的盐田。（张九强 摄）
Saltpans bathed in the morning glow. (Photo by Zhang Jiuqiang)

About salt industry. It is recorded that there were 161 salt ponds in Jinjiang and 129 in Hui'an at that time. Tong'an had four salt fields, including Anren, Shangmalan, Xiamalan, and Zhuangban. Among those salt fields, the ones in Hui'an produced the best salt, which was known for its "clean white color and light taste." Salt production was pretty common along the coastal areas and was vital to the local economy. In 1128, 26.56 million *dan* (a Chinese unit of capacity for grain) of salt were sold from the coastal areas of Fujian exclusively by the central government, including a significant portion from Quanzhou.

There were two methods of producing sea salt adopted by people in Quanzhou: boiling and solar evaporation. Generally, brine was used as the raw material, either boiled over a fire or dried in the sun. After the water evaporated, salt was obtained. The boiling method involved scraping salty soil from the seaside and pouring brine through reed pipes into a storage pool. The concentration of brine was tested to see if it met the standard. (Testing methods were interesting. For example, peach kernels or duck eggs were thrown into the brine. If they floated, it could be concluded that the concentration of brine had reached the standard.) Once the standard was met, one could start burning the firewood to boil the brine for salt. A large pot could produce 200 *jin* (a Chinese unit of weight. One *jin* equals 0.5 kilograms) of salt per day, while a small pot could produce 100 *jin* of salt. The solar evaporation method involved first drawing sea water into an evaporation pool and allowing the water to evaporate in the sunshine until the brine met the standard. And then it was poured into a crystallization pool for further evaporation, and the salt gradually crystallized. Compared to the boiling method, the solar evaporation method was simpler and gave a higher yield. During the Song and Yuan dynasties, solar evaporation was the prevailing method for sea salt production in Quanzhou, having the advantage of greater output at lower costs. The abundant wood resources in the mountainous areas also provided raw materials for making salt utensils.

盐，国家专卖，历代王朝对盐业控制极严，盐税成为政府收入的重要来源之一。北宋时期明确规定“私炼盐者，三斤死”，“严禁民间染指盐利”。但由于“官中煎卖，费多利少”，随后颁布新策，允许商人入钱买钞，到产盐地领盐，自由买卖。由于盐法渐宽，许民纳钱通煎，许商输钱通贩，官商分利原则在制盐业运用日益广泛，宋元泉州的私营盐业迅速发展。制盐专业户与大盐商也逐步增多。据清代《西山杂志》记载，宋代安海李氏家族的盐产品行销于安南，得名“李氏之盐”。李氏通过卖盐在安南获得很高威望，其族人李公蕴甚至做了安南王，可想其势力之大！至于一般商人转贸四方贩盐获利者，更不可胜数。

Salt business was in the charge of the central government. Successive dynasties had strict control over the salt industry, and salt tax was an important source of government revenue. During the Northern Song Dynasty, it was explicitly stipulated that "those who privately refine salt as much as three *jin* shall be sentenced to death," and that "common people are forbidden access to salt profits." However, due to the fact that "the official salt production and sale involved high costs and low profits," a new policy was subsequently issued, allowing merchants to purchase salt certificates and obtain salt from salt-producing areas for free trade. Due to the gradual relaxation of salt regulations, people were allowed to pay for transporting and processing salt, and merchants were allowed to trade salt by paying a charge. Dividing profits between authorities and merchants was increasingly common in the salt industry, leading to rapid development of private salt business in Quanzhou in Song and Yuan dynasties. The number of professional salt producers and prominent salt merchants also gradually increased. According to *Xishan Miscellaneous Records* of Qing Dynasty, salt produced by Li Family in Anhai in the Song Dynasty were sold to Annam and got the name "Li's Salt." The Li Family gained high prestige in Annam through selling salt, and Li Gongyun, one of its clan members, even became the king of Annam, by which one can imagine their great influence. There were countless common businessmen who profited from trading salt in various regions.

盐工们手持盐耙，在盐田劳作。（张九强 摄）
Salt workers are working in the saltpans with rakes. (Photo by Zhang Jiuqiang)

造船业。泉州港成为海上丝绸之路的重要港口，一个重要原因就是拥有发达的造船业和先进的造船技术。隋唐时期，泉州是国内重要的造船基地。宋元时期，泉州所造海船的质量居全国之首。宋朝遣使海外时的船和舟师，很多都到福建招募。南宋建炎三年（1129），监察御史林之平奉命至泉州招募海船，当年十月即有大舟自闽中至明州海域者 200 余艘。宋代泉州也造了许多战船，南宋绍兴年间，黄彦辉在晋江县任职时，朝廷命令东南沿海各县造船，晋江最先完成 9 艘船的造船任务；傅伫在晋江县任职时，亲自督造战船，在按时完成任务的同时还节省了费用。除官营造船外，民营造船业也很发达，宋代泉州、漳州、福州等滨海地区百姓自备财力造船，兴贩获利。绍兴初年，连南夫在泉州任职时，“朝廷下福建造舟”。他建议以度牒向民间买商船 200 艘，可节省缗钱 20 万。

宋代泉州所造海船，在坚固性和适航性上都走在前列，特别是水密隔舱，可增强海船的抗沉性能，加强船体的坚固性，适于远洋航行，如果途中一两个船舱偶然受损，海水不会涌进其他船舱，船仍然可以继续航行。

泉州湾宋代海船的水密隔舱。（成冬冬 摄）
The watertight bulkheads of the Song Dynasty Oceangoing Ship in Quanzhou Bay. (Photo by Cheng Dongdong)

About shipbuilding industry. Quanzhou Port became an important port of the Maritime Silk Road largely due to its advanced shipbuilding industry and technology. During the Sui and Tang dynasties (581—907), Quanzhou was an important shipbuilding base in China. In the Song and Yuan dynasties, the quality of the ships built in Quanzhou surpassed that of any other city in China. During the Song Dynasty, many of the ships and boatmen accompanying the envoys sent overseas were primarily recruited from Fujian. In 1129, Lin Zhiping, an imperial censor, was ordered to recruit ships in Quanzhou, and in October of the same year, over 200 large boats from central Fujian had arrived at Mingzhou waters. Quanzhou also built many warships during the Song Dynasty. During the Shaoxing period of the Southern Song Dynasty, when Huang Yanhui served in Jinjiang County, the imperial court ordered all counties in the southeast coastal areas to build ships, and Jinjiang was the first to complete the construction of 9 ships. Fu Zhu, also once serving in Jinjiang County, personally supervised the construction of warships, and completed the task on time while saving money. Besides the shipbuilding business run by government, private shipbuilding was also highly developed. During the Song Dynasty, people in coastal areas such as Quanzhou, Zhangzhou, and Fuzhou spent money building ships for transporting goods, in order to engage in trade for profit. In the early years of Shaoxing period, when Lian Nanfu was serving in Quanzhou, the court ordered the construction of boats in Fujian. He suggested purchasing 200 merchant ships from the private sector using the money gained by selling monks' or nuns' certificates, which could save money with an equivalent worth of 200,000 strings of copper coins.

The sea vessels built in Quanzhou during the Song Dynasty were at the forefront in terms of robustness and seaworthiness. In particular, the watertight bulkheads made the ship less likely to sink while strengthening its structure, suitable for long-distance voyages. If one or two compartments accidentally got damaged during the journey, sea water would not rush into other compartments, and the ship could continue sailing.

1974 年，泉州湾宋代海船的发现与发掘，是宋代泉州先进造船技术的重要见证。泉州湾宋代海船残长 24.2 米，宽 9.15 米，复原长度可达 34 米，宽 11 米，载重量约 200 吨。船底结构为尖底造型，共有 13 个隔舱，舷侧板为三重木板结构，船底板为二重木板结构。船板上下左右之间都用榫卯衔接，并用铁钉加固，缝隙间堵塞麻丝、竹茹和桐油灰捣成的舱料。这种工艺保证了船体的坚固性与水密性。船壳弯曲弧度大，采用多重板建造，使船壳坚固耐波，经得起风浪，可用于远洋航行。12 道舱壁将全船分成 13 舱，除舱壁近龙骨处留有“水眼”外，所有的舱壁钩联十分严密，密封程度很高。水密隔舱的制造是我国造船史上的一项重大成就。泉州宋船用材是很科学的，凡是需要承担强大压力的构件和部位，都采用坚硬的木材。龙骨由两段松木接合而成，连接龙骨的艏柱用整根樟木制成。在隔舱板与船壳板交接处，贴着用樟木制成的肋骨，其他部分多用杉木。这些木材在福建盛产，就地取材，十分方便。

福船水密隔舱内部结构展示模型。（段燕飞 摄）
A model of internal structure of watertight bulkheads on *Fu-Chuan* for display. (Photo by Duan Yanfei)

In 1974, the discovery and excavation of a Song Dynasty Oceangoing Ship in Quanzhou Bay was an important testament to Quanzhou's advanced shipbuilding technology in the Song Dynasty. The remains of the ship were 24.2 meters long and 9.15 meters wide, reconstructed with a length of up to 34 meters and a width of 11 meters, capable of carrying about 200 tons of goods. Pointed at bottom, the hull was made up of 13 compartments, and the side planks were triple-layered wooden structures, while the bottom planks were double-layered wooden structures. The planks were joined by mortise and tenon joints and reinforced with iron nails, with the seams filled with dunage made of hemp fiber, bamboo stalk, and putty, which ensured the toughness and watertightness of the ship's hull. Due to the large curvature of the hull, multiple layers of planks were used to build a strong hull which could withstand winds and waves, making the ship suitable for long-distance voyages. The 12 bulkheads divided the ship into 13 compartments, with all compartment walls tightly hooked together. The ship was well sealed, except for the scupper in the bulkhead near the keel. The creation of watertight bulkheads was a significant achievement in China's shipbuilding history. Materials for building ships were carefully selected. For components that needed to bear strong pressure, hard wood was used. The keel was made of two sections of pine wood joined together, and the stem post was made of a whole piece of camphor wood. At the junction of the bulkheads and the hull planks, there were ribs made of camphor wood, and other parts were mostly made of Chinese fir. These woods were abundant in Fujian, and it was convenient to collect the materials from local sources.

船上的设备齐全先进，船舵和指南针是远洋商船的标配。工人开始使用升降舵，可根据不同水域环境调节舵的高低。指南针的应用也受到重视。赵汝适在《诸蕃志》中这样描述从泉州到海南的航行，“渺茫无际，天水一色，舟舶来往，惟以指南针为则”。行船时依靠指南针来避免偏航，保障航行安全。

元代海运发达，海外贸易范围覆盖 99 个国家和地区，海船需求量大大增加，泉州造船业进一步发展，泉州成为元代四大海舶建造基地之一。“泉舶”行驶于海道，承担着繁忙的海运业务。元代，朝廷多次命泉州等地造船。

元至元二十八年（1291），马可 · 波罗奉忽必烈之命，护送阔阔真公主出嫁伊儿汗国。忽必烈下令“命备船十三艘，每艘具四桅，可张十二帆”，从泉州启航。这些四桅船是在泉州建造的。

The ships were very well equipped, with rudders and compasses being staple parts on long-distance merchant ships. Workers began using rudders whose height could be adjusted according to different water conditions. The use of compasses was also highly valued. Zhao Rukuo described the journey from Quanzhou to Hainan in his *Records of Foreign Countries*: "The vast and boundless sea, where the sky and water were of the same color, ships came and went, all relying on the use of the compass." People relied on the compass to avoid drift, thus ensuring the safety of navigation.

During the Yuan Dynasty, maritime transportation became more developed, and China had established trade relations with 99 countries and regions. The demand for ships increased greatly, further promoting the development of Quanzhou's shipbuilding industry, making Quanzhou one of the four major shipbuilding bases in the Yuan Dynasty. "Quan Bo" traveled along various sea routes to undertake the busy maritime business. The Yuan court ordered shipbuilding in Quanzhou and other regions many times.

In 1291, Marco Polo was entrusted by Kublai Khan with the task of escorting Princess Kokochin to Ilkhanate. Kublai Khan ordered "thirteen ships to be prepared, each with four masts and capable of hoisting twelve sails." They set sail from Quanzhou. These four-masted ships were built in Quanzhou.

后渚港码头边的马可·波罗出航处石碑。（视觉中国 供图）

The stele marking the departure site of Marco Polo at the dock of Houzhu Port. (Courtesy of VCG.COM)

宋元时期，泉州有许多造船场和修理船舶的船坞，主要分布在滨海地区，即后渚至泉州城南晋江下游沿岸。从造船木料选择来看，主要有松木、樟木、杉木及其他坚韧的杂木。龙骨一般选用尚未出脂的松木，连接在主龙骨前端的艏柱、桅座、舵座则用樟木制成，而舷板、舵叶等由轻便韧耐的杉木制成。造船工序大致如下：首先竖龙骨，龙骨竖好后装配隔舱板，钉上船尾板、船头板和船壳板，再装配肋骨，组成船体结构；然后在船体两侧舷板外再钉上数道船板，以增强船体的坚固程度；船体完成后，用扁木雕出椭圆形的“龙目”，安装在船艏舷墙外侧，这是船的“眼睛”；接着在船头挡浪板顶端钉上一块特制的木板，以防止船体间相互碰撞；随后上涂装，船体各个部位只要有夹缝的地方都要用麻絮填塞，用桐油灰刮缝，还要用火烤一下船的表皮，并且上一层蚝壳灰，以防海蛆，涂装颜色及图案的选择也因区域不同而有所差异，常选红、绿、黑、白、蓝等；涂装完成后立桅杆、安船舵、装缆绳、挂船帆。至此，一艘木制帆船就制成了，可以择吉日下水。造船时每开始一道工序和新船下水都要举行祭祀仪式等活动，以求神明庇护行船平安。

During the Song and Yuan dynasties, there were many shipyards and docks for ship maintenance and repair in Quanzhou, mainly located in the coastal areas from Houzhu to the lower reaches of Jinjiang River in the south of Quanzhou City. As for the selection of shipbuilding materials, pine, Chinese fir, camphor, and other tough woods were chosen. The keels were generally made of pine that had not yet had its resin extracted, while stem posts, mast bases, and rudder bases connected to the front end of the main keel were made of camphor wood, and side planks and rudder blades were made of lightweight and tough fir. The shipbuilding process was roughly as follows: Erect the keel. Assemble the bulkheads, and nail the stern board, the bow board, and the hull board. Then assemble the ribs to form the structure of the ship. After that, nail several extra boards to the outside of the side planks to increase the toughness of the hull. After the hull is completed, carve oval-shaped "loong eyes" out of flat wood and install them on the outer side of the front of the side planks, which are the "eyes" of the ship. Then nail a special piece of wood to the top of the manger board to prevent collisions between ship hulls. Next, apply coatings. Wherever there are gaps, fill them with hemp wadding and scrape them with putty. Roast the surface of the ship with fire and then coat it with oyster shell powder to prevent sea worms. The choice of coating color and pattern varied depending on region, and red, green, black, white, and blue are often chosen. After the coating is finished, erect the mast, install the rudder, position the mooring lines, and hang the sails. With these steps completed, a wooden sailing ship takes shape and can be launched on an auspicious day. Each time when a new step was taken or a new ship was launched, a sacrificial ceremony and other activities would be held, in order to seek the protection of the deities to ensure safe navigation.

泉州湾宋代海船的舵承座。（泉州海外交通史博物馆 供图）
The rudder base of the Song Dynasty Oceangoing Ship in Quanzhou Bay. (Courtesy of Quanzhou Maritime Museum)

食品加工业。农业生产结构的调整是泉州食品加工业发展兴盛的物质基础，而国内外市场需求则是重要的外在因素。拓兴果园广植果树，果品加工业十分兴旺。

当时，荔枝加工不仅有焙干、蜜饯等制法，还有一种以盐梅卤浸佛桑花为红浆，投荔枝腌渍后晒干的“红盐法”。经过“红盐”处理的荔枝，色红而甘酸，可以保存三至四年，采用这种方法，原本只能保鲜数日的荔枝就可以运销东亚与东南亚地区。南安所产的荔枝名品“进贡子”，每年由政府征收入贡，其保鲜法是：择小暑采摘，用黄蜡封住蒂口，然后以锡瓶贮蜜浸之，外用水箱盛之以水，每日更水一次，久而不坏。元代养生家贾铭在《饮食须知》卷四中也提到保存青梅、枇杷、橄榄、橙、李的方法：“以腊水入些少铜青末，密封于净罐内，久留色不变。或用腊水入薄荷、明矾少许，将诸果各浸瓮内，久藏味佳，且不变色。”南方水果的加工制作法当有相通之处。清代《西山杂志》也有记载，南宋晋江东石林氏家族开辟林地，广植水果，并设立果品加工厂和贮货站。

泉州永春，荔枝丰收。（陈小阳 摄）
Lychee harvest in Yongchun, Quanzhou. (Photo by Chen Xiaoyang)

About food processing industry. The adjustment of the agricultural production structure was the material basis for the development and prosperity of the food processing industry in Quanzhou, while domestic and foreign market demand was an important external factor. The expansion of the orchards to plant fruit trees had led to a thriving fruit processing industry.

At the time, as for lychee processing, there were not only methods to make them into dried ones or candied ones, but also a "red salt" method, namely using salted plum brine to soak Chinese hibiscus flowers, where lychees got pickled before they were exposed to sunlight. Lychees processed with "red salt" were red in color, sour and sweet in taste, and could be preserved for three to four years. With this method, lychee, which would have started to go bad a few days after being picked, could be shipped to East Asian and Southeast Asian regions. *Jin gong zi*, a famous lychee product in Nan'an, was collected by the court every year. Its preservation method was as follows: Pick them during the Minor Heat period, and seal the stem ends with beeswax, and then store them in tin bottles filled with honey. Put the bottles into a water tank. Change the water daily to ensure freshness. Jia Ming, a health practitioner of Yuan Dynasty, also mentioned in Volume Four of *Dietary Tips* the methods of preserving green plums, loquats, olives, oranges, and plums: mix brine with patina powder, and seal them with fruits in clean jars. The color will not change even after a long time. One can also mix brine with mint or alum, within which fruits are soaked, and then store them in an urn, and they will have a good taste while retaining their color even after long-term storage. The processing methods of fruits grown in southern China should have similarities. *Xishan Miscellaneous Records* of the Qing Dynasty also recorded that the Lin Family in Dongshi, Jinjiang opened up forest land during the Southern Song Dynasty, planted fruits extensively, and established fruit processing workshops and storage stations.

制糖业。制糖术起源于印度。北宋初年，泉州成为全国产蔗中心之一，制糖业也随之发展，所制之糖有黑糖、白糖、糖霜（又称“冰糖”）三类。黑糖是砂糖的一种。制糖过程中，经加热浓缩后的蔗汁倒入陶制容器，上面铺盖草木灰或石灰以漂白，数月后，糖色上白下黑，最上层为白糖，最下层即为黑糖，统称“砂糖”，还有呈板状的叫“板糖”。宋时，惠安县制糖业特别发达，“诸村皆种蔗煮糖，商贩辐辏，宋置监收其税”。其他各县的产糖规模也不小。

About sugar industry. The sugar making technique originated in India. In the early Northern Song Dynasty, Quanzhou became one of the major centers of sugarcane production, and the sugar industry also grew and developed, producing three types of sugar: brown sugar, white sugar, and icing sugar (also known as "rock candy"). Brown sugar is a type of granulated sugar. In the process of sugar making, the heated and concentrated cane juice was poured into pottery containers for processing, and then it was covered with ash or lime to bleach. After several months, the upper part became white and the lower part became black, forming white sugar and brown sugar respectively. They were collectively known as "granulated sugar." There was also "block sugar," in the shape of a block. During the Song Dynasty, the sugar industry in Hui'an County was particularly developed, with many villages engaging in sugarcane planting and sugar making. Merchants gathered here, and the government set up an agency to tax sugar. The scale of sugar production in other counties was also considerable.

这些蔗糖不仅在国内市场广受欢迎，还大量销往海外，据赵汝适《诸蕃志》记载，泉州产的糖曾运销占城、真腊、三佛齐等国。泉州本地居民对糖制品的需求也因当地制糖业的兴盛而获得满足。雅各·德安科纳在其游记中提到他在刺桐买到“黑糖”的事，看来是可信的。

马可·波罗在他的游记中也提到泉州制糖工艺，他说泉州白砂糖制作技术的引进始于元朝，永春县是当时植蔗制糖的重要基地，来自埃及的制糖匠在这里传授了用木灰净糖脱色的技术，原本生产赤色蔗糖的永春开始扩大白砂糖的生产规模，并且向国内外迅速推广这种新技术。

The cane sugar was not only popular in the domestic market, but also sold in large quantities overseas. According to *Records of Foreign Countries* by Zhao Rukuo, Quanzhou's sugar was once exported to countries such as Champa, Chenla, and Srivijaya. The local residents of Quanzhou also had their demand for sugar products met due to the prosperous local sugar industry. Jacob D'Ancona mentioned in his travel notes that he bought "brown sugar" in Zayton, which seems to be credible.

Marco Polo also mentioned the sugar-making technique in Quanzhou in his travel notes. He said that the introduction of the technique for making white granulated sugar to Quanzhou began in the Yuan Dynasty, and Yongchun County was an important base for sugarcane planting and sugar production at that time. Sugar-making craftsmen from Egypt imparted the technique of using ash to whiten sugar here. Yongchun, formerly engaging in brown cane sugar production, began to expand its production of white granulated sugar and promoted this new technique at home and abroad.

酿酒业。宋代泉州引种推广占城稻，与晚稻配合双季种植，不仅在一定程度上缓解了当地粮食紧张的难题，也为酿酒业的发展提供大量稻米，使酿酒成为广大城乡人民有利可图的家庭副业，时有“千家沽酒万家盐”的盛况。通过海商运往海外的泉州米酒，和丝绸、陶瓷、茶叶一样，成为东南亚诸国最喜爱的商品之一。

近年来，在泉州府后山发现丰厚的炊事工具和饮食废弃物堆积，它们来自同一生活堆积层，并出土大量小口长腹陶瓶残片，随后小口长腹陶瓶残片和酒库造碾在宋代泉州府衙旧址（今泉州中山公园）出土，从而证明了小口长腹陶瓶是宋人用于装酒的酒瓶。宋元磁灶窑系的金交椅山窑、曾竹山窑等几个窑口都生产小口长腹陶瓶（也称“小口瓶”“梅瓶”），曾竹山窑以专烧小口长腹陶瓶为特色，产量也最大；土尾庵窑还生产青釉“清香”罐（罐子的肩部有戳印楷书竖排两字阳文“清香”），即酒瓮。在苏门答腊岛北部，人们将小口长腹陶瓶称为“唐酒壶”。菲律宾华裔陶瓷专家庄良有，日本学者森本朝子、田中克子分别对在菲律宾和日本发现的宋元时期磁灶窑系小口长腹陶瓶作了研究，这些实物遗存是泉州酒外销的体现。

About brewing industry. Quanzhou introduced and promoted Champa Rice, so as to harvest twice a year by combining its cultivation with that of late-maturing rice. In doing so, the local food shortage was alleviated to some extent, and a large amount of rice was readily available for the brewing industry. Brewing became a profitable family sideline for urban and rural people, and there was a sight of "a thousand families selling liquor and ten thousand families selling salt." Quanzhou rice liquor transported by sea merchants became one of the most popular commodities in the Southeast Asian countries, along with silk, ceramics, and tea.

In recent years, a lot of cooking utensils and food waste remains have been found in Fuhou Hill, all of which come from the same deposit layer, and a large number of small-mouthed, long-bellied pottery bottle fragments have been unearthed. There were also small-mouthed, long-bellied pottery bottle fragments and rollers from liquor storehouse found in the site of administrative office of Quanzhou during the Song Dynasty (present-day Zhongshan Park), which has proved that the small-mouthed, long-bellied pottery bottles were liquor bottles used by the Song people. Several kilns within Cizao Kilns, such as Jinjiaoyishan Kilns and Zengzhushan Kilns, produced small-mouthed, long-bellied pottery bottles (also known as "small-mouthed bottles" or "plum bottles"). Zengzhushan Kilns specialized in small-mouthed, long-bellied pottery bottle production, and had the largest output. Tuwei'an Kilns also produced celadon-glazed "Qingxiang" jars (impressed vertically on the upper part with the characters *Qing* and *Xiang*), which were liquor urns. In the northern part of Sumatra, small-mouthed, long-bellied pottery bottles were called "Tang liquor pots." Zhuang Liangyou, a Chinese Filipino ceramic expert, and Japanese scholars Morimoto Asako and Katsuko Tanaka have studied the small-mouthed, long-bellied pottery bottles produced by Cizao Kilns of the Song and Yuan dynasties found in the Philippines and Japan. These material remains are evidence of Quanzhou's liquor being sold overseas.

磁灶窑酱釉小口长腹陶瓶。（成冬冬 摄）
A brown-glazed small-mouthed, long-bellied pottery bottle from Cizao Kilns. (Photo by Cheng Dongdong)

建筑与石雕业。宋元泉州，城市经济发展繁荣，大批番商胡贾侨居于此，泉州人数大增，城区屡次增拓。宋时，游九功筑翼城，真德秀建东南翼城；元时，偰玉立拓建南城垣，与翼城合并为新罗城，大量的居民建筑与公共设施见证了宋元泉州建筑业的兴盛。泉州遍地花岗岩，丰富的石材为城墙、寺观、宫庙、民居、石桥等建筑，以及宗教造像、石刻、石棺、墓碑等提供了材料，石雕业也得到长足发展并达到新高度。“泉州：宋元中国的世界海洋商贸中心”22处世界遗产点中，清净寺、伊斯兰教圣墓、泉州文庙及学宫、开元寺、天后宫、真武庙等寺观宫庙建筑，德济门遗址、江口码头、石湖码头等公共设施，万寿塔、六胜塔等航标石塔，洛阳桥、安平桥、顺济桥遗址等石桥，九日山祈风石刻、老君岩造像、草庵摩尼光佛造像等造像及石刻17处都是泉州建筑工匠、石雕工匠智慧的结晶。除世界遗产点外，宋元时期泉州著名宗教造像和石刻还有很多，留下丰富多彩的文物史迹。

老君岩造像周边发现的宋代石质建筑构件。（成冬冬 摄）

A stone architectural component from the Song Dynasty discovered around the Statue of Lao Tze. (Photo by Cheng Dongdong)

About construction industry and stone carving industry. Quanzhou was experiencing a time of economic prosperity during the Song and Yuan dynasties. A large number of foreign merchants resided here, and the city's population increased rapidly. The urban area was expanded several times. In the Song Dynasty, You Jiugong constructed the city's *yi cheng* (literally meaning a city's wing) and Zhen Dexiu built its southeastern *yi cheng*. In the Yuan Dynasty, Xie Yuli moved the south city wall further south, thus combining the expanded area and *yi cheng* together into a new *luo cheng* (defensive buildings outside the city center). A large number of buildings and public facilities witnessed the remarkable development of the construction industry in Quanzhou. Granite is abundant in Quanzhou, which provided materials for walls, temples, dwellings, stone bridges, religious sculptures, inscriptions, stone coffins, and tombstones. The stone carving industry also reached new heights of development. Among the 22 world heritage sites of "Quanzhou: Emporium of the World in Song-Yuan China," buildings such as Qingjing Mosque, Islamic Tombs, Confucius Temple and School, Kaiyuan Temple, Tianhou Temple, and Zhenwu Temple, public facilities such as Site of Deji Gate, Estuary Docks, and Shihu Dock, stone towers as navigational marks such as Wanshou Pagoda and Liusheng Pagoda, stone bridges such as Luoyang Bridge, Anping Bridge, and Site of Shunji Bridge, sculptures and stone inscriptions such as Jiuri Mountain Wind-Praying Inscriptions, Statue of Lao Tze, and Statue of Mani in Cao'an Temple, a total of 17 sites, are the crystallization of the wisdom of Quanzhou's construction workers and stone carvers. In addition to the world heritage sites, there are many other famous religious sculptures and inscriptions in Quanzhou during the Song and Yuan dynasties, leaving behind rich and colorful cultural heritage.

伊斯兰教在唐代传入泉州，灵山圣墓是来泉州传教的三贤、四贤的陵墓。宋元时期，泉州有六七座清净寺，现仅存涂门街清净寺，是中世纪阿拉伯、波斯流行的伊斯兰教建筑形式。泉州出土 200 多方伊斯兰教墓碑、墓盖石和伊斯兰教建筑石刻，它们是泉州石雕工匠的艺术杰作，也是中阿文化交流的珍贵文物。

泉州已发现的景教石刻有 30 多方，由泉州石匠制作，被称为“刺桐十字架”，它们质地优良、形式多样，有圆拱、尖拱、弧形、长方形四种。雕刻图像富于变化，雕刻的文字有叙利亚文、回鹘文、拉丁文、八思巴文、汉文。

Islam was introduced to Quanzhou during the Tang Dynasty, and the Islamic Tombs in Lingshan Hill are the final resting places of two Muslims who came to Quanzhou to preach. During the Song and Yuan dynasties, there were six or seven Qingjing mosques in Quanzhou. Only the Qingjing Mosque in Tumen Street still exists today, which is a typical Islamic architectural form popular in medieval Arabia and Persia. Over 200 Islamic tombstones, tomb covers, and stone carvings of Islamic buildings have been unearthed in Quanzhou. They are the masterpieces by Quanzhou's stone carvers and precious cultural relics representing China-Arab cultural exchanges.

Over 30 Nestorian stone carvings have been discovered in Quanzhou, all made by Quanzhou craftsmen, which are referred to as "Zayton Crosses." They are of good quality with diverse forms, including circular arch, pointed arch, arc ones and rectangular ones. The carved images are varied, and the carved inscriptions include Syrian, Uighur, Latin, Phags-pa, and Chinese characters.

元至元十八年（1281），印度泰米尔人在泉州建造了印度教寺院番佛寺。泉州发现的印度教石刻有300多方，有故事石刻、龛状石构件、神像、神殿台基石、蛇形图案纹石，以及各种形式的柱头、柱础、楣梁、门楣、门框石、须弥座等。这些石刻是迄今为止在中国发现的唯一一批印度教寺遗存。泉州发现的印度教石雕，其故事内容系出于古代侨居泉州的外国人之授意，而雕刻艺术及风格，则受到泉州石匠的深刻影响。石刻上常可以看到素为我国人民喜爱的传统图案，例如双凤朝牡丹、狮子戏球、海棠、菊花、母鹿教子等；哥林多式柱头石、半人半兽柱础石、半鸟半兽门楣石、人面狮身间柱石则体现了浓厚的古希腊艺术风格；而用蛇作为图案的门框建筑石构件代表着印度风格。这些印度教神庙、祭坛的遗物，是中国与印度、希腊之间文化交流的物证。

In 1281, Tamils from India built Fanfo Temple, a Hindu-style temple, in Quanzhou. Over 300 Hindu stone carvings have been discovered in Quanzhou, including story carvings, niche stone components, sculptures of deities, temple base stones, stones with snake pattern, and various forms of column heads, column bases, architraves, lintels, door frame stones, and sumeru pedestals. These stone carvings are the only relics of Hindu-style temples discovered in China to date. The Hindu stone carvings discovered in Quanzhou depict stories that were inspired by foreigners who once lived in Quanzhou, while their artistry and style were deeply influenced by Quanzhou's stone carvers. Traditional Chinese patterns are common on these stone carvings, such as paired phoenixes and peonies, lions playing with a ball, begonias, chrysanthemums, and deer teaching their babies. Corinthian stone column heads, half-man and half-beast stone column bases, half-bird and half-beast stone lintels, column stones in the shape of a lion's body and a human head exhibit ancient Greek artistic style. One can also see Indian-style door frame architectural components with snake pattern. These relics of Hindu-style temples and altars are tangible evidence of cultural exchanges between China, India, and Greece.

宋代泉州还掀起了史无前例的“造桥热”，江河溪流之上、岛屿陆地之间，从东南海滨到内陆山区，都建起许多石桥，仅宋代就有139座，不仅完善了城乡交通系统，还推动了泉州海外贸易的发展。其中，洛阳桥和安平桥名列中国十大古桥。

“泉州：宋元中国的世界海洋商贸中心”22处世界遗产点中与建筑和石雕业有关的古迹，很多都拥有“世界之最”或是“中国之最”，在宋元中国留下了浓墨重彩的一笔，为泉州赢得“隋唐看西安，宋元看泉州，明清看北京”的美誉。

During the Song Dynasty, Quanzhou witnessed an unprecedented "bridge-building fever." Many stone bridges were built over rivers, streams, and between islands and land, from southeastern coastline to inland mountainous areas. There were 139 stone bridges built during the Song Dynasty alone, which not only improved the urban and rural transportation system but also promoted the development of Quanzhou's overseas trade. Luoyang Bridge and Anping Bridge are among the top ten ancient bridges in China.

Among the 22 world heritage sites in Quanzhou, known as the Emporium of the World in Song-Yuan China, many are related to architecture and stone carving industry, and many of them distinguished themselves as the best of the world or the best of China. They have left a profound impact during the Song and Yuan dynasties, earning Quanzhou the reputation of "knowing Song-Yuan China by looking at Quanzhou," while people are knowing Sui-Tang China by looking at Xi'an, and knowing Ming-Qing (1368—1911) China by looking at Beijing.

文身。宋元泉州的文身深受东南亚居民和印度居民的喜爱，他们不远千里专程到泉州文身。文身是用锐石、动植物的刺或刀、针等工具，在身体某个部位刻画出花纹或符号，再渗入颜色，以便终身保存的一种身体装饰。断发文身是闽越族的习俗之一。古代越人及其后裔，文身的大多是居于海滨水际和操舟弄水之人，古籍中有“断发文身，以避蛟龙之害”的说法。宋元时期，泉州的文身技师技艺出众，吸引了许多外国人来这里文身。汪大渊在《岛夷志略》中曾提到一个和文身有关的故事：菲律宾有一男子曾搭乘远洋商船到泉州经商，喜欢上了泉州文身，就花钱做了。他回国后，国人以尊长之礼对待他，他的身份和地位大大提高。

About tattoos. Quanzhou's tattooing was highly popular among Southeast Asian and Indian people during the Song and Yuan dynasties. They would travel a long distance to get tattoos in Quanzhou. Tattoos are a form of body adornment where patterns or symbols are etched onto a specific part of the body using sharp stones, spines of plants or animals, knives, needles, or other tools, and then colored with ink to last all one's life. The practice of cutting hair and getting tattoos was one of the customs of the Minyue people. As for ancient Yue people and their descendants, those who got tattoos were mainly ones who lived by the sea or operated boats and sailed along waters. There are historical records of the practice of "cutting hair and getting tattoos to avoid being hurt by *jiao long* (a mysterious creature in Chinese mythology)." In the Song and Yuan dynasties, Quanzhou's tattoo artists were highly skilled, attracting many foreigners to the city to get tattoos. Wang Dayuan shared a story related to tattoos in his *A Brief Account of Island Inhabitants*: a man from the Philippines came to Quanzhou to engage in trade and found himself interested in tattooing. He spent money to get one and, when he returned home, he was treated with great respect and his status was greatly elevated.

宋元泉州手工业把握了良好的资源优势和技术优势，因地制宜进行合理布局，陶瓷业、矿冶业、纺织业、制茶业、制盐业、造船业、食品加工业、制糖业、酿酒业、建筑与石雕业、文身等诸多产业齐齐开花，产品种类多、质量好、工艺精，深受喜爱。

雅各·德安科纳、马可·波罗和伊本·白图泰向世界分享了他们眼中这座城市的魅力，他们曾近距离接触陶瓷、丝绸、茶叶这些备受海外市场青睐的外销商品，也曾搭乘出入泉州的海船欣赏沿途风光，见了奇货万种，望了商船千帆，他们将宋元泉州手工业发展的盛况写入游记，是宋元泉州制造的代言人，推动宋元泉州制造扬名世界。

Quanzhou's handcraft industry in Song-Yuan period made good use of its resource advantages and technological advantages, and planned reasonable layout according to local conditions. Many industries such as ceramics industry, mining and smelting, textiles, tea industry, salt production, shipbuilding, food processing, sugar industry, brewing industry, construction and stone carving, tattooing, etc., grew and flourished, making a wide variety of products that were of good quality, showed exquisite craftsmanship, and were deeply loved.

Jacob D'Ancona, Marco Polo, and Ibn Battuta shared the charm of this city with the world. They had once been close to ceramics, silk, and tea which were highly favored by overseas markets. They had also taken ships to and from Quanzhou, admiring the scenery along the way and observing a wide variety of exotic goods and numerous merchant ships. They wrote about the prosperous development of the handcraft industry in Quanzhou during the Song and Yuan dynasties in their travelogues. They were the "brand ambassadors" for Quanzhou products during the Song and Yuan dynasties, making the products known to the world.

陶瓷铜铁饶足过洋

Abundant Ceramics, Copper and Iron Products Had Been Exported

把釉色留给世界的磁灶窑

Cizao Kilns Presenting Glaze Colors to the World

马可·波罗曾代言的德化窑

Dehua Kilns Spoken Highly of by Marco Polo

安溪青阳下草埔冶铁遗址

Xiacaopu Iron Production Site of Qingyang Village in Anxi

走向世界的宋元“泉州造”陶瓷器

Ceramics Made in Song-Yuan Quanzhou Famous Worldwide

安溪青阳下草埔冶铁遗址。（陈晓东 摄）
Xiacaopu Iron Production Site of Qingyang Village in Anxi. (Photo by Chen Xiaodong)

千年前，在中国的东南之滨，有一个海港城市，因城中遍植刺桐树，被前来经商贸易的万国商人称为“刺桐”，这个城市就是泉州。那时，刺桐城是世界海洋商品贸易的中心，是一座“光明之城”；刺桐港是万国商人和旅行家眼中的“东方第一大港”，是繁华的贸易中枢和热火朝天的商品产地，港口与腹地联动发展，繁盛长达 400 年。

走进梅溪之畔，磁灶金交椅山窑址映入眼帘，4 处龙窑遗址和 1 处作坊遗址装点着紫帽山南麓，我们仿佛能看到千年前窑工们摞砖覆土、结穹顶、安窑床的场景。一条条窑炉沿山坡而上，如卧龙般蛰伏于苍翠山林间。脚下厚重的瓷土，被窑工们以巧手化成各种日用器皿，再经过刻划剔花、彩绘点染、施妆补底，最后入窑装烧，繁忙而有序。

About a thousand years ago, there was a seaport on the southeastern coast of China, which was called "Zayton" by foreign merchants who came here for trade due to the abundance of the erythrina variegata trees in the city. This city is Quanzhou. At that time, the city was the center of world maritime trade, known as "the City of Light." The port was considered "the Largest Port in the East" by foreign traders and travelers, and was a bustling commercial hub and a thriving production area of commodities. The port and hinterland developed in tandem, and they continued to flourish for 400 years.

Walking along the Meixi Stream, we can see Jinjiaoyishan Kilns. The ruins of four loong-shaped kilns and one workshop decorate the southern foothills of Mount Zimao. It feels as if we can see the scenes of kiln workers stacking bricks, piling soil, constructing domes, and setting up kiln beds a thousand years ago. Rows of kilns ascended along the mountain slope, hidden among the lush green forests like dormant loongs. The thick porcelain clay under the feet was skillfully transformed by the kiln workers into various daily utensils. After being carved or incised or cut, painted, and coated with engobe, they were finally loaded into the kilns for firing, creating a busy and orderly production scene.

西北部的戴云山雄奇险峻，广袤的山区拥抱着德化龙浔、三班，流水潺潺的上寮溪两侧，尾林窑与内坂窑隔溪相望。溯溪而上，溪南岸宽敞处，水碓坑、淘洗池、臼坑等作坊遗迹清晰可见。“村南村北春雨晴，东家西家地碓声”，担任归德场长的颜仁郁笔下千家万户烧制陶瓷的情景，穿越千年，绽放在眼前。

安溪青阳点缀着五阆山余脉，走进远离尘嚣的安溪青阳下草埔冶铁遗址，思绪便回到千年前的熊熊炉火旁。一拨又一拨铁匠忙前忙后，火星四溅飞蹿，冶炼而出的铁条、铁块等铁器坯件源源不断送出山外，经过短途陆运至渡口上船转水运，由西溪入晋江，抵达泉州港。

The magnificent and steep Mount Daiyun lies in the northwest, with the vast mountainous area embracing Longxun and Sanban in Dehua. Weilin Kilns and Neiban Kilns face each other across the meandering Shangliao Stream. Going upstream, wide open areas on the south bank of the stream reveal the clear remnants of workshops such as base pits of husking machine, washing pools, and mortars. The scene of thousands of households producing ceramics in Guide (former name of Dehua), described by Yan Renyu, the magistrate of Guide, as "the sky clearing after the spring rain in the south and north of the village, the sound of pounding rose from households in the east and west," is now unfolding before our eyes after a thousand years.

Qingyang of Anxi decorated part of the mountain range of the Mount Wulang. Entering Xiacaopu Iron Production Site of Qingyang Village in Anxi, away from the hustle and bustle of the world, one's thoughts fly back to a thousand years ago, when the furnace fire was roaring. Wave after wave of blacksmiths worked tirelessly, sparks flying. Iron bars, iron blocks, and other iron products, which were then transported by land to the ferry, and transferred to water transport. They entered the Jinjiang River from the Xixi Stream, and arrived at Quanzhou Port.

把釉色留给世界的磁灶窑

泉州晋江的磁灶窑是中国古代著名的民窑，也是宋元时期华南沿海重要的外销陶瓷产地。陶瓷生产始于南朝晚期，兴于唐五代，宋元时达到鼎盛，明清时衰落。产品比较粗放，但生产工艺博采众长，因地制宜，独具特色。磁灶窑业在宋元时期生产水平最高，规模也最大，并以泉州港为依托，以海外低端市场为导向，“粗瓷”产品乘着从泉州港启程的商船，大量远销东亚、东南亚、南亚、西亚，最远到达东非。磁灶窑由一处普通的内销民窑，“甚饶足并过洋”，一跃成为宋元时期泉州重要的外销陶瓷生产基地，蜚声海内外。

Cizao Kilns Presenting Glaze Colors to the World

Cizao Kilns in Jinjiang, Quanzhou, are famous ancient folk kilns in China and an important production site for exported ceramics along the southern coast of China during the Song and Yuan dynasties. Their ceramic production began in the late Southern Dynasties, flourished during the Tang Dynasty and Five Dynasties, and reached its peak during the Song and Yuan dynasties, but declined during the Ming and Qing dynasties. The products were relatively rough, but the production process drew on the strengths of many and adjusted according to local conditions, with its own characteristics. During the Song and Yuan dynasties, Cizao Kilns reached their highest production level and the largest scale. They relied on Quanzhou Port and were oriented toward the low-end overseas markets. The "coarse porcelain" products were exported in large quantities to East Asia, Southeast Asia, South Asia, West Asia, and even as far as East Africa, riding on merchant ships departing from Quanzhou Port. Cizao Kilns, originally ordinary kilns oriented toward domestic market, quickly became an important production base for export ceramics in Quanzhou during the Song and Yuan dynasties, gaining fame both domestically and internationally.

磁灶窑址是泉州城郊规模最大的古窑址群，拥有陶瓷生产得天独厚的自然资源。地处紫帽山南麓的丘陵地带，地势由西北向东南倾斜，适于建窑；瓷土资源丰富，可取地土开窑；植被茂密，可就地取柴；梅溪穿境而过，可解决陶瓷生产用水；梅溪流自西北，东折而去，汇于晋江入海，水上交通便捷，舟楫运量大、运费低，低成本解决原材料的供给和产品运输，使得磁灶窑的产品更具市场竞争力。考古调查共发现南朝至清代窑址 26 处，其中宋元时期窑址 12 处，均分布于梅溪两岸的小山坡上。2006 年，磁灶窑址被国务院列入第六批全国重点文物保护单位名单，包含土尾庵窑址、蜘蛛山窑址、童子山窑址和金交椅山窑址 4 处宋元时期的代表性窑址。

The Sites of Cizao Kilns are the largest ancient kiln site group in the suburbs of Quanzhou, richly endowed with natural resources for ceramic production. Located in the hilly area at the southern foot of Mount Zimao, the land slopes southeastward, which was suitable for kiln construction. The clay resources were abundant, allowing of local clay collection. The area was densely forested, providing ample supply of firewood. Meixi Stream flowed through the site, providing water for ceramic production. Meixi Stream flowed from the northwest, turned east, and merged with the Jinjiang River before flowing into the sea, which formed a convenient water transportation route that allowed of large transport capacity and low transportation costs. Cheap raw materials and transportation enabled Cizao Kilns products to be more competitive in the market. A total of 26 kiln sites from the Southern Dynasties to the Qing Dynasty have been discovered in archaeological explorations, among which 12 kiln sites are from the Song and Yuan dynasties, all of which are distributed on the small hillsides on both sides of the Meixi Stream. In 2006, the Sites of Cizao Kilns were listed among the sixth batch of national key cultural relics protection units by the State Council, including four representative kiln sites from the Song and Yuan dynasties, namely Tuwei'an Kilns, Zhizhushan Kilns, Tongzishan Kilns, and Jinjiaoyishan Kilns.

金交椅山窑址及其相连环境全景。（郑文桂 摄）
A panoramic view of the Site of Jinjiaoyishan Kilns and its surroundings. (Photo by Zheng Wengui)

金交椅山窑址。金交椅山窑址在沟边村的金交椅山坡地，东北临梅溪上段，东邻沟边村，西接南安，南靠邱山，山上的草木丛中，宋代青瓷片及窑具散布成堆。金交椅山窑址于20世纪60年代考古调查时发现，当时的窑址遗物堆积主要分布于金交椅山的北坡和西坡，面积达万余平方米。金交椅山窑址的考古发掘分两期进行，第一期的发掘时间为2002年6月至8月，第二期的发掘时间为2003年2月至6月，两期发掘面积共计约1,500平方米，发现和揭露有叠压打破关系的龙窑遗址4条（Y1—Y4）和作坊遗址1处（F1）。金交椅山窑址的作坊、密集分布的4条龙窑及其所在的山体和水系，构成陶瓷生产的完整体系。

About the Site of Jinjiaoyishan Kilns. The Site of Jinjiaoyishan Kilns is located on the slope of Jinjiaoyi Hill in Goubian Village, with its northeastern part facing the upper reaches of Meixi Stream, its eastern part close to Goubian Village, its western part bordering Nan'an, and its southern part adjacent to Qiushan Hill. In the tussocks of the hill, there are scattered piles of celadon shards and kiln facilities from the Song Dynasty. The Site of Jinjiaoyishan Kilns was discovered during the archaeological investigations in the 1960s. At that time, the relics of the kiln site were mainly distributed on the north and west slopes of Jinjiaoyi Hill, spanning an area of more than 10,000 square meters. The archaeological excavation of the Site of Jinjiaoyishan Kilns was carried out in two phases. The first phase was in 2002, from June to August, and the second phase was in 2003, from February to June. The total excavation area of the two phases was about 1,500 square meters, where four overlapping loong-shaped kilns (labeled "Y1—Y4") and one workshop (labeled "F1") were found and exposed. The workshop, the densely spaced four loong-shaped kilns, and the hill and waters where they were located formed a complete system for ceramic production.

金交椅山窑址局部。（成冬冬 摄）
Part of the Site of Jinjiaoyishan Kilns. (Photo by Cheng Dongdong)

Y1 位于金交椅山西坡北侧，平面呈直长条形，窑头方向 310°；窑头、窑尾均遭破坏，仅存中段残斜长 13.6 米，水平残长 13 米，宽 2.2—2.3 米；窑壁由红砖或土坯砖砌成，窑壁残高 0—0.36 米，窑底烧结层厚 0.04—0.06 米；窑门共发现 7 处（北侧 3 处，南侧 4 处）；护窑墙以石块叠砌于窑壁外侧，保存较好的有 4 段；西南侧的上窑路保存稍好；窑壁内侧还保存数处可判明是投柴孔位置的痕迹。推断其龙窑窑炉经两期使用，烧造青瓷、酱黑釉器，年代约为北宋末至南宋。

Y2 位于金交椅山西北侧，平面呈长条状，窑头方向 333°；窑炉受损程度较重，水平残长 58.78 米，残斜长 60.88 米，宽 0.78—2.28 米；窑墙残高 0.04—0.68 米，窑底前、中段坡度约 16°，窑顶是楔形砖横向错缝立砌；窑头残存火膛后壁、两侧窑墙（有 3 重，为早晚 3 期）；窑门共发现 12 处，护窑墙为大石垒砌，南侧窑墙外的上窑路为红褐土、瓷片堆垫；窑壁内侧保存 5 处可判明是投柴孔的痕迹。Y2 分为三期，烧造青瓷、酱黑釉器，年代约为北宋末至南宋。

Y3 位于金交椅山西坡中北部，平面呈直长条形，窑头方向 292°，窑头、窑尾及中段被破坏，水平残长 40.02 米，残斜长 41.12 米，宽 2—2.36 米，窑底坡度均为 14°，尚存出烟室的一小段前壁，残长 0.5 米，厚 0.12—0.14 米，高 0.18 米；共发现 7 处窑门；护窑墙较完整的有 5 段，为石块、残砖砌成；南侧的上窑路保存较好。推断 Y3 为两期使用，烧造青瓷、酱黑釉器，约为五代末至北宋末。

Y4 位于西北坡，窑炉呈长条形、方向 284°，窑头被破坏，窑尾保存北侧的一部分，残斜长 44.5 米，水平长 42.7 米，宽 1.6—2.2 米；窑壁残高 0.1—0.3 米，窑底平均坡度 15°；窑门共计 14 处（北侧 8 处，南侧 6 处）；窑炉南侧用石块垒成护窑墙；窑旁路面均为红褐色窑沙杂少量瓷片、瓦片。Y4 为两期，烧造青瓷、酱黑釉器，年代约为北宋末至南宋。

Kiln Y1 is located on the north slope of Jinjiaoyi Hill, with a straight rectangular shape in plan view and a kiln head at an angle of 310°. Both ends of the kiln had been damaged, with only an extant section being 13.6 meters in oblique length, 13 meters in horizontal length, and 2.2 to 2.3 meters in width. The kiln wall was made of red bricks or adobe bricks, with its remaining part being 0 to 0.36 meters in height, and its sintered layer at the bottom of the kiln being 0.04 to 0.06 meters in thickness. There are 7 kiln doors found in total (3 on the north side and 4 on the south side). The protective wall was built with stones outside the kiln wall, with 4 well-preserved sections. The road beside the kiln furnace on the southwest side is relatively better preserved. Several traces of the firewood entrance can be identified on the inner side of the kiln wall. It is inferred that the furnace of the loong-shaped kiln was used for two phases to produce celadon and brownish-black glazed ware (fired with iron-containing glaze at high temperatures), dated from the late Northern Song Dynasty to the Southern Song Dynasty.

Kiln Y2 is located on the northwest side of Jinjiaoyi Hill, with a rectangular shape in plan view and a kiln head at an angle of 333°. The furnace is heavily damaged, with the extant section being 58.78 meters in horizontal length, 60.88 meters in oblique length, and 0.78 to 2.28 meters in width. The remaining part of the kiln wall is 0.04 to 0.68 meters in height. The front and middle sections of the bottom of the kiln is at an angle of about 16°. The top of the kiln was constructed with wedge-shaped bricks laid horizontally and in an interlaced way. As for the front part of the kiln, the back wall of the kiln entrance and the kiln walls on both sides (3 layers, representing three different periods) remain. A total of 12 kiln doors have been found, and the protective wall was constructed with large stones. The road beside the kiln furnace on the south side of the kiln wall was built with reddish-brown soil and ceramic shards. Five traces of the firewood entrance have been identified on the inner side of the kiln wall. Y2 was used for three phases of production to make celadon and brownish-black glazed ware, dated from the late Northern Song Dynasty to the Southern Song Dynasty.

Kiln Y3 is located in the middle and north section of the west slope of Jinjiaoyi Hill, with a straight rectangular shape in plan view and a kiln head at an angle of 292°. The kiln head, the smoke outlet, and the middle section are damaged, with the extant part being 40.02 meters in horizontal length, 41.12 meters in oblique length, and 2 to 2.36 meters in width. The kiln bottom slopes at an angle of 14°, with a small segment of the front wall of the smoke chamber still remaining, 0.5 meters in length, 0.12 to 0.14 meters in thickness, and 0.18 meters in height. A total of seven kiln doors have been found, and there are five relatively intact sections of the protective wall, constructed with stones and bricks. The road beside the kiln furnace on the south side is relatively well-preserved. It is inferred that Y3 was used for two phases to produce celadon and brownish-black glazed ware, dated from the late Five Dynasties to the late Northern Song Dynasty.

Kiln Y4 is located on the northwest slope, with the kiln furnace in the shape of a long strip and at an angle of 284°. The kiln head was damaged, while a part of the north side of the smoke outlet was preserved. The extant part is 44.5 meters in oblique length, 42.7 meters long horizontally, and 1.6 to 2.2 meters in width. The remaining part of kiln walls are 0.1 to 0.3 meters high. The kiln bottom slopes at an angle of 15° averagely. There are 14 kiln doors (8 on the north side and 6 on the south side) found in total. A stone wall was built on the south side of the kiln furnace for protection. The road beside the kiln is covered with reddish-brown kiln sand mixed with a small number of porcelain shards and tiles. Y4 was used for two phases and produced celadon and brownish-black glazed ware, dated from the late Northern Song Dynasty to the Southern Song Dynasty.

Y1、Y2、Y3、Y4出土遗物以陶瓷器和窑具标本为主，还有少量制瓷工具。出土的陶瓷器主要有青釉、酱釉、素胎三种，器类不多，皆为生活用器。胎质大多夹有细砂，胎色多呈浅灰色或灰白色。其中，青釉器占了半数以上，釉色以青灰、青绿、青黄为主，大多数釉面莹润，玻璃质感强，开细碎冰裂纹。器型以执壶为主，还有水注、罐、碗、碟、盒、瓶、器盖、灯盏、盏托、网坠、砚台、香薰、漏斗、陶车零件等。装饰技法有划花、印花，花纹有弦纹、宽条纹、草叶纹、篦划纹、卷叶纹、菊花纹、瓜棱纹、卷草缠枝纹、莲瓣纹等。金交椅山窑址出土的窑具多数有刻划符号或文字，如1至4道的竖条以及“吴”“李”“王二”等。

金交椅山窑址出土的酱釉梅瓶。（晋江博物馆 供图）
A brown-glazed plum bottle unearthed from the Site of Jinjiaoyishan Kilns. (Courtesy of Jinjiang Museum)

Unearthed artifacts from Y1, Y2, Y3, and Y4 are mainly ceramic ware and kiln facilities samples, besides a small number of porcelain-making tools. The unearthed ceramics mainly include celadon, brown-glazed ware, and unglazed ware, and there are not many types, all of which are daily utensils. Most of them contain fine sand, and their colors are mostly light gray or grayish white. Among them, celadon ware accounts for more than half of the total, with glaze colors mainly being bluish gray, bluish green, and bluish yellow. Most of them boast a lustrous surface with a strong glass-like texture, bearing fine, scattered ice crack patterns. They are mainly pitchers, besides water injectors, jars, bowls, dishes, boxes, bottles, utensil covers, lamp stands, cup stands, weights, inkstones, incense burners, funnels, pottery cart parts, and so on. Decorative techniques include incising and molding, and the patterns include string patterns, wide stripe patterns, grass-leaf patterns, incised comb patterns, scrolling leaf patterns, chrysanthemum patterns, melon ridge patterns, interlocking leaf scroll patterns, lotus petal patterns, etc. Most kiln facilities unearthed from the Site of Jinjiaoyishan Kilns have carved and incised signs or characters, such as vertical stripes from one stripe to four stripes, and characters like "Wu," "Li," "Wang Er," and so on.

金交椅山窑址出土的青釉碗。（晋江博物馆 供图）
A celadon-glazed bowl unearthed from the Site of Jinjiaoyishan Kilns. (Courtesy of Jinjiang Museum)

金交椅山窑址出土的酱釉罐。（晋江博物馆 供图）
A brown-glazed jar unearthed from the Site of Jinjiaoyishan Kilns. (Courtesy of Jinjiang Museum)

作坊遗址（F1）位于金交椅山北坡西侧的坡地上，介于 Y1 与 Y3 之间，面积约 250 平方米。地势东高西低、分 6 个梯状台地，发掘总面积约 200 平方米，发现贮泥池 1 处、沉淀池 1 处、柱洞 3 个、磉墩 4 个、灰坑 6 处、陶缸 10 口、路面 1 段；推断该作坊是拉坯、上釉的工作场所，使用年代约为五代至南宋。出土遗物以陶瓷器及窑具标本为主，还有少量的制瓷工具。出土的陶瓷器主要有青釉器、酱釉器、素胎器和少量陶器，种类不多，皆为生活用器。胎质大多夹有细砂，胎色多呈浅灰色或灰白色。器形主要有执壶、水注、碗、盏、碟、钵、小罐、器盖、灯盏、灯托、漏斗、瓷塑等。装饰技法主要是刻划和模印，纹样主要有凹、凸弦纹，螺旋形弦纹，宽条纹，六瓣花形，十瓣花形，八瓣瓜棱形，宝相花等。

The workshop site (F1) is located on the west side of the northern slope of Jinjiaoyi Hill between Y1 and Y3, with an area of about 250 square meters. The land is higher in the east and lower in the west, terraced into six platforms. The excavation area is about 200 square meters, where one mud storage pool, one precipitation tank, three holes for column placement, four column bases, six ash pits, ten pottery vats, and one section of road were revealed. It is inferred that the workshop was a place for shaping and glazing, dated from the Five Dynasties to the Southern Song Dynasty. The unearthed artifacts are mainly ceramic ware and kiln facilities, with a small number of porcelain-making tools. The unearthed ceramics mainly include celadon, brown-glazed ware, greenware, and a small amount of pottery, with not many types. All of them are daily utensils. Most of them contain fine sand, and their colors are mostly light gray or grayish white. They are mainly pitchers, water injectors, bowls, cups, dishes, small jars, utensil covers, lamp stands, lamp holders, funnels, and porcelain sculptures. The decorative techniques mainly include carving, incising and stamping, and the patterns mainly include concave and convex string patterns, spiral string patterns, wide stripe patterns, six-petal flower shapes, ten-petal flower shapes, eight-petal melon ridge shapes, and auspicious composite flower shapes.

金交椅山窑址作坊遗址。（成冬冬 摄）

The workshop site of the Site of Jinjiaoyishan Kilns. (Photo by Cheng Dongdong)

土尾庵窑址。土尾庵窑址在岭畔村的梅溪南岸小山坡，东邻后宅村，西接水尾宫，南接蜘蛛山。1995 年，福建省博物馆考古部选择在山顶部及其东北角发掘，布探方 4 个，尺寸均为 5m×5m，发掘面积共 100 平方米，发现龙窑遗址一处，出土一批陶瓷器和窑具标本。出土陶瓷器的器类以日常生活用品为主，供器、陈设器亦有相当数量。除常见的生活用品如碗、盘、碟、盏、杯、钵、盆、罐、壶、盏托、水注、执壶之外，还有灯、炉、瓶、枕、砚、急须、军持、花盆、扑满、香炉、鸟食罐、腰鼓以及神像（如力士）、动物模型等。釉色有青黄釉，绿釉或黄、绿釉兼施，青、黑釉兼施（如青口黑釉盏、内青釉外黑釉的碗等）以及青釉褐斑、釉下褐彩等。装饰技法有刻划、剔刻、模印、堆贴、雕塑、绘画等多种。纹样和图案有龙、凤、龟、蟾、狮、莲花、牡丹、寿桃、蔓草、荷叶、卷云、云雷、几何形、弦纹等，其中以各式龙纹最有特色。推断土尾庵窑址的年代为南宋晚期至元代。

About the Site of Tuwei'an Kilns. The Site of Tuwei'an Kilns is located on a small slope on the south bank of Meixi Stream in Lingpan Village, with its eastern part facing Houzhai Village, its western part adjacent to Shuiwei Palace, and its southern part close to Zhizhu Hill. In 1995, the department of archaeological studies of the Fujian Provincial Museum conducted excavations on the top of the hill and its northeast corner, with four excavation units measuring 5m by 5m each and a total excavation area of 100 square meters. A loong-shaped kiln site was discovered and a batch of ceramic artifacts and kiln facilities were unearthed. The unearthed ceramic artifacts are mostly daily utensils, besides a considerable number of ceremonial utensils and decorative artifacts. In addition to common household items such as bowls, plates, dishes, cups, basins, jars, pots, cup stands, water injectors, and pitchers, there are also lamps, stoves, bottles, pillows, inkstones, *ji xu* (teapots), kendis, flower pots, moneyboxes, incense burners, bird food jars, waist drums, and deity figurines (such as warriors) and animal models. The glaze colors include bluish yellow, green, or yellow combined with green, and celadon combined with black (such as black-glazed tea cups with celadon lip, bowls with celadon glaze on the inner side and black glaze on the outer side, etc.), and one can also see celadon-glazed ware with brown spots, ware in underglaze brown, etc. Decoration techniques include carving and incising, cutting, molding, embossing, sculpting, and painting. Patterns include loongs, phoenixes, tortoises, toads, lions, lotuses, peonies, longevity peach buns, weeds, lotus leaves, rolling clouds, clouds and thunders, geometric designs, and strings, among which various loong patterns were the most distinctive. It is inferred that the Site of Tuwei'an Kilns existed from the late Southern Song Dynasty to the Yuan Dynasty.

蜘蛛山窑址。蜘蛛山窑址在梅溪南畔的岭畔村蜘蛛山上，与土尾庵窑毗邻。至20世纪80年代，遗物堆积范围仅存600余平方米。其出土器物风格与土尾庵窑的产品较接近，有青釉器、酱黑釉器、绿釉器以及素胎器等，胎质基本相同，一般质地较粗松，胎色呈灰、灰褐，施釉不到底。器形种类较多，有碗、盏、碟、钵、盅、杯、罐、执壶、水注、盆、炉、盏托、器盖、瓶、腰鼓等。装饰技法有刻划、模印、绘画、贴塑等，纹样有弦纹、曲线纹、水波纹、直条纹、莲瓣纹、菊花纹、荷花纹、牡丹纹、瓜棱纹、缠枝花纹、草叶纹、云雷纹等。此外，多次发现器物中有“程”姓的铭文，如瓦板和托钵刻划有“程干”“程二”字样，外销军持的底部记有“程家工夫”等，这种窑工记号说明宋元时期已经出现了搭烧和生产责任制的管理模式。蜘蛛山窑址的黑釉盏、青釉碟、军持等，皆为宋元时期磁灶窑址的典型器物，因此推断蜘蛛山窑址的年代为南宋至元代。

About the Site of Zhizhushan Kilns. The Site of Zhizhushan Kilns is located on the Zhizhu Hill in Lingpan Village on the south bank of Meixi Stream, adjacent to the Site of Tuwei'an Kilns. In the 1980s, the area of the debris pile was only over 600 square meters. The style of artifacts excavated is similar to those produced in the Tuwei'an Kilns. They are mainly celadon-glazed ware, brownish-black glazed ware, green-glazed ware, and unglazed ware. Their textures are basically the same, generally being coarse and loose, and their colors are gray or grayish brown, with partial glazing. There are many types of vessels, including bowls, cups, dishes, jars, pitchers, water injectors, basins, stoves, cup stands, vessel covers, bottles, waist drums, and so on. Decoration techniques include carving and incising, molding, painting, and embossing, with patterns such as strings, curved lines, water ripples, straight stripes, lotus petals, chrysanthemums, lotuses, peonies, melon ridges, interlocking vegetal scrolls, grass leaves, and clouds and thunders. In addition, inscriptions bearing the surname "Cheng" havc been found on several artifacts, such as "Cheng Gan" and "Cheng Er" on tile plates and bowls, and "Cheng Jia Gong Fu" on the bottom of exported kendis. These kiln worker marks demonstrate that cooperative firing and production responsibility system had appeared during the Song-Yuan period. Black-glazed cups, celadon-glazed dishes, and kendis from Zhizhushan Kilns are typical artifacts of the Sites of Cizao Kilns during Song-Yuan period, so it is inferred that the Site of Zhizhushan Kilns existed from the Southern Song Dynasty to the Yuan Dynasty.

蜘蛛山窑址出土的绿釉执壶。（成冬冬 摄）
A green-glazed pitcher unearthed from the Site of Zhizhushan Kilns. (Photo by Cheng Dongdong)

童子山窑址。童子山窑址位于梅溪北岸，东南距横跨梅溪的下板桥约100米。窑址依山傍水，山高约40米，窑址遗物散布面积达万余平方米。童子山窑址历经多次考古调查。1977年，泉州海外交通史博物馆的磁灶窑考古调查小组对童子山窑址进行小规模的试掘，发掘一条长4米、宽2米的探沟。采集到的陶瓷器标本主要是青釉器和素胎器，二者的胎质类似，均为陶质，较粗松，呈灰或深灰色；釉色多偏青黄，一般器内满釉，器外施半釉，底部露胎，有的在釉下用褐彩绘画或标文字等。主要器形是各式盆，其他还有缸、罐、壶、洗、枕、陶拍、器盖、器座和建筑材料等。釉色有黄、绿、青、青黄、青绿、青灰、黑和酱色等。装饰技法有划花、印花、堆花和绘花等，花纹有龙纹、缠枝花纹、莲瓣纹、牡丹花纹等。童子山窑的产品大量外销，居各窑之首。其中，釉下彩黄釉铁绘花纹大盆（盘）、军持、青釉碟等器物专供外销，值得一提的是，釉下彩黄釉铁绘花纹盆（盘）开创了泉州釉下彩绘之先河，闻名海内外。根据考古调查和试掘结果，推断童子山一号窑的年代为宋元时期。

童子山窑址出土的釉下彩黄釉铁绘大盆。（吴金鹏 摄）
A large basin with underglaze yellow using iron-containing colorant unearthed from Site of Tongzishan Kilns. (Photo by Wu Jinpeng)

About the Site of Tongzishan Kilns. The Site of Tongzishan Kilns is located on the north bank of Meixi Stream, about 100 meters away from the Xiaban Bridge that spans Meixi Stream in the southeast. The site is cuddled by the hill and the stream. The hill is about 40 meters high and the debris of the kiln site scattered covers an area of over 10,000 square meters. Several archaeological investigations of the site have been conducted. In 1977, a small-scale exploratory trench, 4 meters long and 2 meters wide, was opened up by Cizao Kilns Archaeological Investigation Team from Quanzhou Maritime Museum. The specimens of the ceramic artifacts mainly consist of celadon-glazed ware and unglazed ware. They have similar clay bodies that were relatively coarse and loose, and gray or deep gray in color. Most of them are bluish-yellow glazed, with the interior of the vessel fully glazed and the exterior partially glazed, leaving the bottom of the clay body exposed. Some vessels are decorated with underglaze brown paintings and texts. They are mainly basins of various types, besides tanks, jars, pots, pillows, pottery boards, vessel covers, base stands and building materials. Their glaze colors include yellow, green, celadon, bluish-yellow, bluish-green, bluish-gray, black, and brown, etc. The decorative techniques include incising, molding, embossing, and painting, and the patterns included loongs, interlocking vegetal scrolls, lotus petals, and peonies. The products of Tongzishan Kilns were widely exported, and the quantity of the exports ranked first among all kilns. Large basins (plates) with underglaze yellow using iron-containing colorant and floral pattern, kendis, and celadon-glazed dishes were exclusively for export. It is worth mentioning that the basins (plates) with underglaze yellow using iron-containing colorant and floral pattern pioneered the underglaze method in Quanzhou, and became famous both at home and abroad. According to the results of archaeological investigations and exploratory excavations, it is inferred that the Tongzishan Kiln No. 1 existed during the Song and Yuan dynasties.

经营理念和商业模式。勤劳智慧的泉州人充分利用优势资源，创新窑业技术和经营管理模式，提升磁灶窑产品的市场竞争力和占有率。窑场科学选址，有效利用本地丰富的自然资源降低了产业链成本。磁灶窑的考古资料表明，宋元时期的 12 处窑址，都分布于梅溪两岸的小山坡且相对集中在三大片区，布局具有科学性，同一片区窑场之间和不同片区形成相对分工又紧密联系的生产格局，便于技术交流，生产特色产品，成功地扩大了影响。

About business philosophy and business model. The hardworking and intelligent people of Quanzhou fully utilized their advantageous resources, and innovated new kiln technology and management models, thus enhancing the market competitiveness and market share of their Cizao Kilns products. Scientific site selection for kilns and effective use of abundant local natural resources had lowered the costs. Archaeological data on Cizao Kilns indicates that 12 kiln sites in the Song and Yuan dynasties were distributed on the small hills on the both sides of Meixi Stream, relatively concentrated in three major areas, and with a scientific layout. Between different production areas as well as different kiln sites within the same area, a production pattern with a relatively clear division of labor and close connections was formed, making it easy for technological exchange and production of specialties. They successfully made their name.

金交椅山窑址总平面图。（泉州市文物考古研究所 供图）
The site plan of the Site of Jinjiaoyishan Kilns. (Courtesy of Quanzhou Institute of Cultural Relics and Archaeology)

例如，同属今岭畔村片区的蜘蛛山窑、土尾庵窑、童子山一号窑和山坪窑四处窑场，风格较接近，生产的产品种类多样、釉色丰富、工艺水平较高，而且在海外发现的外销产品也最多，应是同一时期同一片区窑业技术相互影响的缘故。又如，在同属今前埔村片区的金交椅山窑、曾竹山窑和溪墘山窑三处窑场中，金交椅山窑主要烧制执壶，曾竹山窑烧制碗，溪墘山窑烧制小口瓶，产品生产相对分工，各有特色。这种模式下，主打产品优势明显，有助于提高市场占有率；同时，单一产品专业化有利于形成更高的劳动效率，并降低成本。可以说，这种相对集中的选址布局就是今天工业园区的雏形。

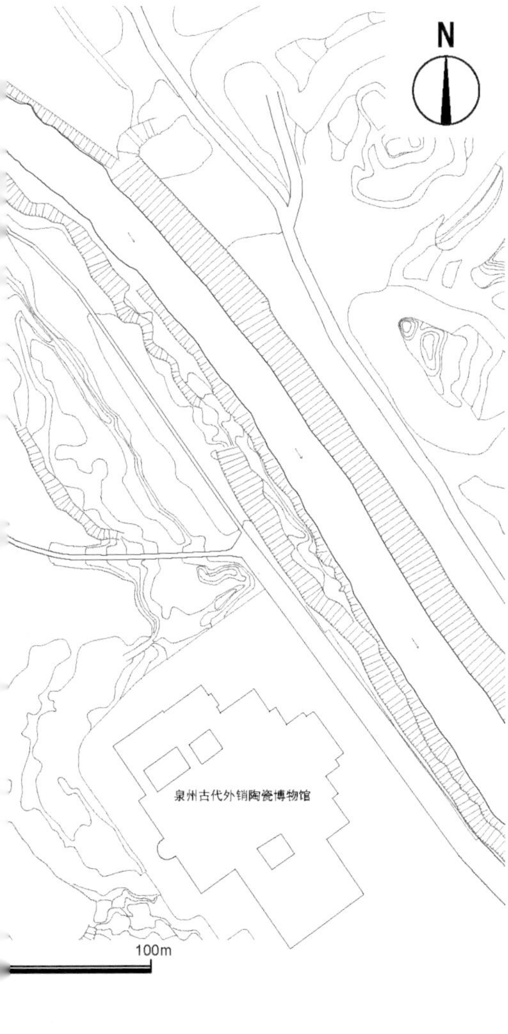

For example, the four kiln sites in present-day Lingpan Village area, namely Zhizhushan Kilns, Tuwei'an Kilns, Tongzishan Kiln No. 1 and Shanping Kilns, were similar in style, and all of them produced a wide range of products with rich glaze colors and high craftsmanship, as well as the largest number of exports found overseas. This is probably because they had applied similar techniques, existing during the same period and in the same region. Similarly, in present-day Qianpu Village area where Jinjiaoyishan Kilns, Zengzhushan Kilns, and Xiqianshan Kilns were located, pitchers were mainly produced by Jinjiaoyishan Kilns, bowls were mainly produced by Zengzhushan Kilns, and small-mouthed bottles were mainly produced by Xiqianshan Kilns. The production was relatively specialized, each with its own characteristics. Under this model, the advantages of their featured products were obvious, which was conducive to the increase of market share. At the same time, specializing in a single product is helpful in boosting productivity and reducing costs. We can safely say that this kind of layout is the prototype of today's industrial park.

因“取地土开窑”，磁灶窑存在着本地瓷土质量不高的先天不足，胎质颗粒较粗，不够致密，容易吸水，制作出的产品可以说是“半陶半瓷”。宋代以来，磁灶窑扬长避短、博采众长，探索窑业技术创新，提升市场竞争力。

磁灶窑吸收了名窑的先进工艺，并结合自身特点，在产品种类、釉色和装饰技法上都进行了创新，而不是简单地照搬照抄。例如，土尾庵窑在装饰技法上吸收北方磁州窑的剔花和黄绿釉传统工艺，龙泉窑流行的青釉加点彩工艺，也吸收进来；在产品造型上，借鉴建窑和龙泉窑，黑釉碗主要模仿了建窑建盏，青釉莲瓣碗又与龙泉窑器物相仿。童子山一号窑烧制的釉下彩黄釉铁绘大盆，使用的釉下彩绘工艺融合了唐代长沙铜官窑的技术，在泉州窑业属首创。在福建众多的宋元窑址中，兼收并容多种窑业技术的窑址并不多，磁灶窑是其中最典型的代表。博采众长使磁灶窑克服了当地无优质瓷土的弱势，不仅生产出了琳琅满目的各类瓷器，在装饰技艺上也尽显泉州匠人的聪明才智，使产品能在强手如林的窑业竞争中独树一帜，并凭借靠近泉州港的地理优势远销海外，在外销瓷史上写下了浓墨重彩的一笔。

童子山窑址出土的釉下彩黄釉铁绘大盆。（吴金鹏 摄）

A large basin with underglaze yellow using iron-containing colorant unearthed from the Site of Tongzishan Kilns. (Photo by Wu Jinpeng)

Using local soil to build kilns, Cizao Kilns had an inherent disadvantage, that is, the local porcelain clay was of low quality, with coarse clay particles and low particle density, leading to high moisture absorption. In other words, the products they made were semipottery-semiporcelain. Since the Song Dynasty, Cizao Kilns workers had made use of their strengths and avoided weaknesses, learned from others, and explored technological innovation, so as to enhance their market competitiveness.

Cizao Kilns had learned advanced techniques from famous kilns, while developing their own characteristics, and innovated new product types, glazes, and decoration techniques, rather than simply copying others. Take Tuwei'an Kilns as an example. In terms of decoration techniques, they absorbed the traditional cutting and yellow-and-green glazing of Cizhou Kilns in northern China, and also learned from Longquan Kilns to make celadon-glazed wares with colored splashes. As for product modeling, they learned from Jianyao Kilns and Longquan Kilns, with black-glazed bowls mainly imitating *jian zhan* teacups of Jianyao Kilns, and celadon-glazed bowls with lotus petals pattern resembling Longquan Kilns wares. In addition, the large basins with underglaze yellow using iron-containing colorant from Tongzishan Kiln No. 1 integrated the underglaze painting technique of Tongguan Kilns in Changsha during the Tang Dynasty, which was a pioneering effort in Quanzhou's kiln industry. Among the many Song and Yuan kiln sites in Fujian, Cizao Kilns were one of the few kilns that had integrated multiple kiln technologies. The practice of incorporating various techniques had enabled Cizao Kilns to overcome the limitation of lacking premium porcelain clay. They had not only produced a dazzling array of porcelain, but also applied distinctive decoration techniques which showcased the wisdom of Quanzhou craftsmen. Their products stood out in the fiercely competitive kiln industry and, with the geographical adjacence to Quanzhou Port, had been exported overseas, leaving a splendid chapter in the history of export porcelain.

制坯、施釉和装烧技术也有很大改进。在坯体制作上，除沿袭轮制的技术外，运用了小器形直接模制、大中器形分段模制再粘接等新的制坯技术，坯体的成品率和统一性大大提高，产量得以满足巨大的市场需求；在施釉工艺上，为解决胎质致密性不够、易吸水，以致增加釉料成本的问题，研发了在素胎上施一层白色化妆土再施釉的工艺，减少釉料的吸附，这一工艺成为磁灶窑产品的一大特色；在装烧方面，采用长条形斜坡底龙窑装烧，窑室两侧筑有护窑墙，从原先的明火裸烧发展到部分产品开始采用 M 字形匣钵为主的匣钵装烧，提高了瓷器成品率，同时广泛应用垫具（垫柱、垫圈、垫座等）和间隔器（支钉、垫饼等）等多种窑具，提高了窑内空间利用率，满足扩大产量的需要，提高了经济效益。

There were also significant improvements in the techniques of greenware making, glazing and firing. In terms of greenware making, in addition to the conventional technique of using a pottery wheel, new techniques such as direct modeling of small utensils and segmented modeling of large and medium utensils before bonding components together were used. These techniques greatly improved the yield and helped to make the appearances of the products look more uniform, meeting the enormous market demand. In terms of glazing, to overcome low clay density and high moisture absorption which cost more glaze material, a technique of applying a layer of white engobe on the greenware before glazing was developed, reducing its adsorption of the glaze material, which was what distinguished Cizao Kilns from other kilns. In terms of firing, a long slope-bottomed loong-shaped kiln with protective walls on both sides was used for firing. Some products had been fired by being placed in M-shaped saggers, instead of being exposed to flames, which had increased the yield of porcelain. Various kiln facilities like firing stands (such as cushion pillars, ring-shaped firing stands, support bases, etc.) and spacers (such as support nails, support dishes, etc.) were widely used, which allowed of more efficient use of space, thus meeting the need to increase output and achieve better economic return.

新颖的经营管理模式也是宋元窑场的制胜法宝。在蜘蛛山窑址中，多次发现器物上有“程”姓的铭文，专家认为这是窑工的记号。关于窑工记号有两种说法：一是搭烧的可能，即某个窑工自己生产的产品集中在标有自己记号的托座上装烧，标明自己对这些产品的所有权，可见窑内产品由一家或数家统一搭烧；另一种可能是实行生产责任制，产品质量责任到人，可以对陶瓷质量进行跟踪监督，有助于鼓励窑工提高制瓷技术。

A novel management model was also the winning formula of Song-Yuan kilns. At the Site of Zhizhushan Kilns, inscriptions bearing the surname "Cheng" were frequently found on the utensils, which experts believe were carved to mark their producer. There are two explanations for these kiln worker marks. One possibility is that collaborative firing presented the demand for marks, indicating that each kiln worker had their wares fired on their own firing stands bearing their marks to show the ownership. A kiln was used by one manufacturer or jointly used by several manufacturers. Another possibility is that a production responsibility system was implemented, which means that each individual worker should assume responsibility for the quality of his products, so that effective product traceability could be achieved, thus encouraging kiln workers to improve their ceramics-making techniques.

海外发现的部分磁灶窑军持，底部记有“程家工夫”或“陈家工夫”，垫柱刻划有“程干”字样。专家认为，与程姓相关的不同铭文应该是为作区别而刻划的，分别代表着不同的身份和对象。磁灶窑已注重打造品牌，以提升知名度，标记“程家工夫”或“陈家工夫”的产品就是磁灶窑的高端产品，在海外也受到追捧。“程干”并非窑工名，“干”指的是“干人”，即替官员和大地主（在泉州可能是南外宗正司皇族）经营私人产业的人。这一职业在宋元时期大受欢迎，官员和大地主让“干人”代为“管库”“管米谷”，及从事商业活动，他们就相当于今天的职业经理人。“干人”主导代替官府督造的全新模式由此诞生。

For example, some kendis discovered overseas bear inscriptions like "Cheng Jia Gong Fu" or "Chen Jia Gong Fu" on the bottom, and the characters "Cheng Gan" incised on the cushion pillars. Experts believe that the different inscriptions associated with the Cheng Family were carved to distinguish between different products owned by different people. Cizao Kilns had attached importance to building its brand to enhance its visibility. The products marked with "Cheng Jia Gong Fu" or "Chen Jia Gong Fu" were the high-end products of Cizao Kilns, also much sought-after overseas. "Cheng Gan" is not the name of a kiln worker, but refers to a *gan ren* surnamed Cheng. *Gan ren* was someone who helped officials and large landlords (In Quanzhou, they were possibly members of the Southern Clan Office) to operate their businesses. This occupation was highly popular during the Song and Yuan dynasties. The officials and large landlords asked *gan ren* to manage their warehouses, grain depots and engage in commercial activities. *Gan ren* is akin to present-day professional managers. The brand-new model of *gan ren* management replacing official supervision arose.

磁灶窑通过创新窑业技术和管理模式来提高产品质量，降低成本；临近梅溪水道和通达海外的泉州港，解决了产品运输问题；而为了扩大产品在海外市场的销售，主要依靠的则是泉州海商，他们既了解海外市场需求又熟悉磁灶窑业，他们提供关于海外市场需求的信息，引导磁灶窑产品生产，是磁灶窑产品供销大军的重要力量。

宋元时期的泉州海商由本地海商、外地海商和外国番商构成，本地海商又有舶商、南外宗子海商、僧人海商、海员水手。他们开展贸易的范围相当广泛，据《诸蕃志》记载，当时与泉州通商的国家和地区多达 58 个；《岛夷志略》提到与泉州通商的国家和地区已达 99 个，提到的地名更达 220 个。

Cizao Kilns improved their product quality and reduced costs by fostering innovations in kiln technology and management models. Located near the Meixi waterway and Quanzhou Port which provided easy access to going overseas, Cizao Kilns found a solution to product transportation problem. To expand their sale in overseas markets, Cizao Kilns mainly sought help from sea merchants in Quanzhou, who understood the overseas market demands and were familiar with Cizao Kilns manufacturing. They provided information on overseas market demands and guided Cizao Kilns production, making themselves an essential force of Cizao Kilns' supply and marketing workers.

During the Song and Yuan dynasties, sea merchants in Quanzhou consisted of local merchants, merchants who were out-of-towners, and foreign merchants. Local merchants included ship merchants, merchants from Southern Clan Office, monk merchants and sailors. They traded extensively. According to *Records of Foreign Countries,* there were 58 countries and regions that had dealings with Quanzhou. *A Brief Account of Island Inhabitants* recorded 99 countries and regions that traded with Quanzhou, with up to 220 place names mentioned.

宋磁灶窑“陈家工夫”款绿釉龙纹军持，印度尼西亚回流，泉州古代外销陶瓷博物馆藏。（泉州古代外销陶瓷博物馆 供图）

A Song Dynasty green-glazed kendi carved with characters "Chen Jia Gong Fu" with loong pattern produced in Cizao Kilns, returning from Indonesia, is housed in Quanzhou Ancient Exported Ceramics Museum. (Courtesy of Quanzhou Ancient Exported Ceramics Museum)

泉州海商了解海外市场需求的途径有两条。

其一，住番经商。在季风气候条件下，每年冬季十月、十一月或十二月刮北风，商舶从泉州港顺风南下，隔年夏季四月刮南风，商舶从南番回航。泉州海商候风住番，就地进行商业贸易，渐渐通晓当地语言，熟悉风土人情，沟通上层人物。住番经商是宋代出洋贸易的典型模式，这种模式延续到了元代，并且又有了新的发展。曾出使真腊的周达观在《真腊风土记》中提到“（真腊）国人交易，皆妇人能之，所以唐人到彼，必先纳一妇人者，兼亦利其能买卖故也”。他们与当地人杂居，深入掌握了海外商情。这些海商便是早期的华侨。

Sea merchants in Quanzhou had two ways of knowing overseas market demands.

One is to engage in business activities while staying in foreign countries. During winter from October to December when the monsoon winds blew, ships departing from Quanzhou Port sailed downwind, and sailed back northward the following year in April when the monsoon winds had changed direction. Sea merchants in Quanzhou would stay in foreign lands and conduct trade. They grew familiar with the local language and customs, and got in touch with people with high status. Staying in foreign lands while carrying on trade was a typical model of overseas trade in the Song Dynasty, which continued to exist in the Yuan Dynasty and fostered further developments. Zhou Daguan, who had been sent on a mission to Chenla, mentioned in *A Record of Cambodia: The Land and Its People* that women in Chenla were capable of trading. Tang people would, therefore, marry a woman after they arrived there, which also benefited their business transactions. They lived with the locals and gained a deep understanding of overseas business situations. These sea merchants were the early overseas Chinese.

其二，接触来泉番商。他们与来泉州经商的外国番商取得联系，在来往中了解到对方所在国家的方位、山川、途程、风土、物产，从中定位海外市场需求。赵汝适的《诸蕃志》就是在这一背景下成书于宋代泉州的。

《诸蕃志》提到，登流眉国“饮食以葵叶为椀，不施匕筯，掬而食之”；苏吉丹“饮食不用器皿，缄树叶以从事，食已则弃之”；渤泥国“无器皿，以竹编贝多叶为器，食毕则弃之”。这样的情况，为磁灶窑的碗盘等日用粗瓷远销东南亚赢得了广阔的市场空间，这些产品着眼于实用价值，价格低廉，一般人都用得起，它们进入当地市场后，人们便趋之若鹜。

The other is to make contact with foreign merchants who came to Quanzhou to do business. They learned about the location, mountains, rivers, routes, customs, and local products of the foreign traders' homeland, so as to pinpoint the overseas market demands. Zhao Rukuo's *Records of Foreign Countries* was written against this background in Quanzhou during the Song Dynasty.

In *Records of Foreign Countries*, it is mentioned that in Dengliumei (probably present-day Nakhon Si Thammarat in Thailand), people used sunflower leaves as bowls and scooped the food to eat it instead of using chopsticks or spoons; in Sujidan (a vassal of ancient Java), people tied leaves together as bowls without using any other utensil for eating, and they would discard the leaves after eating; in Borneo, there were no utensils, and people wove bamboo and many leaves together as containers, which they discarded after finishing their meal. This situation allowed coarse porcelain products such as bowls and plates from Cizao Kilns to gain a large market in Southeast Asia. These products focused on practical value, with low prices, affordable for common people. Once they entered the local market, people eagerly sought after them.

宋元时期，生活在泉州的穆斯林广泛使用军持。“军持”即“水瓶”之意，是佛教僧侣和伊斯兰教穆斯林随身携带用于贮水饮用和净手的器物。宋末元初侨居泉州的穆斯林蒲寿宬曾在《山中井》一诗中写道：“明月照我牖，独起携军持。”磁灶窑由此获知军持是穆斯林圣物，看到了其中蕴藏的市场前景，生产了各种装饰、各种釉色的军持，通过泉州海商远销东南亚地区，其中，龙纹军持最受欢迎。故宫博物院原顾问韩槐准先生在《军持之研究》中提到东南亚信奉伊斯兰教的人“对于传统习惯应用之军持，需要尤多……除日常拜功当备此类水壶为小净之用处。同时古代到天方朝觐之最大重典时，亦当备此类水壶一个或数个，以为搭船时船主配给淡水之用……至将归时，当以所携带之壶，汲麦加阿必渗渗井之泉……马来人称为圣水……归赠戚友，以备家用。”

During the Song and Yuan dynasties, kendi was widely used by Muslims living in Quanzhou. Kendi means "water bottle." It is a utensil carried by Buddhist monks and Muslims for storing and drinking water, as well as washing hands. In his poem *Mountain Well*, Pu Shoucheng, a Muslim who lived in Quanzhou during the late Song Dynasty and early Yuan Dynasty, wrote, "The bright moon shines through my window, and I arise alone taking the holy water bottle with me." From this line, Cizao Kilns workers learned that kendi was a sacred object for Muslims, and saw the market potential it held. They had, therefore, produced kendis with various decorations and various glaze colors, which were exported to Southeast Asia through sea merchants in Quanzhou. Among them, the kendi with loong pattern was the most popular product. Mr. Han Huaizhun, the former consultant of the Palace Museum, mentioned in the *Research on Kendi* that the people who embraced Islam in Southeast Asia needed a large number of kendis for observing traditional customs ... In addition to daily worship, they would prepare such water bottles for washing. When ancient people went on a pilgrimage to Mecca, they would also prepare one or several such water bottles for the ship's owner to provide fresh water ... When they returned, they would carry the water from Bir Zam Zam in the bottle ... Malaysians called it holy water ... After they returned, it could be given to their relatives or friends for household use.

在菲律宾的土著民族中，有“瓮棺葬”或称“洗骨葬”的习俗。另外，菲律宾和加里曼丹岛的一些土著居民还有“瓮崇拜”的习俗，对龙瓮的崇拜尤为突出。据记载，这里的人们“所藏之瓦瓮，或来自中国，上雕龙形，视为传家之宝。土人谓瓦瓮有神呵护，对之极恭敬”。他们每年都要举行一次“圣瓮节”，即在每年农作物收成后举行拜瓮的祭典。瓮还有其他功用，有用作酿造的酒瓮，还有盛水的水瓮。这些与瓮有关的习俗，为泉州海商带来了巨大的商机，磁灶窑生产的龙瓮便是经由他们大量销往东南亚。

Among the indigenous people in the Philippines, there was a custom of "urn burial" (also known as "bone washing burial"). In addition, some indigenous people in the Philippines and Kalimantan Island had the custom of "urn worship," with particular emphasis on the worship of urns with loong pattern. According to records, the earthen urns there, probably made in China, were carved with loong pattern, and they were considered family heirlooms. The indigenous people believed that there was a god guarding the urns and treated them with the utmost respect. They held a "sacred urn festival" every year, which was a ceremony to worship the urns after the annual harvest. Urns also had other uses, such as brewing liquor and holding water. These urn-related customs brought tremendous business opportunities to sea merchants in Quanzhou, and the urns with loong pattern produced by Cizao Kilns were sold in large quantities to Southeast Asia through them.

磁灶窑绿釉双龙抱珠军持。（成冬冬 摄）
A green-glazed kendi with the design of double loongs embracing a pearl from Cizao Kilns. (Photo by Cheng Dongdong)

宋磁灶窑龙瓮。（吴金鹏 摄）
An urn with loong pattern from Cizao Kilns in the Song Dynasty. (Photo by Wu Jinpeng)

在宋代，对日贸易的主要港口虽然是明州，泉州港的商舶需要在明州办理出境手续即“公凭”，才能航海东渡日本，但这并不影响泉州海商对日贸易的积极性，泉州的对日贸易十分活跃。李充是专门从事对日贸易的泉州本地海商，可以说是泉州陶瓷（包括磁灶窑产品）日本市场供销大军中的先锋人物。据记载，他曾于宋徽宗崇宁元年至四年（1102—1105）先后两次从泉州出发，在明州启航，泛海日本经商。北宋崇宁四年（1105）明州市舶司发给李充的“公凭”上记载的贸易品除丝织品外，还有瓷碗200床、瓷碟100床。（“床”在闽南方言中可以表示计量单位。）如按当时一床200个单位计算，那么就有瓷碗40,000个、瓷碟20,000个。这批瓷器应该都是泉州本地生产的。

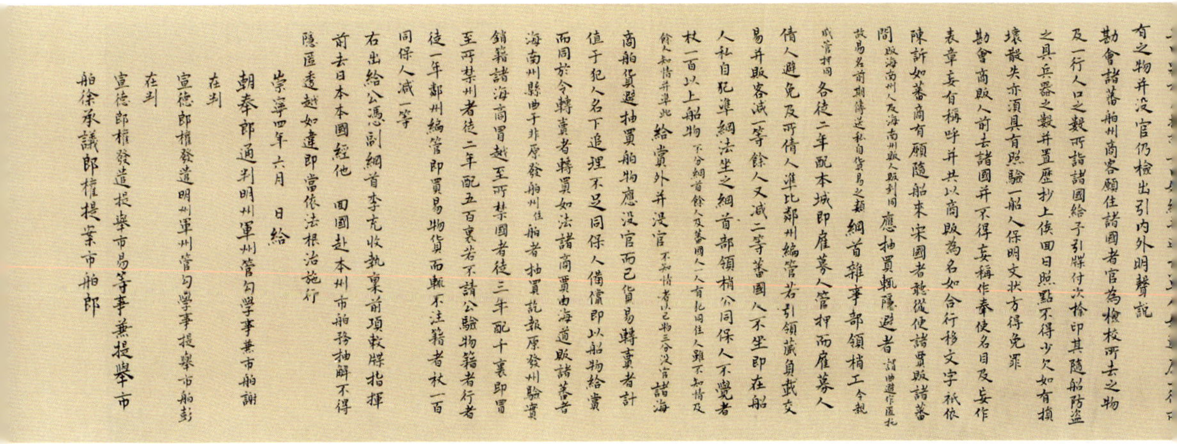
有之物并沒官仍檢出引內外明聲說
勘會諸蕃舶州商客願往諸國者官為檢校所去之物
及一行人口之數所詣諸國給予引牒付次捺印其隨船防盜
之具兵器之數并置歷抄上候回日照點不得少欠如有損
壞散失亦須具有照驗一船人保明文狀方得免罪
勘會商販人前去諸國并不得妄稱作奉使名目及妄作
表章妄有稱呼并共以商販為名如合行移文字祇依
陳訴如蕃商有願隨船來宋國者聽從便諸買販諸蕃
間（販海南州人及海南州販人販到同）應抽買輒隱避者（謂曲避作匿報
故易名前期傳送私自貨易之類）綱首雜事部領梢工（令親
戚管押同）各徒二年配本城即雇募人管押而雇募人
倩人避免及所倩人準比鄰州編管若引領藏負載交
易并販客減一等餘人又減二等蕃國人不坐即在船
人私自犯準綱法坐之綱首部領梢公同保人不覺者
杖一百以上船物（下分綱首餘人及蕃國人一人有犯同住人雖不知情及
餘人知情并準此）給賞外并沒官（不知情者以己物三分沒官）諸海
商船貨避抽買舶物應沒官而已貨易轉賣者計
值于犯人名下追理不足同保人備償即以船物給賞
而同於令轉賣者轉買如法諸商賈由海道販諸蕃
海南州縣曲于非原發舶州（住）舶者抽買訖報原發州驗實
銷籍諸海商冒越至所禁國者徒三年配千裏即冒
至所禁州者徒二年配五百裏若不請公驗物籍者行者
徒一年鄰州編管即買易物貨而輒不注籍者杖一百
同保人減一等
右出給公憑副綱首李充收執稟前項敕牒指揮
前去日本國經他　回國赴本州市舶務抽解不得
隱匿透越如違即當依法根治施行
崇寧四年六月　日給
朝奉郎通判明州軍州管勾學事兼市舶謝
在判
宣德郎權發遣明州軍州管勾學事提舉市舶彭
在判
宣德郎權發遣提舉市易等事兼提舉市
舶徐承議郎權提案市舶郎

李充赴日贸易的公凭（复制件）。（泉州海外交通史博物馆 供图）
A replica of the official document approving a trade trip to Japan led by Li Chong, a merchant in Quanzhou. (Courtesy of Quanzhou Maritime Museum)

Although the main port for trade with Japan during the Song Dynasty was Mingzhou, and merchant ships from Quanzhou port were required to obtain an "official document" from Mingzhou before they sailed to Japan, this did not affect the enthusiasm of Quanzhou's maritime merchants for engaging in trade with Japan, and trading activities were vigorous. Li Chong was a local Quanzhou sea merchant who specialized in trade with Japan, and could be considered a pioneer in the Quanzhou ceramics (including products from Cizao Kilns) market in Japan. According to the records, he had twice departed from Quanzhou for Mingzhou, and then sailed to Japan to engage in trade during the period from 1102 to 1105. In addition to silk fabrics, there were 200 *chuang* of porcelain bowls and 100 *chuang* of porcelain dishes for trade, as shown by the "official document" issued by the Mingzhou Maritime Trade Office to Li Chong in 1105. (*Chuang* is a unit of measurement in Minnan dialect.) If calculated based on 200 items per *chuang* at that time, there would be 40,000 porcelain bowls and 20,000 porcelain dishes. These porcelain products were very likely to be made in Quanzhou.

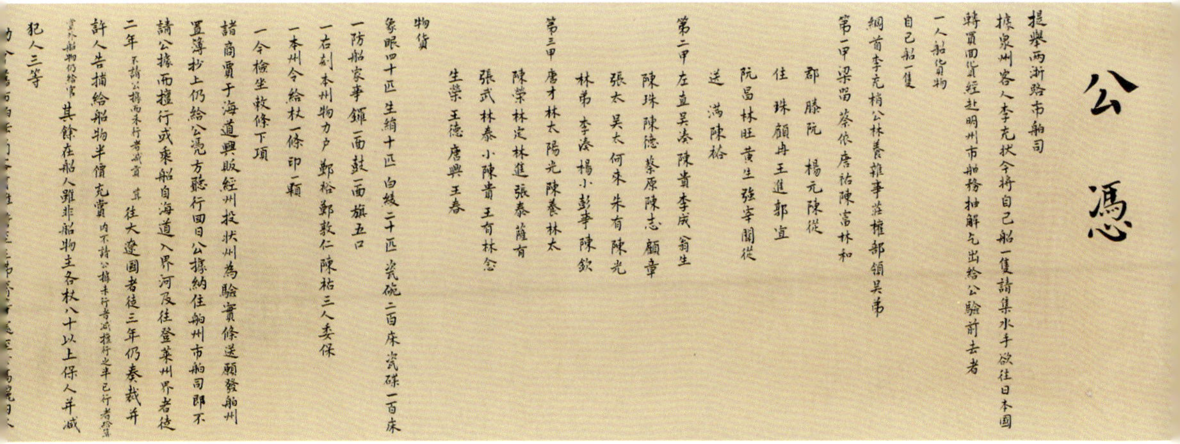
公憑
提舉兩浙路市舶司
據泉州客人李充狀今將自己船一隻請集水手欲往日本國
轉買回貨經赴明州市舶務抽解乞出給公驗前去者
一人船貨物
自己船一隻
綱首李充 梢公林養 雜事莊權 部領吳弟
第一甲 梁留 蔡依 唐祐 陳富 林和
郡 滕阮 楊元 陳從
佳 珠 顧冉 王進 郭宜
阮昌 林旺 黃生 強宰 關從
送 滿 陳裕
第二甲 左直 吳湊 陳貴 李成 翁生
陳珠 陳德 蔡原 陳志 顧章
張太 吳太 何来 朱有 陳光
林弟 李添 楊小 彭事 陳欽
第三甲 唐才 林太 陽光 陳養 林太
陳榮 林定 林進 張泰 薩有
張武 林泰 小陳 貴王 有林 念
生榮 王德 唐興 王春
物貨
象眼四十匹 生絹十匹 白綾二十匹 瓷碗二百床 瓷碟一百床
一防船家事 鑼一面 鼓一面 旗五口
一石刻本州物力户 鄭裕 鄭敦仁 陳祐三人委保
一本州令給杖一條 印一顆
一今檢坐敕條下項
諸商賈于海道興販經州投狀州為驗實條送願發船州
置簿抄上仍給公憑方聽行回日公據納住舶州市舶司即不
請公據而擅行或乘船自海道入界河及往登萊州界者徒
二年 不請公據而未行者減貳等 往大遼國者徒三年仍奏裁并
許人告捕給船物半價充賞 內不請公據未行者減擅行之半已行者從笞
其餘在船人雖非船物主各杖八十以上保人并減 實外船物仍給官
犯人三等

磁灶窑以市场为导向，按订单烧制（亦称定烧），由客户根据自身需要就某种产品的款式、釉色、装饰、数量、交货日期等方面提出具体要求，并指定磁灶某窑场生产。产品的内销与外销都采用了这种模式。内销产品中，土尾庵窑出土的瓷器里，几件黑釉茶碗的内腹部发现剔刻的文字，可辨认的有“济”“庙”等，可能是寺庙庵观定烧的；1979 年，在晋江草庵前古井曾出土 1 件宋代碗内壁阴刻“明教会”三个字的黑釉碗，学术界把它称为“宋‘明教会’黑釉碗”，被誉为继草庵摩尼光佛造像之后世界摩尼教研究的第二大发现，属于国家一级文物。后来，在磁灶窑系宋代大树威窑址，发现了有“明”“教”等字样的黑釉碗残片。这些都是定烧经营模式的鲜活证明。外销产品中，蜘蛛山窑的堆贴兽首衔环瓶、孔雀印纹盘，土尾庵窑的绿釉花口碟、堆贴兽首衔环瓶和二彩、三彩小罐等，这些器形和我国传统造型装饰有所不同，目前在国内发现的很少，它们可能是专供外销的，这些具有浓郁的异域风情的磁灶窑产品，可以说属于海外定烧器。

草庵前出土的“宋‘明教会’黑釉碗”。（成冬冬 摄）
The black-glazed bowl carved with characters "Ming Jiao Hui" of the Song Dynasty excavated in front of Cao'an Temple. (Photo by Cheng Dongdong)

Cizao Kilns operated under a market-oriented model. Products were made according to customers' need (also known as "customized production"). Customers set requirements on style, glaze color, decoration, quantity, and delivery date for a certain product, and they also specified which kiln made their products. This model was used for both domestic and foreign sales. As for domestic market, among the unearthed porcelain products produced by Tuwei'an Kilns, several black-glazed tea bowls with carved inscriptions within have been found, identified characters including "Ji" and "Miao," indicating that they were custom orders from temples or monasteries; in 1979, a black-glazed bowl with Chinese characters "Ming Jiao Hui" (Society of the Religion of Light) engraved on the inner side was discovered from the ancient well in front of the Cao'an Temple in Jinjiang, referred to as "black-glazed bowl carved with characters 'Ming Jiao Hui' of the Song Dynasty" by scholars and considered to be the second largest discovery in the world of Manichaeism research after the statue of Mani in Cao'an Temple. It is a Grade One Cultural Relic. Later, at the Dashuwei kiln site within Sites of Cizao Kilns, fragments of black-glazed bowls with the characters "Ming" and "Jiao" were found. They are vivid proof of the customized production. Among the exported products, there are the bottle attached with sculptured animal head holding a ring in its mouth, and the plate with peacock pattern from Zhizhushan Kilns, the green-glazed dish with flower-shaped edge, the bottle attached with sculptured animal head holding a ring in its mouth, and bi-color, tri-color small jars from Tuwei'an Kilns, etc. They differ from traditional Chinese products in decorative styles, and are rarely found domestically at present. They might be specially made for export. These exotic products made in Cizao Kilns, can be considered as customized kiln products for export.

千年的时光把海内外一艘艘古老的沉船连缀在一起，古代海上丝绸之路便清晰地展现在世人面前。磁灶窑是宋元时期泉州外销瓷窑址的杰出代表，作为外销产品的军持、釉下彩黄釉铁绘大盆、绿釉花口碟、龙瓮等典型器物，近 50 年来在宋元时期的海上丝绸之路航线上的沉船中越来越多地被发现，如位于中国的“南海 I 号”沉船、“华光礁 I 号”沉船，位于韩国的新安沉船，位于印度尼西亚的爪哇沉船及哲帕拉沉船，位于菲律宾的吕宋沉船等，让泉州制造一次又一次惊艳世界。它们不仅仅是贵重的古董，更是宋元泉州制造行销世界的沉甸甸的历史见证。

The ancient sunken ships at home and abroad were witnesses to the history spanning a thousand years, presenting the ancient Maritime Silk Road to the world. Cizao Kilns are an outstanding representative of the export porcelain kiln sites of Quanzhou in the Song and Yuan dynasties. The typical export products such as kendis, large basins with underglaze yellow using iron-containing colorant, green-glazed dishes with flower-shaped edge, and urns with loong pattern, have been discovered in increasingly large quantities from sunken ships along the Maritime Silk Road during the Song and Yuan dynasties over the past 50 years, like the "Nanhai No. 1" Shipwreck and the "Huaguang Reef No. 1" Shipwreck in China, the Xin'an sunken ship in the Republic of Korea, the Java sunken ship and the Jepara sunken ship in Indonesia, the Luzon sunken ship in the Philippines, etc., which continuously impress the world with Quanzhou's manufacturing prowess. They are not only precious antiques, but also eloquent testimonies to the worldwide popularity of Quanzhou products in the Song and Yuan dynasties.

泉州古代外销陶瓷博物馆的展区里生动再现了宋代民间制陶的方法。（中新图片 供图）
The vivid reproduction of the folk pottery making methods of the Song Dynasty in the exhibition area of Quanzhou Ancient Exported Ceramics Museum. (Courtesy of CNSphoto.com)

在金交椅山窑址发现了大量碎瓷片。（陈英杰 摄）
A large number of porcelain shards discovered at the Site of Jinjiaoyishan Kilns. (Photo by Chen Yingjie)

马可·波罗曾代言的德化窑

德化窑是中国陶瓷文化发祥地之一，在中国陶瓷史上占有重要地位。德化窑位于泉州市西北部的德化县，这里地处戴云山区，拥有丰富的瓷土矿、水系和森林资源，瓷土品质优良，瓷器生产条件优越。德化陶瓷生产历史悠久，始于夏商，兴于宋元，盛于明清。早在新石器时代末期至青铜时代早期，德化就已使用龙窑烧制印纹硬陶和原始青瓷；唐五代烧制青瓷；宋代始烧青白瓷；元代出现分室龙窑，烧制白瓷；明代创烧的乳白釉瓷色泽莹润、器形精巧，达到白瓷工艺的顶峰，被誉为“中国白”。据《德化县文物志》记载，目前德化县境内发现的古窑址多达 239 处，其中宋元时期 42 处。这些窑址遍布德化全境，很多窑址规模大、延烧时间长，有的从宋元时期一直延续到明清时期。

Dehua Kilns Spoken Highly of by Marco Polo

Dehua Kilns are one of the birthplaces of Chinese ceramic culture and occupy an important position in Chinese ceramic history. Located in Dehua County, northwest of the city of Quanzhou, Dehua Kilns lie in the Mount Daiyun, with abundant porcelain clay mines, water systems, and forest resources. The porcelain clay is of excellent quality, and the porcelain production conditions are superb. Dehua ceramic production has a long history, dating back to the Xia and Shang dynasties, flourishing in the Song and Yuan dynasties, and reaching its peak in the Ming and Qing dynasties. As early as the late Neolithic period and the early Bronze Age, Dehua used the loong-shaped kilns to fire hard pottery with impressed patterns and primitive celadon. During the Tang Dynasty and Five Dynasties, it fired celadon. And during the Song Dynasty, it began firing bluish-white glazed porcelain. In the Yuan Dynasty, it began firing white porcelain in multi-chambered loong-shaped kilns. In the Ming Dynasty, it created milky-white glazed porcelain, with translucent features and exquisite shapes, reaching the peak of white porcelain craftsmanship, and its products made their name as "Blanc de Chine." According to *Records of Dehua County Cultural Relics*, there are currently 239 ancient kiln sites discovered in Dehua County, including 42 sites from the Song and Yuan dynasties. These kiln sites are spread throughout Dehua, with many large-scale kiln sites in operation for a long time, some being functional from the Song and Yuan dynasties to the Ming and Qing dynasties.

德化窑作坊区的瓷土加工区。（刘纵横 摄）
Processing area for porcelain clay in the workshop of Dehua Kilns. (Photo by Liu Zongheng)

宋元时期，得益于泉州海洋贸易的繁荣，德化窑迅速崛起，窑场林立，瓷器品种丰富多样，尤以青白瓷、白瓷为代表，是重要的外销陶瓷生产基地，在器形与纹饰上满足了海外中高端市场需求。屈斗宫德化窑遗址包括三班、盖德、龙浔、浔中四个乡镇的宋至明代窑址。

大量产品从泉州港出发，沿着海上丝绸之路，销往东亚、东南亚、南亚的国家和地区，对输入国的社会生活产生了深远的影响，加深了我们同这些国家和地区在政治、经济、文化等方面的交流和联系；窑业技术传播到海外，在国际陶瓷业发展繁荣的过程中厥功至伟。

1988 年，屈斗宫德化窑遗址被公布为第三批全国重点文物保护单位；2006 年，南安市的寮仔窑址、南坑窑址并入屈斗宫德化窑遗址，同列入这一名录；2021 年 7 月，德化窑址（尾林—内坂窑址、屈斗宫窑址）作为“泉州：宋元中国的世界海洋商贸中心”系列遗产之一，列入《世界遗产名录》。德化窑址（尾林—内坂窑址、屈斗宫窑址）和磁灶窑址（金交椅山窑址）成为世界上首批瓷窑类的世界文化遗产。

屈斗宫古窑址。（陈小阳 摄）
Site of Qudougong Kiln. (Photo by Chen Xiaoyang)

During the Song and Yuan dynasties, against the background of thriving maritime trade, Dehua Kilns rose rapidly, with numerous kiln sites and a wide variety of porcelain products, featuring bluish-white glazed porcelain and white-glazed porcelain. Dehua Kilns became an important production base for export-oriented ceramics, meeting the demands from middle- and high-end overseas markets. The Site of Qudougong Dehua Kilns include kiln sites from the Song Dynasty to the Ming Dynasty in Sanban, Gaide, Longxun, and Xunzhong.

A large quantity of products departed from Quanzhou Port, and were marketed to countries and regions in East Asia, Southeast Asia, and South Asia along the Maritime Silk Road. The products deeply influenced the social lives of those countries and regions, deepening our exchanges and communication with them in politics, economics, culture, and other fields. The ceramics-making technique spread overseas, playing a significant role in the development of the international ceramic industry.

In 1988, the Site of Qudougong Dehua Kilns was included in the third batch of national key cultural relics protection units; in 2006, the Liaozai kiln site and Nankeng kiln site in Nan'an were included among those of Qudougong Dehua Kilns, and were, therefore, protected at the national level; in July 2021, Sites of Dehua Kilns (Weilin-Neiban Kilns and Qudougong Kiln) were included in the World Heritage List as part of "Quanzhou: Emporium of the World in Song-Yuan China" serial property. Sites of Dehua Kilns (Weilin-Neiban Kilns and Qudougong Kiln) and Sites of Cizao Kilns (Jinjiaoyishan Kilns) became the first batch of ceramic kiln sites to be recognized as World Cultural Heritage.

屈斗宫窑址。屈斗宫窑址位于德化县龙浔镇宝美村破寨山的南坡上。1976 年，揭露一处元代窑炉遗址，窑炉方向 195°，窑床坡度 12°—22°。窑炉全长 57.1 米，宽 1.4—2.95 米。该窑为分室龙窑，共有 17 间窑室，发现 14 处窑门，部分窑壁和窑室间的隔墙保存了下来，窑壁外还有护墙。窑室多呈长方形，纵长 2.45—3.95 米，底部斜平，分室但不分阶级。这种分室龙窑是龙窑向阶级窑转化的过渡形式，反映了宋元时期窑炉技术的发展。窑床上发现了大量烧瓷所用窑具，可见生产规模之大。产品以青白瓷、白瓷为主，多是碗、盘、盒、洗、执壶、军持、瓶等日用器型。刻花、划花、模印等装饰手法比较流行。在东亚、东南亚、南亚、西亚和东非等地区，出土了大量高足杯、粉盒、军持、壶、花瓶、碗等，在“华光礁 I 号”和“南海 I 号”等水下沉船中，这样的产品有许多，可见德化窑瓷器在海上丝绸之路上的重要地位。

屈斗宫窑址出土的青白瓷高足杯。（成冬冬 摄）
A bluish-white porcelain stem cup unearthed from the Site of Qudougong Kiln. (Photo by Cheng Dongdong)

About the Site of Qudougong Kiln. The Site of Qudougong Kiln is located on the southern slope of Pozhai Hill in Baomei Village, Longxun Town, Dehua County. In 1976, a Yuan Dynasty kiln site was excavated with the kiln furnace at an angle of 195° and the kiln bed at an angle of 12° to 22°. The kiln is a multi-chambered loong-shaped one with a total length of 57.1 meters and a width of 1.4 to 2.95 meters. There are 17 chambers in the kiln, with 14 kiln doors found. Some of the kiln walls and partition walls between the chambers have been preserved, and there are also protective walls outside the kiln walls. The chambers are mostly rectangular, with a length of 2.45 to 3.95 meters and a sloping bottom. The kiln is divided into chambers, but not into different steps. This type of multi-chambered loong-shaped kiln is a transitional form from loong-shaped kiln to ascending kiln and reflects the development of kiln technology during the Song and Yuan dynasties. A large number of kiln facilities used for porcelain production were found on the kiln bed, indicating a large production scale. Its main products were bluish-white glazed porcelain and white-glazed porcelain, mostly bowls, plates, boxes, washbasins, pitchers, kendis, bottles and other daily utensils. Decorative techniques such as carving, incising, and molding were popular. In East Asia, Southeast Asia, South Asia, West Asia and East Africa, a large number of stem cups, powder boxes, kendis, pots, vases, bowls and other products have been unearthed. There are many found in sunken ships such as "Huaguang Reef No. 1" Shipwreck and "Nanhai No. 1" Shipwreck, indicating the important position of Dehua porcelain on the Maritime Silk Road.

屈斗宫窑址出土的白瓷"长寿新船"款盒盖。（成冬冬 摄）

A white porcelain box lid engraved with characters "Chang Shou Xin Chuan" unearthed from the Site of Qudougong Kiln. (Photo by Cheng Dongdong)

屈斗宫窑址出土的白瓷花卉纹洗。（成冬冬 摄）
A white porcelain basin with floral pattern unearthed from the Site of Qudougong Kiln. (Photo by Cheng Dongdong)

屈斗宫窑址出土的青白瓷蔗段洗。（成冬冬 摄）
A bluish-white porcelain basin in the shape of segments of sugarcane unearthed from the Site of Qudougong Kiln. (Photo by Cheng Dongdong)

尾林—内坂窑址。尾林—内坂窑址位于德化县三班镇西北，至今仍是德化陶瓷的主要生产基地。窑址分布于上寮溪的南北两岸，窑址总面积577,373.37平方米。这里瓷土原料和烧窑材料丰富，适于建窑。窑场沿溪流分布，便于利用水碓等水力工具进行瓷土加工，同时为部分原料和产品的运输提供了条件。已发掘部分窑炉、作坊、废品堆积等窑业遗存。其中，南宋至元代窑炉遗迹7座，窑室内宽1.7—2.7米，最长的一座残长90米。出土了青白瓷、白瓷两类产品和各类窑具，以及2组瓷土加工作坊遗迹，包括约800平方米的尾林瓷土加工作坊和约900平方米的内坂瓷土加工作坊，分别分布在上寮溪两岸，多处水碓坑、水池、臼坑、垒石水渠、石坝等都保存了下来。这两处加工作坊后代长期沿用。窑炉周边的瓷片堆积总面积约8,000平方米，以废弃瓷器与窑具碎片为主，最厚处达2米。此外，遗址周边的梅岭等区域还发现部分明清时期的窑址，可见这一区域的瓷器烧造持续繁荣。

About the Site of Weilin-Neiban Kilns. The Site of Weilin-Neiban Kilns are in the northwest of Sanban Town, Dehua County, and are still the main production base for Dehua ceramics. Distributed along both sides of the Shangliao Stream, they cover a total area of 577,373.37 square meters. The porcelain clay and firewood are abundant here, which is suitable to build kilns. The kilns are distributed along the stream, making it convenient to use helve hammers and other hydraulic tools for porcelain clay processing. The stream also provides an effective means for transporting some raw materials and products. Some kiln remains, workshops, and waste dumps have been excavated. Among them, there are seven sites of kiln remains from the Southern Song Dynasty to the Yuan Dynasty, with kiln chambers ranging from 1.7 meters to 2.7 meters in width, and the longest kiln remains being 90 meters long. What have been excavated includes bluish-white glazed porcelain, white-glazed porcelain, various kiln facilities, and two sites of porcelain clay processing workshops, including the one in Weilin covering approximately 800 square meters and the other in Neiban covering approximately 900 square meters which are located on both sides of Shangliao Stream. Many helve hammer foundation pits, ponds, mortars pits, stone channels, and dams have been preserved. These two processing workshops have been used for generations. The porcelain shard piles around the kilns cover an area of approximately 8,000 square meters, mainly consisting of waste wares and kiln facilities fragments, with a maximum thickness of 2 meters. In addition, some kiln sites existing during the Ming and Qing dynasties have been found in the surrounding areas such as Meiling, indicating the sustained prosperity of porcelain production in this region.

尾林窑全景。（刘纵横 摄）
A panoramic view of Weilin Kilns. (Photo by Liu Zongheng)

尾林窑东南隔上寮溪与内坂窑相望。2019 年，发现并确认 3 处窑炉遗迹。2020 年，对一号窑进行考古发掘，发掘面积 242 平方米，发现有叠压打破关系的 1 座宋元龙窑、1 座元明分室龙窑以及 2 座明清横室阶级窑。此外，还试掘 2 处作坊遗迹。出土瓷器标本主要是宋元明时期的青白瓷、白瓷以及少量清代青花瓷。青白瓷、白瓷装饰技法有模印、刻划、捏塑、堆贴等。纹饰主要有莲花、牡丹花、菊瓣、缠枝花卉等，部分器物底部模印、刻划文字。青花瓷主要有碗、盘，图案有松鼠葡萄纹、龙纹、花卉等。窑具有伞状支烧具、支圈、垫柱、匣钵等。

Weilin Kilns face Neiban Kilns across Shangliao Stream to the southeast. In 2019, three sites of kiln remains were discovered and confirmed. In 2020, excavation was conducted in the Kiln No. 1, with an excavation area of 242 square meters. A loong-shaped kiln in Song-Yuan period, a multi-chambered loong-shaped kiln in Yuan-Ming period (1271—1644), and two flat-chambered ascending kilns in Ming-Qing period were found, overlapping each other. In addition, two workshop sites were also excavated. The unearthed porcelain specimens are mainly bluish-white glazed porcelain and white-glazed porcelain from the Song, Yuan, and Ming dynasties (960—1644), as well as a small amount of blue-and-white porcelain in the Qing Dynasty. The decorative techniques of bluish-white glazed porcelain and white-glazed porcelain include molding, carving and incising, kneading, and embossing. The patterns mainly include lotuses, peonies, chrysanthemum petals, interlocking vegetal scrolls, etc. Some objects have impressed, carved or incised characters underneath. The blue-and-white porcelain mainly includes bowls and plates, with patterns such as squirrels and grapes, loongs, and flowers. The kiln facilities include umbrella-shaped burner stands, ring-shaped firing stands, cushion pillars, saggers, etc.

已揭露的 4 座窑炉横跨宋、元、明、清 4 个朝代，十分罕见，可以说是“一眼千年”，第一次较为完整地揭示了德化窑从宋元时期龙窑至明清时期横室阶级窑的发展演变过程，填补了德化窑古代窑业技术史的缺环，为展示德化古代制瓷工艺技术提供了重要的实物材料。产品以碗、盘、盒、瓶等日常生活用品为主，在保证实用功能的同时，还注重造型艺术和审美情趣，最具代表性的是荷口花瓶、鼓腹长流喇叭口的执壶，以及形式繁多、大小不一、制作精美的瓷盒等。这些器物胎质洁白细腻，薄而坚硬；釉色白中泛青或青中泛白，色调深浅不一，深者呈湖绿色，淡者接近白色；纹饰线条之流畅，构图形象之简练雅致，题材内容之丰富，国内少见。

The four kilns that have been uncovered span four dynasties from the Song Dynasty to the Qing Dynasty, which is extremely rare and can be described as "a thousand years at a glance." This is the first time that the evolution of Dehua Kilns from the loong-shaped kilns in Song-Yuan era to the flat-chambered ascending kilns in Ming-Qing era has been displayed in a relatively complete way, which fills the void of the history of ancient kiln technology in Dehua Kilns and provides important material evidence for the ancient ceramic technology of Dehua. The products mainly include daily utensils such as bowls, plates, boxes, and bottles. They were both aesthetic and functional. The most typical ones are the vases with lotus-shaped edge, the round-bellied pitchers with long spout and trumpet-shaped mouth, and exquisitely crafted porcelain boxes in all shapes and sizes. The greenware is pure white, delicate, thin yet tough, and the glazes are white with a celadon tint or celadon with a whitish tint. They vary in tone, with darker shades appearing lake green and lighter shades closer to white. The smooth lines form decorative patterns which are concise and elegant, and the rich content of the themes is rare in China.

内坂窑址位于上寮溪南岸，西北距尾林一号窑约 230 米，面积约 3,600 平方米。经考古研究，已确认 4 处龙窑、分室龙窑遗迹。2020 年，对二号窑进行考古发掘，发掘面积 113 平方米。揭露 2 道残存的隔墙，都仅存最底部一层立砖；发现 7 处窑门，均位于西侧，窑门底部与窑底平；另外，还有 5 处护窑墙，主要位于西侧中前段地势较低处，平面多近似圆角长方形、弧形等；窑尾破坏较严重，出烟室仅存倒塌堆积等少量痕迹。出土器物以青白瓷为主，主要是碗、盘、盏、盒、瓶等器型。大部分器物的表面模印缠枝花纹、莲瓣纹等。窑具多为支圈、伞状支烧具、垫柱，还有少量匣钵。内坂二号窑的窑炉结构较为简单，窑墙未发现多次修补现象，出土产品风格以南宋中晚期为主。初步认定内坂二号窑年代为南宋中期至元代初期。

The Neiban kiln site is located on the south bank of Shangliao Stream, about 230 meters southeast of Weilin Kiln No. 1, covering an area of approximately 3,600 square meters. Through archaeological research, four loong-shaped and multi-chambered loong-shaped kiln sites have been identified. In 2020, excavation was carried out in Kiln No. 2, with an excavation area of 113 square meters. Two remaining partition walls were uncovered, each with only the bottom layer of bricks; seven kiln doors were found, all located on the west side, with the bottom of the doors level with the kiln floor. In addition, there were five protection walls, mainly in the low-lying area of the middle and front part on the west side, with planar shapes similar to rounded rectangles, arcs, and so on. The smoke outlet was severely damaged, with only a small amount of debris in the collapsed smoke chamber. Excavated artifacts consisted mainly of bluish-white porcelain products, such as bowls, plates, cups, boxes, and bottles, most of which have impressed patterns of interlocking vegetal scrolls, lotus petals and so on. The kiln facilities mostly consisted of ring-shaped firing stands, umbrella-shaped burner stands, cushion pillars, and a few saggers. The structure of Neiban Kiln No. 2 is relatively simple and no evidence of multiple repairs to the kiln walls has been found. The style of the products unearthed mainly dates back to the mid-to-late Southern Song Dynasty. Preliminary findings conclude that Neiban Kiln No. 2 existed from the mid-Southern Song Dynasty and the early Yuan Dynasty.

尾林—内坂窑址出土的青白瓷莲瓣纹小瓶。（成冬冬 摄）

A small bluish-white porcelain vase with lotus petals decoration unearthed from the Site of Weilin-Neiban Kilns. (Photo by Cheng Dongdong)

尾林—内坂窑址出土的青白瓷莲瓣纹炉。（成冬冬 摄）

A bluish-white porcelain stove with lotus petals decoration unearthed from the Site of Weilin-Neiban Kilns. (Photo by Cheng Dongdong)

尾林—内坂窑址出土的青白瓷菱花口花卉纹大碗。（成冬冬 摄）
A large bluish-white porcelain bowl with water chestnut flower-shaped rim and floral pattern unearthed from the Site of Weilin-Neiban Kilns. (Photo by Cheng Dongdong)

尾林—内坂窑址出土的青白瓷芒口斗笠碗。（成冬冬 摄）
A bluish-white porcelain bamboo hat-shaped bowl with unglazed rim unearthed from the Site of Weilin-Neiban Kilns. (Photo by Cheng Dongdong)

尾林—内坂窑址出土的青白瓷菊瓣纹粉盒。（成冬冬 摄）
A bluish-white porcelain powder box with chrysanthemum petal decoration unearthed from the Site of Weilin-Neiban Kilns. (Photo by Cheng Dongdong)

尾林—内坂窑址出土的青白瓷芒口花卉纹盘。（成冬冬 摄）
A bluish-white porcelain plate with unglazed rim and floral pattern unearthed from the Site of Weilin-Neiban Kilns. (Photo by Cheng Dongdong)

碗坪仑窑址。碗坪仑窑址位于盖德村北面山包的东南侧，南距溪约 200 米，西南距公田仑窑约 300 米，海拔 583 米，相对高度约 40 米。窑址面积 10,000 平方米。1976 年 4 月至 7 月，对该窑址进行了考古发掘，发掘面积 87.25 平方米，揭露 2 处有叠压打破关系的窑炉遗迹；窑址为东北—西南走向，东西长 200 米，南北宽 150 米。堆积层厚度约 2 米。早期窑炉保存窑头和部分窑室，残长 3.7 米，最宽处 1.4 米；晚期窑炉首尾均被破坏，仅存中间一段，残长 12 米，宽 2.6—2.8 米。文化层堆积分上、下 2 层，上层为南宋龙窑，下层为北宋龙窑，出土 1,700 多件瓷器及窑具。下层出土青白瓷，包括碗、盘、碟、炉、瓶、执壶、盒等器型，年代为北宋晚期至南宋中期；上层出土青瓷和少量酱黑釉瓷，有碗、盘、碟、瓶、军持、盏等器型，年代为南宋中晚期。釉色以白釉和青白釉为主，多刻划花卉、水波纹、云雷纹等，是宋代德化最具特色的古窑遗址之一。

About the Site of Wanpinglun Kilns. The Site of Wanpinglun Kilns is located on the southeast side of a hill north of Gaide Village, about 200 meters north of the creek, and about 300 meters northeast of Gongtianlun Kilns. At an elevation of 583 meters, the site height is about 40 meters. The site covers an area of 10,000 square meters. From April to July in 1976, archaeological excavations were carried out on the site, with an excavation area of 87.25 square meters, revealing two kiln ruins overlapping each other. The kiln site runs from northeast to southwest and is 200 meters long from east to west and 150 meters wide from north to south. The thickness of the deposit layer is about 2 meters. The early kiln has its kiln head and part of the kiln chamber preserved, with a length of 3.7 meters and 1.4 meters at its widest. The later kiln was damaged at both ends, leaving only the middle section, 12 meters long and 2.6 to 2.8 meters wide. The cultural deposit consists of two layers, with the upper layer being the remains of Southern Song Dynasty loong-shaped kiln and the lower layer being the remains of Northern Song Dynasty loong-shaped kiln. More than 1,700 porcelain artifacts and kiln facilities were unearthed. From the lower layer, bluish-white glazed porcelain wares were unearthed, including bowls, plates, dishes, stoves, bottles, pitchers, boxes, and other utensils, dating from the late Northern Song Dynasty to the mid-Southern Song Dynasty. From the upper layer, celadon and a small amount of brownish-black glazed porcelain were unearthed, including bowls, plates, dishes, bottles, kendis, and cups dating back to the mid-to-late Southern Song Dynasty. The glazes are mainly white and bluish-white. And there are many carved and incised decorations of flowers, water waves, and clouds and thunders. It is one of the most distinctive ancient kiln sites in Dehua during the Song Dynasty.

宋碗坪仑窑青白釉云纹军持。（德化陶瓷博物馆 供图）
A bluish-white glazed kendi with cloud decoration from Wanpinglun Kilns in the Song Dynasty. (Courtesy of Dehua Ceramics Museum)

甲杯山窑址。甲杯山窑址位于宝美村东部的甲杯山山坡，甲杯山属中低山地形，山顶海拔 520 米，高差约 25 米。山体浑厚，坡形连续，窑址主要分布于坡腰至山脚平台上，范围约 1,700 平方米。2001 年，投入将近两个月的时间对甲杯山窑址进行抢救性考古发掘，总发掘面积 120 平方米，揭露有叠压打破关系的窑炉遗迹 3 座，出土了一批陶瓷器标本及窑具。其中，Y3 出土标本有青白瓷和白瓷，主要是碗、盘、碟、洗、盒等器型，年代为元代；Y2、Y1 出土标本大部分为乳白色瓷器，以杯、碗、盘、盏、碟、洗、炉、罐、灯、盒、砚滴等器型为主，有些堆贴梅花，有些刻划花草、文字、人物等，年代为明代。大量白瓷烧造技术的宝贵资料在甲杯山窑址面世，出土了大量有代表性的白瓷精美器物标本，尤其是发现了一批罕见的器型，为德化白瓷研究提供了宝贵的田野资料，意义重大。

About the Site of Jiabeishan Kilns. The Site of Jiabeishan Kilns is located on the slope of Mount Jiabei in the east of Baomei Village. Mount Jiabei is of medium-low height, with its peak at an elevation of 520 meters and a height difference of about 25 meters. The mountain is thick and the slope is rolling. The kiln site mainly extends from the mountainside to the foothills and covers an area of about 1,700 square meters. In 2001, a nearly two-month rescue excavation of the Site of Jiabeishan Kilns was carried out, with a total excavation area of 120 square meters, revealing three kiln ruins overlapping each other. A batch of ceramic samples and kiln facilities were unearthed. Among them, samples unearthed from the Kiln Y3 include bluish-white glazed porcelain and white-glazed porcelain. They are mainly bowls, plates, dishes, washbasins, boxes, and other utensils, dating back to the Yuan Dynasty. Samples unearthed from the Kiln Y2 and the Kiln Y1 are mostly milky-white ceramics. They are mainly cups, bowls, plates, dishes, washbasins, stoves, jars, lamps, boxes, water injectors, etc., some of which are embossed with plum blossom decoration, and some are carved or incised with patterns of flowers, grass, characters, figures, etc., dating back to the Ming Dynasty. A large amount of valuable material on the production techniques of white porcelain has been discovered at the Site of Jiabeishan Kilns. A large number of typical samples of exquisitely made white porcelain were unearthed, and a batch of vessels in rare shapes were discovered, providing valuable field data for the study of Dehua white porcelain, with profound significance.

宋元以来，德化陶瓷随着泉州港的崛起而兴盛，销往海外，在日本、菲律宾、泰国、马来西亚、印度尼西亚等地都成为热销产品。德化窑瓷土优势显著。“泥产山中，穴而伐之，绠而出之”，高岭土、长石、石英等分布极广，质地极佳，它们“皆由石英斑岩或长英岩等富含长石之岩石风化而成。多呈脉状或其他不规则之形状，大都生于白垩纪火山岩系中”。可根据风化程度的深浅，将其用作胎土或长石瓷釉，它们细腻、柔软，颜色洁白，不须调和其他原料，即可直接制坯作器，是上好的制瓷原料。这也是为什么德化窑能生产满足中高端市场需求的产品，进而闻名于世。

Since the Song and Yuan dynasties, Dehua ceramics have prospered with the rise of Quanzhou Port and have been sold overseas. They have become hot selling products in countries such as Japan, the Philippines, Thailand, Malaysia, Indonesia, etc. Dehua has a distinct advantage of good porcelain clay. The clay takes shape in the mountains. It was dug and obtained from caves. Kaolin, feldspar, quartz and other resources are widely distributed and of excellent quality. They are all formed by weathering of rocks rich in feldspar such as quartz porphyry or felsic rock, and they are mostly distributed in the form of veins or other irregular shapes, mostly in Cretaceous volcanic rock formations. According to the extent of weathering, they can be used as clay for the greenware or feldspar glaze, with a fine and soft texture and a pure white color. As excellent materials for ceramics making, they can be directly used to make ceramic products without the addition of other raw materials. That is why Dehua Kilns can make products that met the needs from the middle- and high-end market and thus became famous around the world.

俯瞰屈斗宫窑址。（郑永集 摄）
An aerial view of the Site of Qudougong Kiln. (Photo by Zheng Yongji)

马可·波罗代言德化瓷。马可·波罗在中国生活 17 年之久，回国前曾来到泉州，到过德化。在游记中，他提到“刺桐城附近有一别城，名称迪云州。制造碗及磁（瓷）器，既多且美”。“迪云州”是德化的古称。随着《马可·波罗游记》的广泛流传，“迪云州”这三个字也蜚声于世。马可·波罗还把德化窑青白釉瓷罐带回欧洲，被欧洲人称为“马可·波罗罐”，这是有文字记载的第一件到达欧洲的德化瓷，目前收藏在马可·波罗的故乡意大利威尼斯的圣马可大教堂。

《马可·波罗游记》中还记述了德化瓷器的生产和销售情况，“这些瓷器的制作工艺如下：人们首先从地下挖取一种泥土，将其堆成一堆，在三四十年间，任凭风吹雨淋日晒，都不翻动它。经过这种处理的泥土变得十分精纯，适合烧制瓷杯、瓷碗和瓷碟等器皿。然后工匠们在土中加入合适的颜料，再放入窑中烧制。因此，那些掘土的人只是替自己的子孙准备原料。烧制好的瓷器在城中出售，一个威尼斯银币可以买八个瓷杯。”

马可·波罗代言德化瓷器，吸引了西方人的目光，直接推动了德化瓷器在海外市场的销售。

Marco Polo spoke highly of Dehua porcelain. Marco Polo lived in China for 17 years. Before returning home, he visited Quanzhou, including Dehua. In his travelogue, he mentioned a small town near Zayton called Tiunguy where beautiful bowls and ceramics were produced on a large scale. Tiunguy was the ancient name for Dehua. As *The Travels of Marco Polo* spread widely, the name of the town became famous. Marco Polo also brought back to Europe a bluish-white glazed porcelain jar made in Dehua Kilns. It was called "Marco Polo Jar" by Europeans. This was the first documented piece of Dehua porcelain to reach Europe, and is currently housed in the Saint Mark's Basilica in Venice, Italy, Marco Polo's hometown.

The Travels of Marco Polo also described the production and sale of Dehua porcelain: the process of making these porcelain wares is as follows: people dig for a type of clay from the ground, pile it up into a large heap, and leave it exposed to wind, rain, and sun for thirty to forty years without disturbing it. After this process, the clay was much refined, suitable for making porcelain cups, porcelain bowls, porcelain dishes, and other kinds of vessels. Then craftsmen add glaze with appropriate colors to the clay and fire the ceramics inside a furnace. People dig for the earth and pile it up for the purpose of stockpiling materials for their descendants. Porcelain wares are sold in the city, and people can buy eight porcelain cups for a Venetian silver coin.

Marco Polo's description of Dehua porcelain attracted the attention of Westerners and directly promoted the sales of Dehua porcelain in overseas markets.

日本“陶祖”德化学艺。南宋时，德化制瓷技术传入日本，甚至有日本人专程来德化取经。据木宫泰彦《日中文化交流史》一书记载，南宋嘉定十六年（1223），日本人加藤四郎曾随永平寺的禅僧道元入宋，到德化窑学习建窑、制瓷技术，回国后在日本濑户设窑烧制陶瓷，开辟了日本制陶技术发展的新纪元，后世尊加藤四郎为日本“陶祖”。加藤四郎将德化制瓷技术带至日本，也谱写了中日文化交往史上的一段佳话。另据铃木已代《窑炉》一书记载，日本将连室型窑称为“串窑”，大概也是借鉴了德化窑的形式。

Father of Japanese Pottery learned crafts in Dehua. During the Southern Song Dynasty, Dehua porcelain-making techniques were introduced to Japan. Some Japanese even came to Dehua specially to learn about the craft. According to the book *History of Cultural Exchange Between Japan and China* by Yasuhiko Kimiya, in 1223, a Japanese man named Shiro Kato followed Dogen, a monk from Eiheiji, to Dehua Kilns to study how to build kilns and make ceramics. After returning to Japan, he established a kiln in Seto to produce ceramics, which opened a new era of the development of Japanese pottery-making techniques. Later generations revered Shiro Kato as the father of Japanese pottery. Shiro Kato brought Dehua porcelain-making techniques to Japan, which created a beautiful chapter in the history of cultural exchange between China and Japan. Additionally, as stated in the book *Kilns* by Iyo Suzuki, Japanese referred to multi-chambered kilns as "Continuous Kilns," and they were possibly modeled on the form of Dehua Kilns.

安溪青阳下草埔冶铁遗址

位于泉州西部山区的安溪，自然条件得天独厚，矿藏种类多、储量大、品位高，有铁、煤、铅、锌、锰、银、石墨、稀土、石灰石、高岭土、花岗岩等20多种，其中铁矿、煤矿、花岗岩、石灰石、高岭土的储量居福建省前列。宋元时期，冶铁场在安溪县遍地开花，除了青阳铁场所在的尚卿乡，湖头、长卿、祥华、剑斗、福田、感德等乡镇也有冶铁遗存共20余处，下草埔冶铁遗址是其中规模最大、最为典型的遗址，是泉州地区宋元时期块炼铁冶炼的代表。下草埔冶铁遗址面积大，选址科学合理，具有较好的整体规划性。

早在五代时，就有安溪"冶有银铁，税有竹木之征"的说法。北宋时期，安溪已有官方设置的青阳铁场，据成书于北宋元丰年间的地理总志《元丰九域志》卷九记载："下清溪州西一百五里四乡青阳一铁场"；《宋史》中亦有北宋庆历五年（1045）"泉州青阳铁冶大发"的相关记载。宋代冶铁的规模和产量较之前有较大发展，全国遍设"监""冶""务""坑""场"组织冶铁业生产或进行监管。

安溪青阳下草埔冶铁遗址考古发掘现场。（成冬冬 摄）
The archaeological excavation site of Xiacaopu Iron Production Site of Qingyang Village in Anxi. (Photo by Cheng Dongdong)

Xiacaopu Iron Production Site of Qingyang Village in Anxi

Anxi, located in the western mountainous area of Quanzhou, has unique natural conditions, with large reserves of different kinds of mines of high ore grade. There are more than 20 types of mines, including iron, coal, lead, zinc, manganese, silver, graphite, rare earths, limestone, kaolin, granite and so on. The reserves of iron ore, coal mine, granite, limestone and kaolin rank among the largest in Fujian Province. During the Song and Yuan dynasties, iron smelting flourished all over Anxi County, with over 20 iron smelting sites found in towns such as Hutou, Changqing, Xianghua, Jiandou, Futian, and Gande in addition to Shangqing Town where the Qingyang ironworks was located. Among these remains, the Xiacaopu Iron Production Site is the largest and the most typical one, a representative of the sponge iron production sites of the Song-Yuan period in Quanzhou. The site covers a large area, and a scientific and reasonable approach to site selection was taken, achieving good overall planning.

As early as the Five Dynasties, Anxi was believed to have engaged in silver and iron smelting, and bamboo and wood were collected as a way of taxation. During the Northern Song Dynasty, Qingyang iron plant was set up by the government. According to *Nine Regions in the Yuanfeng Reign*, a geographical treatise written during the Yuanfeng period (1078—1085) of the Northern Song Dynasty, Volume Nine, traveling from Quanzhou to Anxi, one would find an ironworks in Qingyang, one of the four towns 150 *li* away west of Quanzhou; *History of Song* also records the significant advance of iron smelting in Qingyang, Quanzhou in 1045 during the Northern Song Dynasty. The scale and output of iron smelting in the Song Dynasty was huge compared to previous times, and production and supervision of iron smelting industry was organized nationwide through the establishment of a series of institutions.

安溪青阳下草埔冶铁场“选址有道，冶铁有术”。这里地处五阆山余脉，与安溪县城直线距离 30 千米，地势北高南低，三面背山，南面缺口，冶铁场就选址在峡谷中，便于冶炼活动的开展。遗址位于一处梯田上，北为现代铁矿坑，南为荒废田地，东西两侧均为山地。下草埔冶铁遗址面积 50,000 平方米，遗址的西、南侧各有一河流，在遗址东南交汇流向谷口，其中，发掘区西侧北南流向的河流跟北侧的池塘相通。冶炼遗址东北侧的山坡是矿山，铁矿资源丰富；周边的山地有茂密的树林，是冶炼所需燃料的来源；遗址的东部有一条古道通往西溪，是产品外运的路线，由此形成了从原料到加工再到运输的产业链条。

The site of the Xiacaopu ironworks in Qingyang, Anxi was carefully chosen, and its iron smelting techniques were well-developed. Located in the lower area of the Mount Wulang, 30 kilometers away from the county town as the crow flies, the region is high in the north and low in the south, surrounded by mountains on three sides except for its southern part. The iron smelting site was chosen in the canyon, convenient for smelting activities. The site is located on a terrace, with a modern iron mining pit in the north, abandoned fields in the south, and mountains in the east and the west. The site covers an area of 50,000 square meters. There are two rivers on the west side and south side of the site respectively which meet on the southeast side and flow toward debouchure. One of the rivers which flows from north to south on the west side of the excavation area is connected to the pond on the north side. The mountain slope in the northeast of the smelting site is a mine lot, with rich iron ore resources. There are dense forests on the surrounding mountains, providing fuel wood for smelting. To the east of the site, there is an ancient road leading to the Xixi Stream, forming a route for product transportation. In this way, an industrial chain extending from raw materials collecting to processing and then transport is formed.

2019 年 10 月至 2020 年 8 月，在国家文物局的统筹下，经过前期反复调研，北京大学考古文博学院、泉州市文化广电和旅游局、安溪县人民政府组成联合考古队，对下草埔冶铁遗址进行了为期 10 个月的考古发掘。这是福建首个大规模考古发掘的冶铁遗址，生产集中于宋元时期。生铁和块炼铁生产集为一处，有着清晰的技术体系，其中块炼铁冶炼炉结构完整、炉型多样、保存状况较好，系国内首次正式考古发掘出土，意义重大。

From October 2019 to August 2020, led by the National Cultural Heritage Administration, a joint archaeological team composed of the experts from School of Archaeology and Museology of Peking University, the Quanzhou Municipal Bureau of Culture, Radio, Television and Tourism, and the People's Government of Anxi County conducted a 10-month archaeological excavation at the Xiacaopu iron production site, based on extensive preliminary research. This is Fujian's first large-scale excavation of an iron-smelting site where smelting activities were mainly undertaken in the Song and Yuan dynasties. The production of pig iron and sponge iron was at the same site, and a clear technical system was built. It is worth noting that the structure of the bloomery for producing sponge iron was intact, with a variety of furnace types and in good condition. This is the first time that such a smelting site has been found in China, which is of considerable significance.

炼铁炉遗迹。（成冬冬 摄）
Iron smelting furnace remains. (Photo by Cheng Dongdong)

青阳村冶铁遗迹分布图。（中国建筑设计研究院 供图）

A map of iron smelting sites in Qingyang Village. (Courtesy of China Architecture Design & Research Group)

中国古代传统钢铁冶炼技术以生铁及生铁制钢技术为核心，中原地区以生铁体系为主，边疆地区则多见块炼铁技术。在下草埔冶铁场中，生铁冶炼和块炼铁冶炼两种冶炼模式并存，以块炼铁冶炼为主导。块炼铁冶炼，指的是直接还原出固态铁的冶炼过程，由于还原气氛不如生铁冶炼，渣铁分离不完全，其产物常呈海绵状，炉渣含量较高。遗址中块炼炉渣大量存在而生铁渣相对较少，可见块炼铁冶炼确实占主导地位，由此形成当地的冶铁传统。

Chinese traditional iron and steel smelting techniques in ancient times mainly focused on pig iron production and turning iron into steel. The Central Plains region mainly produced pig iron, while the border regions often produced sponge iron. Those two kinds of products coexisted at the Xiacaopu smelteries, with sponge iron production being dominant. Sponge iron smelting refers to the smelting process that directly produces solid iron. Due to the less reducing atmosphere compared to that of pig iron production, the separation of slag and iron is incomplete, resulting in a sponge-like product with a higher slag content. A large amount of bloomery slag and relatively less pig iron slag were discovered at the site, indicating that the sponge iron production indeed held a dominant position in local iron smelting traditions.

古铁矿洞外景。（成冬冬 摄）
The exterior of an ancient iron mine cave. (Photo by Cheng Dongdong)

在下草埔冶铁遗址发现了各式各样的冶铁炉，这些小高炉都是用石块垒砌而成的。其中，一号炉、二号炉是用于冶炼块炼铁的半地穴式碗状小高炉，依傍山坡的原生面而修筑。三号炉为平地砌筑，先用大块的冶炼炉渣围住，然后再修筑冶炼炉；它是由原来两侧的四个炉子废弃后改筑而成的，可以生产块炼铁、生铁以及钢。这三架冶铁炉炉型比较完整，有投料口、出渣口、鼓风口以及操作平台等。明代宋应星《天工开物》记载了冶铁炉的修造方法：“凡铁炉用盐做造，和泥砌成。其炉多傍山穴为之，或用巨木匡围，塑造盐泥，穷月之力不容造次。盐泥有罅，尽弃全功。”四号炉为锻炉，是在平地起建的地上炉型，炉体呈方形，西侧的薄胎磁灶窑缸是淬火缸。五号炉原为南宋中期的冶铁炉，南宋末至元代被改造成灶。六号炉的性质尚待进一步研究。

Various kinds of furnaces have been discovered at the Xiacaopu iron production site. The small blast furnaces were all constructed with stones. Furnace No. 1 and Furnace No. 2 were semi-subterranean bowl-shaped furnaces used for producing sponge iron, and were built against the original slope of the mountain. Furnace No. 3 was built on level ground, based on structures enclosed with large pieces of slag. It was rebuilt from four abandoned furnaces on both sides, and could produce sponge iron, pig iron, and steel. These three furnaces are relatively well-preserved, with feeding mouth, slag discharging mouth, air supply mouth, and operating platforms, etc. The method of constructing iron furnaces was recorded by Song Yingxing, a Chinese scientist who lived during the Ming Dynasty, in his book *The Exploitation of the Works of Nature*: all iron furnaces were made of salt mixed with mud, many of which were built near mountain caves, or enclosed with giant logs, where salt mud was made. One month of hard work was put in. No imperfection was allowed. If there were cracks in the salt mud, the entire structure would be abandoned. Furnace No. 4 was a forging furnace and was built on the level ground with a square furnace body. The thin-walled tank made in Cizao Kilns on the west side was used for quenching. Furnace No. 5 was originally a mid-Southern Song Dynasty iron smelting furnace, and was transformed into a range from the late Southern Song Dynasty to the Yuan Dynasty. Further research is needed to determine the nature of Furnace No. 6.

下草埔冶铁遗址周边铁矿蕴藏丰富，森林茂密，为冶场提供了丰富的铁矿和木炭资源。《天工开物》中“治（冶）铁”条记载：“凡炉中炽铁用炭，煤炭居十七，木炭居十三。凡山林无煤之处，锻工先择坚硬条木，烧成火墨（俗名火矢，扬烧不闭穴火），其炎更烈于煤。即用煤炭，亦别有铁炭一种，取其火性内攻，焰不虚腾者，与炊炭同形而分类也。”青阳村庵坑两座近现代烧炭窑，可能沿袭了宋元时期烧炭窑的样式。

There are rich iron deposits and dense forests near the Xiacaopu iron production site, providing abundant iron ore and charcoal resources for iron smelting. According to the record of "iron smelting" in the book *The Exploitation of the Works of Nature*, in the furnace, charcoal was used for smelting iron, with coal accounting for seventy percent and wood charcoal accounting for thirty percent. In places where there was no coal in the mountains and forests, metalsmiths first selected hard and straight wood, and burnt it into hard charcoal (commonly known as fire arrows, burning without closing the hole). Its flame was even more raging than coal. If coal was used, a particular type of broken coal making low flames would be chosen. It produced internal power and its flame was truly strong. It differentiated itself from the charcoal for kitchen use, though they were similar in shape. There are two modern charcoal kilns in Ankeng of Qingyang Village. They may have inherited the style of charcoal kilns in the Song and Yuan dynasties.

安溪青阳下草埔冶铁遗址出土的扇形排出渣。（何康 摄）
Fan-shaped slag excavated from Xiacaopu Iron Production Site of Qingyang Village in Anxi. (Photo by He Kang)

宋元时期安溪冶铁业已有合理处理冶炼垃圾的意识。在下草埔冶铁遗址发现了有规划的板结层，这一独特现象在世界上还是首次发现。遗址发掘区包含 14 级台地，在台地 1、台地 2、台地 4、台地 6、台地 7、台地 8、台地 9 和台地 11 都发现了板结层。板结层主要包含的是黏土、块炼铁颗粒、碎炉渣、方解石颗粒等，质地坚硬，可能是单质铁含量较高的炉渣锈结，是与人类活动相关的硬结层。板结层间距大致等同，在 60 厘米至 80 厘米之间。每当冶炼垃圾堆积到一定的高度时，会进行泼水冷却、细碎、平整，并结合炉渣、炉灰堆积位置和次序进行合理规划处理，板结层由此形成。板结层一方面起到压实、固定冶炼垃圾的作用，这也是就地处理冶炼垃圾的简易有效的办法；另一方面，也可以作为后来者进行冶炼的操作平台。因此，安溪宋元冶铁场多呈现自下而上、依靠山坡修筑冶炉的面貌，一旦达到一定高度，冶铁场也就随之弃用，另择其他场所。在安溪长坑乡青苑宋代冶铁遗址、南斗宋代冶铁遗址等处也发现了板结层。

安溪青阳下草埔冶铁遗址人类活动面遗迹。（成冬冬 摄）
Traces of human activities at Xiacaopu Iron Production Site of Qingyang Village in Anxi. (Photo by Cheng Dongdong)

During the Song and Yuan dynasties, people who engaged in iron smelting in Anxi had already been conscious of disposing of waste in a rational way. Layers of hardened soil were discovered at the Xiacaopu iron production site, a unique discovery for the first time in the world. The excavation area of the site includes 14 terraces, and layers of hardened soil were found on Terrace No. 1, Terrace No. 2, Terrace No. 4, Terrace No. 6, Terrace No. 7, Terrace No. 8, Terrace No. 9 and Terrace No. 11. The layers mainly consist of clay, particles of sponge iron, slag, and particles of calcite, with a hard texture. They might be formed by the rust slag with a high content of elemental iron, and are hard layers related to human activities. The distances between the hard layers are roughly the same, about 60 centimeters to 80 centimeters. When the smelting waste was piled to a certain height, it would be cooled by splashing water, crushed, and leveled, and then rationally dealt with according to the position and piling time of slag and ash. The layers of hardened soil were thus formed. On the one hand, the layers played a role in compacting and fixing the smelting waste. It was a simple and effective method for disposing of the waste on the spot. On the other hand, the layers also served as platforms for later smelting operations. Therefore, the iron smelting sites in Anxi during the Song and Yuan dynasties created a sight of furnaces constructed from the bottom up against the slope. Once the layers reached a certain height, the site would no longer be used and another site would be chosen. Such layers have also been found at the iron smelting sites of the Song Dynasty in Qingyuan and Nandou in Changkeng Town of Anxi.

下草埔冶铁遗址出土遗物，按照材质可分为冶炼遗物、钱币、金属器、陶瓷、石块 5 大类。其中，冶炼遗物主要包括炉渣、矿石、烧土、炉衬 4 大类，炉渣数量最为丰富，可分为排出渣、挂渣、炉内渣 3 类，排出渣又有槽形排出渣和扇形排出渣。它们是冶场长时间冶铁活动的见证者。金属器大致分为铁制品和铜制品，铁钉是遗址目前仅见的锻打铁制品，这也进一步证明了当时锻造活动的存在；铁片、铁块为块炼铁粗加工的产品，是遗址性质的直接证据。出土陶瓷可分为建筑构件、陶器和瓷器，建筑构件主要有筒瓦和板瓦，其中板瓦有黄、红、白 3 色，在数量上多于筒瓦，另有滴水、瓦当残件及地表采集的花纹陶砖，这些建筑构件是已发现的 4 处工匠或管理人员居所房屋的遗存，其中一处屋内南间东南角还发现 1 座灶台，推测这里是生活用宅。

The unearthed relics from the Xiacaopu iron smelting site can be divided into five categories based on material: smelting relics, coins, metal wares, ceramics, and stones. Smelting relics mainly include slag, ore, burnt soil, and furnace linings. Among them, slag is the most abundant and can be divided into three types: discharged slag, hanging slag, and furnace slag. Discharged slag can be further divided into trough-shaped and fan-shaped slag. They are witnesses to the long-term iron smelting activities at the site. Metal wares are roughly divided into iron products and copper products. Iron nails are the only forged iron product found at the site, which further proves the existence of forging activities at the time. Iron sheets and iron blocks are products from rough processing in bloomery, which are direct evidence of the nature of the site. Unearthed ceramics can be divided into building components, pottery, and porcelain. The building components mainly include cylinder tiles and flat tiles. There are yellow, red, and white flat tiles, and flat tiles outnumber cylinder tiles. There are also *di shui* (literally meaning "water drops") tiles for draining the rainfall from the roof, eaves tile remnants, and bricks with floral pattern collected from the surface of the ground. These building components are remains of the four discovered homes of craftsmen or managers. In addition, a cooker was found in the southeast corner of the south room of one house, indicating that it was likely to be a residential house.

下草埔冶铁遗址出土的陶瓷器以南宋中晚期至元代的安溪窑、磁灶窑产品为主，兼有多种福建地区宋元时期其他窑口的产品。陶器包括罐、执壶、盆、缸、盏、器盖、器耳、勺、纺轮等，大件器居多。瓷器包括碗、碟、盏、盘、瓶、罐、壶、水注、器盖、杯、洗等，以碗为大宗，有青釉、青白釉、白釉、黑釉等釉色。其中25件陶瓷器带有墨书，如“朱佰伍”“置”“四伍”“吴”“朱”“胡五”“十”“郭□”等，墨书瓷器集中出土于冶炼炉和建筑遗迹周边区域，墨书很可能是冶铁工匠的姓氏；其他没有墨书的日用陶瓷器，很可能是大量伐木、烧制木炭、矿石提炼与材料运输等非冶铁技术工种人员使用的。表面平整、不见任何遗物的地面很可能是冶铁作坊工人主要的日常活动场所。

The ceramics unearthed from the Xiacaopu iron smelting site mainly include products from Anxi Kilns and Cizao Kilns between the middle- to-late Southern Song Dynasty and the Yuan Dynasty, as well as products from other kilns in Fujian during the Song-Yuan period. Pottery includes jars, pitchers, basins, tanks, cups, lids, lugs, spoons, and spindle whorls, the majority of which were larger items. Porcelain includes bowls, dishes, cups, plates, bottles, jars, pots, water injectors, lids, and washbasins. Bowls are in the majority, with glazes including celadon, bluish-white, white, and black. Among them, there are 25 pieces bearing ink writing, such as "Zhu Bai Wu," "Zhi," "Si Wu," "Wu," "Zhu," "Hu Wu," "Shi," "Guo (?)," etc. Porcelain wares bearing ink writing are mainly unearthed near the smelting furnaces and architectural remains. Those marks are very likely to be the surnames of iron smelting workers. Other daily-use ceramics without ink writing were possibly owned by a large number of workers engaging in logging, charcoal burning, ore refining, and material transportation. The flat ground without any relics on the surface is likely to be the main place for daily activities for iron smelting workers.

安溪青阳下草埔冶铁遗址出土的铜钱。（何康 摄）

Copper coins unearthed from Xiacaopu Iron Production Site of Qingyang Village in Anxi. (Photo by He Kang)

安溪青阳下草埔冶铁遗址出土的瓷器碗底。（何康 摄）

Porcelain bowl bottoms unearthed from Xiacaopu Iron Production Site of Qingyang Village in Anxi. (Photo by He Kang)

安溪青阳下草埔冶铁遗址出土的花纹砖。（何康 摄）
Bricks with floral pattern unearthed from Xiacaopu Iron Production Site of Qingyang Village in Anxi. (Photo by He Kang)

安溪青阳下草埔冶铁遗址出土的矿石。（何康 摄）
Ores unearthed from Xiacaopu Iron Production Site of Qingyang Village in Anxi. (Photo by He Kang)

冶铁业采用官办与民办相结合的生产模式。宋代泉州最主要的铁产地是安溪的青阳铁场、永春的倚洋铁场和德化的赤水铁场与五华铁场。《宋史》记载：“（庆历）五年，泉州青阳铁冶大发，转运使高易简不俟诏，置铁钱务于泉，欲移铜钱于内地。”

除了以块炼铁冶炼为主的冶铁场之外，晋江下游还有铸铁和灌钢的冶炼作坊。经下草埔冶铁场小高炉冶炼后的产品经过锻打形成铁块、铁片等后，再加工或运输至晋江下游梧宅铸铁冶炼作坊和曾炉寺灌钢冶炼作坊等其他地区进行锻造再成型，制成铁器，共同构成泉州完整的冶铁业生产链条，成为海上丝绸之路贸易的重要商品之一。

铁制品是重要的外销产品。宋元时期，安溪茶叶、瓷器、铁制品通过晋江西溪水路运到泉州，再通过泉州刺桐港出口到海外，在中外贸易中占据优势长达数百年。安溪冶铁制品可分为熟铁（块炼铁）、生铁和钢三部分。一部分产品县内自销，其余的除了销往邻近地区之外，大部分“兴贩入海”“远泛蕃国”，通过泉州源源不断销往东南亚等国家和地区，“取金贝而还，民甚称便”。

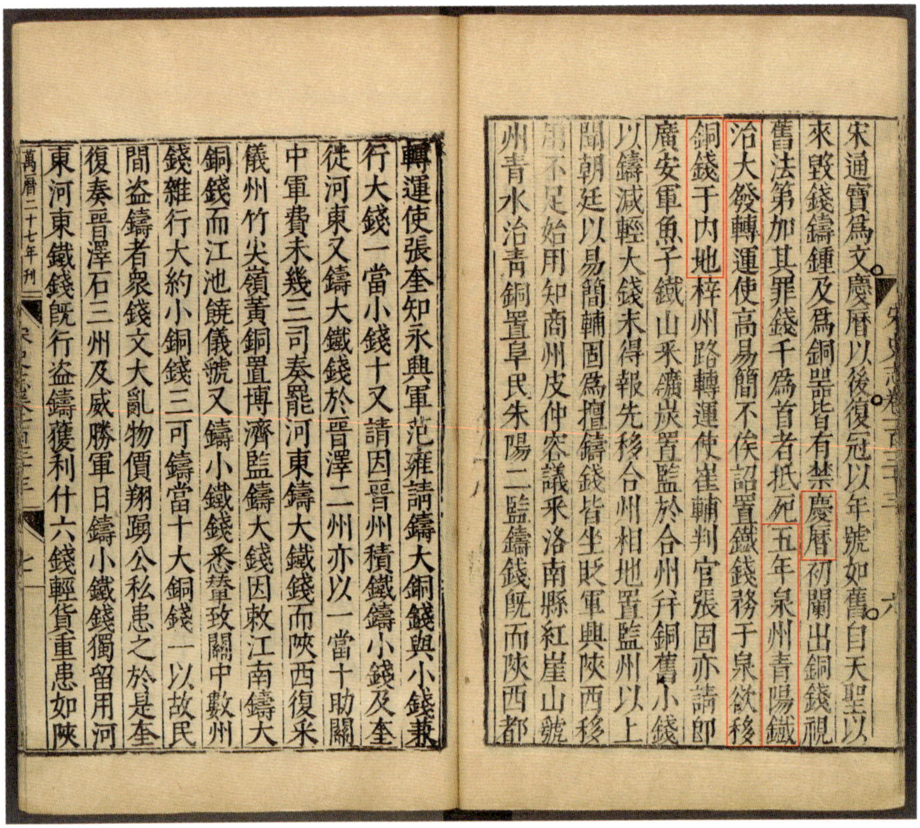
宋通寶爲文慶曆以後復冠以年號如舊自天聖以
來毀錢鑄鍾及爲銅器皆有禁慶曆初闌出銅錢視
舊法第加其罪錢千爲首者抵死五年泉州青陽鐵
冶大發轉運使高易簡不俟詔置鐵錢務于泉欲移
銅錢于內地梓州路轉運使崔輔判官張固亦請即
廣安軍魚子鐵山采礦炭置監於合州并銅舊小錢
以鑄減輕大錢未得報先移合州相地置監州以上
聞朝廷以易簡輔固爲擅鑄錢皆坐貶軍興陝西移
用不足始用知商州皮仲容議采洛南縣紅崖山虢
州青水冶青銅置阜民朱陽二監鑄錢既而陝西都
轉運使張奎知永興軍范雍請鑄大銅錢與小錢兼
行大錢一當小錢十又請因晉州積鐵鑄小錢及奎
徙河東又鑄大鐵錢於晉澤二州亦以一當十助關
中軍費未幾三司奏罷河東鑄大鐵錢而陝西復采
儀州竹尖嶺黄銅置博濟監鑄大錢因敕江南鑄大
銅錢而江池饒儀虢又鑄小鐵錢悉輦致關中數州
錢雜行大約小銅錢三可鑄當十大銅錢一以故民
間盜鑄者衆錢文大亂物價翔踴公私患之於是奎
復奏晉澤石三州及威勝軍日鑄小鐵錢獨留用河
東河東鐵錢既行盜鑄獲利什六錢輕貨重患如陝
萬曆二十七年刊

《宋史》中关于青阳冶铁的记载。（黄明珍 供图）
The record of iron smelting in Qingyang in *History of Song*. (Courtesy of Huang Mingzhen)

The iron smelting industry adopted a production mode that combined official and private ownership. The main iron production areas in Quanzhou during the Song Dynasty were the Qingyang iron field in Anxi, the Yiyang iron field in Yongchun, and the Chishui iron field as well as the Wuhua iron field in Dehua. According to *History of Song*, in 1045, there was a large-scale development of iron smelting in Quanzhou's Qingyang iron field, and Gao Yijian, the Transport Commissioner, set up the iron money mint in Quanzhou without waiting for the imperial decree, intending to move copper money mint to the hinterland.

In addition to the smelting yards that focused on sponge iron production, there were also iron casting workshops and steel making workshops near the lower reaches of Jinjiang River. Products obtained from the smelting process in small blast furnaces in Xiacaopu ironworks were struck into iron blocks and iron sheets, which were further processed or transported downstream to areas like Wuzhai iron casting workshops and Zenglu Temple steel making workshops to be forged and shaped, and then made into ironware. These steps together form a complete iron production chain in Quanzhou, and its products became one of the important commodities in the trade activities along the Maritime Silk Road.

Iron products were important export products. During the Song and Yuan dynasties, Anxi's tea, porcelain, and iron products were transported along the Xixi Stream of Jinjiang river system to Quanzhou, and then exported overseas through the Zayton Port. They held an advantageous position in foreign trade for hundreds of years. Iron products in Anxi could be divided into three main categories: wrought iron (sponge iron), pig iron, and steel. Some of the products were sold to local and neighboring areas, while the rest were sold overseas, like countries and regions in Southeast Asia. They were traded for gold and shells, and people enjoyed the convenience.

生铁产品。用生铁铸造的锅、釜，在宋元明时期被海外大量购置。铸造锅釜用于对外商贸，是宋代冶铁业的一项重要业务。大锅难得，可以用于制造军器，甚或装炮，因此十分抢手。“南海Ⅰ号”沉船出水了十几万件文物，其中有大量的铁质凝结物（铁锅）、铁锭、铁条，还有银锭、铜环等。元代汪大渊《岛夷志略》中也记载了当时海外贸易中有铁锅、铁条等货物。到了明代，这种货物仍是海外贸易中的重要物品，例如，在明代“南澳Ⅰ号”沉船出水文物中，可以见到铁锅、铜钱、铜板以及锡壶等物品。

About pig iron products. Iron pots and cauldrons made of pig iron were extensively purchased overseas during the Song, Yuan, and Ming dynasties. Casting iron pots and cauldrons for foreign trade was an essential business of the iron smelting industry during the Song Dynasty. Large pots were rare but highly sought after as they could be used to make armaments, and even carry cannons. Over 100,000 artifacts were recovered from the "Nanhai No. 1" Shipwreck, including a large number of iron condensates (iron pots), iron ingots, iron bars, as well as silver ingots, copper rings, and other objects. Wang Dayuan's *A Brief Account of Island Inhabitants* of the Yuan Dynasty also mentioned iron pots and iron bars as commodities in overseas trade at the time. In the Ming Dynasty, these goods remained important in foreign trade. For example, in the artifacts recovered from the "Nan'ao No. 1" Shipwreck in the Ming Dynasty, there are iron pots, copper coins, copper plates, and tin kettles.

炼银中间产品。《旧唐书》卷四十八记载："夫铸钱不杂以铅铁则无利，杂以铅铁则恶。"这一现象可能与唐以后一种炼银的技术手段有关，即铁还原沉淀熔炼法，利用铁的亲硫性，将含银铅从其硫化物中置换出来。这种方法的一大优势是，不需要对含银硫化铅矿石进行焙烧，因而减少了银在焙烧步骤中的损失，提高了银的提取效率。当时多利用铁还原沉淀熔炼法炼含银铅，再结合利用灰吹法提炼含银铅中的银。灰吹法是一种冶炼、提取银的工艺，始见于南宋赵彦卫《云麓漫钞》和洪咨夔《大冶赋》。该技术利用铅易氧化的特点，将炼银工艺中间产物（银铅合金）中的铅氧化成"灰"（密陀僧）而将银分离出来。《天工开物》中亦有关于这种技术的记载。其操作简单，金属收得率与银的纯度均较高。离下草埔冶铁遗址不远的尚卿福林银场遗址是宋代一处官办的银场，采集到的炉渣属于排出渣类型，是典型的铁还原沉淀熔炼法炼铅渣。结合炉渣宏观形貌特征，初步判断福林银场炼银遗址系修筑高炉，使用了铁还原沉淀熔炼法炼含银铅。

About intermediate products for silver refining. According to Volume 48 of *The Old Book of Tang*, if money was minted without adding lead and iron, the industry was not profitable; if mixed with lead and iron, it would be despised. This phenomenon might be related to a silver refining technique that emerged after the Tang Dynasty i.e. iron reduction precipitation smelting. The technique utilizes iron's sulfur-philic nature to displace silver-containing lead from its sulfide. One major advantage of this method is that it does not require roasting silver-containing lead sulfide ores, reducing the loss of silver, thereby improving its extraction efficiency. At that time, iron reduction precipitation smelting method was often used to refine silver-containing lead, along with the use of cupellation method to separate silver from lead. The cupellation method is used in silver smelting and silver refining. It was first seen in *Zhao Yanwei's Historical Notes* and Hong Zikui's *The Ode to Mining and Smelting.* This technique takes advantage of the fact that lead is easily oxidized, oxidizing the lead in silver-lead alloy, the intermediate product in silver smelting. The oxidized lead, called lithargyrum, were thus separated from silver. *The Exploitation of the Works of Nature* also records this technique. The method allows of easy operation, and both the yield and purity of the silver are relatively high. The silver plant site of Fulin Village, Shangqing, not far from the Xiacaopu iron production site, was an official silver refining plant during the Song Dynasty. The slag collected from the site belongs to the discharged slag. To be specific, it is a typical slag of iron reduction precipitation smelting. Based on the form of the slag, initial judgement was reached that the silver plant of Fulin Village built blast furnaces and applied the iron reduction precipitation smelting method for silver-containing lead refining.

块炼铁产品。下草埔冶铁场使用石块垒砌小高炉进行冶炼，炉容量远大于地炉冶炼，排出渣产量大，生产的海绵铁可能具有一定含碳量。这种海绵铁经过初锻形成铁块、铁片等初加工产品，再加工或运输至国内外其他地区。

铁钉等钢产品。铁钉等钢产品是兵器的重要构件，对船只建造也是不可或缺的。元代周达观《真腊风土记》“舟楫”条记载：“船亦用铁钉，上以茭叶盖覆，却以槟榔木破片压之。此船名为‘新拏’，用棹。所粘之油，鱼油也；所和之灰，石灰也。”随着造船业逐步发展，铁钉等钢产品的需求量也不断扩大。

About sponge iron products. The Xiacaopu ironworks used small blast furnaces for smelting. The furnace capacity was much larger than that of traditional ground furnaces, resulting in higher slag output. The sponge iron from these furnaces might have contained a certain amount of carbon. The sponge iron was initially struck into iron blocks and iron sheets, and then further processed or transported to other regions home and abroad.

About steel products like iron nails. Steel products like iron nails are important components of weapons and indispensable for shipbuilding. According to Zhou Daguan's *A Record of Cambodia: The Land and Its People* written in the Yuan Dynasty, iron nails were used for shipbuilding, covered with Zizania leaves and pressed with broken betel wood. This type of ship was called *xin na* and was propelled by oars. The adhesive used was fish oil, and lime was added. With the gradual development of shipbuilding industry, the demand for steel products such as iron nails had also continuously expanded.

生产经营实现了“采、产、运、销”一体化。下草埔冶铁遗址及周边相关遗址均分布于古道或水系周围，贯穿其间的陆路、水路运输系统，将区域内外密切联结，呈现高度一体化的乡村腹地手工业体系和海港经济体的空间布局和整体形态。宋元时期，安溪冶铁场的产品运上竹排，经郭埔至金谷源口渡上船，可一路顺流至泉州，且下草埔冶铁场东侧有运送货物的古道，源口渡处进入清溪，上游与蓬莱的新林渡相连，下游经过县治西北的吴埔渡后，可顺流而下一直通向晋江入海。这样，从安溪到泉州便形成了比较完整的生产经营模式。

An integrated system connecting mining, production, transportation, and sale was formed. The Xiacaopu iron production site and its surrounding remains were distributed around old roads or waterways, and the land and water transportation systems connecting the region with the outside world established a highly integrated spatial layout and overall form of the rural handcraft industry and port economy. In the Song and Yuan dynasties, the products of the iron smelting plants in Anxi were transported up the bamboo rafts, and then carried to Guopu, before being shipped to Yuankou wharf in Jingu, where ships could sail downstream to Quanzhou. To the east of the Xiacaopu iron production site, there is an ancient road for transporting goods. From Yuankou wharf, the boats entered Qingxi Stream whose upper reaches connected with the Xinlin wharf in Penglai and whose lower reaches was where Wupu wharf, northwest of the county seat, was located. The boats reached Jinjiang River which flows into the sea. A relatively complete production and management model from Anxi to Quanzhou was thereby established.

安溪青阳下草埔冶铁遗址生动展现了宋元泉州冶炼场生产与生活的图景，是中国东南地区经济史、手工业技术史、海洋贸易史的缩影。这里发现的冶炼遗迹、遗物承载着丰富的信息，融合了多样的技术，冶铁技术体系比较完整，是重要的实物资料。冶场采用板结层的方式就地处理掩埋冶炼垃圾，充分展现了冶场管理者和工匠在处理人地关系上的超常智慧。包括生铁产品、块炼铁产品、钢产品以及用于炼银的中间产品这 4 类主要外销铁制品，通过陆路和内河航运紧密相连的、便捷的运输系统，运送到泉州并随同其他地方的铁制品汇入海上丝绸之路，完成了“采、产、运、销”的高度整合，推动当地冶铁经济与文化融入世界海洋文明。

安溪青阳下草埔冶铁遗址展示馆内生动还原了宋元时期青阳下草埔冶铁场景。（陈晓东 摄）
The vivid reconstruction of the iron smelting scene at Xiacaopu of Qingyang Village during the Song and Yuan dynasties in the Exhibition Hall of Xiacaopu Iron Production Site of Qingyang Village in Anxi. (Photo by Chen Xiaodong)

The Xiacaopu Iron Production Site of Qingyang Village in Anxi vividly presents the production activities and life in Quanzhou smelting fields in Song-Yuan era, and is a microcosm of the development of economy, handcraft technology, and maritime trade of southeastern China. The smelting relics and artifacts found at the site carry rich information, having incorporated various technologies. The iron smelting technology system was relatively complete. The remains constitute important archaeological materials. The smelteries dealt with smelting waste on the spot by constructing hard layers, fully demonstrating the extraordinary wisdom of the managers and craftsmen in handling the relationship between humans and the environment. There were mainly four kinds of iron products for export, including pig iron products, sponge iron products, steel products, and intermediate products used for silver refining. They were transported to Quanzhou through a convenient transportation system with land routes and waterway closely connected, and joined other iron products from different places to become commodities along the Maritime Silk Road. A highly integrated system combining mining, production, transportation, and sale was formed, and the site promoted the integration of local iron production economy and culture into the world maritime civilization.

走向世界的宋元“泉州造”陶瓷器

日本著名古陶瓷学家三上次男说：“古代东西方的文明交流是写在中国陶瓷上的。”

宋元时期，泉州陶瓷生产遍及泉州城郊和山区腹地，窑场密布，可谓盛况空前。各窑场依托资源优势，以海外市场为导向，生产各具特色的产品，形成了德化窑、永春窑、安溪窑、南安窑、磁灶窑、东门窑和同安窑等数量众多的窑口，磁灶窑、德化窑两大窑系的产业规模最大、产品品种和产品数量也最多，共同供应着海内外市场不同层次的消费需求，“泉州造”陶瓷由此风靡世界。今天，在东亚、东南亚、南亚、西亚和东非的国家和地区，都有大量的“泉州造”陶瓷在大海沉船中、在港口城市的地下地层里相继出水或出土，是海上丝绸之路商贸活动这一古代人类伟大壮举的重要历史见证，这些宝藏弥足珍贵，被当地的国家博物馆、美术馆和私人收藏家收藏和珍视。

世界手工艺理事会专家组授予福建德化县“世界陶瓷之都”称号。图为专家组考察德化瓷。（中新图片 供图）
The World Crafts Council bestowed the title of "World Ceramics Capital" upon Dehua County, Fujian Province. The photo shows the expert panel examining Dehua porcelain. (Courtesy of CNSphoto.com)

Ceramics Made in Song-Yuan Quanzhou Famous Worldwide

Tsugio Mikami, a renowned Japanese ceramic scholar, once said that the exchange of civilizations between ancient East and West was written on Chinese ceramics.

During the Song-Yuan period, Quanzhou ceramics production spread throughout the outskirts of Quanzhou and the mountainous areas, with densely distributed kilns. The industry had developed on an unprecedented scale. Oriented toward overseas market, each one of them made good use of its resources, and made unique products. Many kilns, such as Dehua Kilns, Yongchun Kilns, Anxi Kilns, Nan'an Kilns, Cizao Kilns, Dongmen Kilns, and Tong'an Kilns, were built. Cizao Kilns and Dehua Kilns had the largest production scale, the most product varieties and the largest number of products. They met different levels of consumer demand from domestic and foreign markets, and ceramics made in Quanzhou gained worldwide popularity. Today, a large number of ceramics made in Song-Yuan Quanzhou have been discovered in sunken ships in the sea and in underground layers of port cities in countries and regions in East Asia, Southeast Asia, South Asia, West Asia, and East Africa. These ceramics are important historical evidence of the great accomplishments by ancient people who engaged in trade activities along the Maritime Silk Road. These treasures are extremely precious and are collected and cherished by national museums, art galleries, and private collectors.

单是日本东京国立博物馆《日本出土的中国陶瓷》一书所搜集的日本各地出土的中国瓷器就达数百件，其中有不少是泉州一些窑场烧造的产品，如：在日本的福冈、长野等地，出土了磁灶窑系童子山窑生产的釉下彩黄釉铁绘花纹盘，安溪窑的素面青瓷碗、青瓷执壶和折沿青瓷洗等；在奈良出土了磁灶窑绿釉瓷片标本；在镰仓、博多海岸也发现了日本镰仓时代由中国运输到日本的瓷器，其中就有磁灶窑生产的绿釉瓶、青釉执壶、青釉褐彩盆、黄绿釉盆等陶瓷器，以及同安窑系汀溪窑生产的青黄釉刻花篦纹碗，日本人称之为“珠光青瓷”；在对马出土的绿釉器（印花盘、盆）是磁灶窑系蜘蛛山窑、土尾庵窑的产品……

蜘蛛山窑出土的绿釉上面画黄釉斑点的黄绿釉划花器，在日本也发现不少。1981 年 4 月底，日本日中贸易史学者友好访华团来到泉州，访华团团长三上次男教授谈到，晋江土尾庵的绿釉瓷器，在日本到处都有……在日本的山口等地出土有宋代德化窑白釉盒子、青白釉撇口平底洗。日本学者森村健一、田中克子等在参观磁灶金交椅山窑址的泉州古代外销陶瓷博物馆时，也提到日本京都、博多等地区出土的急须就有磁灶窑同类器物造型。

宋同安汀溪窑青釉划花碗。（成冬冬 摄）
A celadon-glazed bowl with incised floral pattern in the Song Dynasty from Tingxi Kilns of the Tong'an kiln system. (Photo by Cheng Dongdong)

Just in the book *Chinese Ceramics Excavated in Japan* by the Tokyo National Museum, hundreds of pieces of Chinese porcelain unearthed in various parts of Japan have been mentioned, many of which were products from Quanzhou kilns. For example, plates with underglaze yellow using iron-containing colorant produced by Tongzishan Kilns, and plain celadon bowls, celadon pitchers, as well as celadon basins with foliated edge produced by Anxi Kilns, have been unearthed in Fukuoka and Nagano. In Nara, there are also shards of green-glazed porcelain from Cizao Kilns. On the coast of Kamakura and Hakata, porcelain imported from China during the Kamakura period in Japanese history was also discovered, including green-glazed bottles, celadon-glazed pitchers, celadon-glazed basins with brown splashes, as well as yellow-and-green glazed basins produced in Cizao Kilns, and bluish-yellow glazed bowls with carved decoration and comb patterns, also known as "celadon with pearly luster," produced in Tingxi Kilns, part of the Tong'an kiln system. In Tsushima, the green-glazed wares produced in Zhizhushan Kilns and Tuwei'an Kilns, including plates and basins with impressed flower pattern, were unearthed...

Quite a few green-glazed utensils with yellow splashes and incised floral patterns, produced in Zhizhushan Kilns, have also been discovered in Japan. In late April, 1981, a delegation of Japanese scholars studying Japan-China trade history made a friendly visit to Quanzhou, and Tsugio Mikami, the head of the delegation, mentioned that the green-glazed porcelain from Tuwei'an Kilns in Jinjiang could be found in many places in Japan, and that white-glazed boxes and bluish-white basins with a spreading mouth and a flat bottom from Dehua Kilns in Song Dynasty had been unearthed in Yamaguchi and other places in Japan. Japanese scholars Kenichi Morimura and Katsuko Tanaka mentioned during their visit to the Quanzhou Ancient Exported Ceramics Museum at the site of Jinjiaoyishan Kilns that some teapots found in Kyoto, Hakata, and other regions of Japan were similar to those unearthed in Cizao Kilns in shape.

有学者通过查阅菲律宾的大量考古记录得出结论，在菲律宾的 12 世纪至 13 世纪的遗址普遍出土的两种宋代瓷器，是泉州外销的，其中，一种是影青牙白凸纹瓷瓶，是德化窑烧制的，另一种是双鱼纹和螺纹的青瓷，是同安窑烧制的。除此之外，在菲律宾出土的不少中国宋元时期的瓷器中，青釉盖罐和瓜形盒器物是南安窑系东田窑的产品，青釉执壶、八棱盒、瓜瓣罐、瓜瓣杯等都是安溪窑产品，双龙抢珠或缠枝牡丹绿釉军持、黑釉军持、刻花瓷炉、刻花瓷瓶等都是磁灶窑产品。值得一提的是，出土的绿釉菱花盘、绿釉长颈瓶、剔花玉壶春瓶、青釉瓜棱腹执壶、酱釉粗颈执壶、酱釉直口执壶、青釉铁斑执壶、酱釉粗颈罐、黄绿釉六系罐、蟠龙军持、黄绿釉军持、绿釉军持等是磁灶土尾庵窑的产品。

Based on extensive archaeological records in the Philippines, scholars concluded that there were two major types of Song Dynasty porcelain unearthed from sites dating back to the 12th century and the 13th century in the Philippines which were bought from Quanzhou. One is shadowy blue and ivory white porcelain bottles with raised design, produced in Dehua Kilns, and the other is celadon ware with double-fish pattern and spiral design, made in Tong'an Kilns. Except for that, among many porcelain objects made in China during Song-Yuan era unearthed in the Philippines, there were celadon-glazed lidded jars and melon-shaped boxes from Dongtian Kilns in the Nan'an kiln system, celadon-glazed pitchers, octagonal boxes, jars and cups in the shape of melon pieces, and other products of Anxi Kilns, as well as green-glazed kendis with double loong playing with pearl design or interlocking scrolls of peonies decoration, black-glazed kendis, porcelain burners and bottles with carved floral pattern, and other products of Cizao Kilns. It's worth mentioning that products from Tuwei'an Kilns, such as green-glazed plates with water chestnut flower pattern, green-glazed bottles with long neck, *yu hu chun* (literally meaning "spring in a jade bottle," a pear-shaped bottle with flaring lip) bottles with carved floral pattern, celadon-glazed pitchers with melon-shaped belly, brown-glazed thick-necked pitchers, brown-glazed straight-mouthed pitchers, celadon-glazed iron-spotted pitchers, brown-glazed thick-necked jars, yellow-and-green glazed jars with six lugs, kendis with coiling loong design, yellow-and-green glazed kendis, green-glazed kendis have been unearthed in the Philippines.

在菲律宾发现的宋元磁灶窑黄绿釉军持。（栗建安 供图）
A yellow-and-green glazed kendi from Cizao Kilns in Song-Yuan era discovered in the Philippines. (Courtesy of Li Jian'an)

著名古陶瓷专家冯先铭在菲律宾进行外销陶瓷相关考察时，发现了磁灶窑生产的低温绿铅釉印花盘、军持等器，认为军持应属定烧器。在菲律宾发现的德化窑瓷器也确实不少，种类也十分丰富。1964 年以来，在菲律宾圣安娜、民都洛等古代文化遗址和墓葬中发现了数千件德化窑瓷器，例如，在圣安娜出土了青白釉小瓶、青白釉碗、青白釉大盖盒，在民都洛出土了青白釉尊形壶、青白釉注壶。此外，德化窑军持、玉壶春瓶、青白釉盖罐、青白釉小盖盒、青白釉飞凤碗、高足杯、青白釉墩式碗等在菲律宾也有出土。

Feng Xianming, an expert in ancient ceramics, discovered products of Cizao Kilns, including plates with impressed floral pattern and kendis under green lead-containing glaze fired at low temperatures, during his investigation into the porcelain products in the Philippines, and he believed that kendis should be customized products. Indeed, there are also many Dehua Kilns porcelain wares found in the Philippines, with a wide variety of types. Since 1964, thousands of Dehua Kilns porcelain products have been unearthed from ancient cultural sites and tombs in locations such as Santa Ana and Mindoro. For example, small bluish-white glazed bottles, bluish-white glazed bowls, as well as large bluish-white glazed lidded boxes were found in Santa Ana, and bluish-white glazed pots as well as bluish-white glazed liquor containers were found in Mindoro. In addition, kendis, *yu hu chun* bottles, bluish-white glazed lidded jars, small bluish-white glazed lidded boxes, bluish-white glazed bowls with flying phoenix pattern, stem cups, and stump-like bluish-white glazed bowls produced in Dehua Kilns have also been unearthed in the Philippines.

在菲律宾发现的宋元磁灶窑绿釉军持。（栗建安 供图）

A green-glazed kendi from Cizao Kilns in Song-Yuan era discovered in the Philippines. (Courtesy of Li Jian'an)

1947 年至 1967 年，在马来西亚沙捞越发现数以万计的中国唐宋时期瓷器，其中有大量磁灶器物。沙捞越博物馆收藏的中国瓷片达 100 万片，其中有德化窑的军持、覆仰莲瓣纹小瓶，德化窑和安溪窑的印纹盒子、折沿刻花大盘，南安窑的瓢形盒，磁灶窑的绿釉花口盘等。磁灶窑的绿釉陶器在沙捞越州大量出土，但完整器物较少。此外，还出土了不少德化窑阳文印花青白瓷器。

在著名的世界文化遗产地吴哥古迹，日本上智大学吴哥古迹国际调查团在考古发掘过程中，发现了一件磁灶窑的堆贴龙纹、刻划水波图案的青釉四系瓮，也就是磁灶窑龙瓮。

在泰国的海底，经常能打捞出泉州生产的宋代瓷器。泰国曼谷大学博物馆就收藏并展出宋元磁灶窑生产的青釉瓮和龙瓮产品。湄公河及附近水域也出水许多瓷器，其中就有元代同安窑生产的产品。

Tens of thousands of porcelain wares of Tang and Song dynasties (618—1279), including a large number of Cizao Kilns products, were discovered in Sarawak, Malaysia between 1947 and 1967. The Sarawak Museum houses one million pieces of Chinese ceramic shards, including kendis and small bottles with the pattern of lotus petals facing downward and upward from Dehua Kilns, boxes with impressed pattern, and large plates with carved floral pattern and foliated edge from Dehua Kilns and Anxi Kilns, gourd-shaped boxes from Nan'an Kilns, and green-glazed plates with flower-shaped mouth from Cizao Kilns. Huge quantities of green-glazed pottery from Cizao Kilns were unearthed in Sarawak, but intact artifacts were rare. In addition, a significant number of bluish-white porcelain wares with floral pattern in raised design produced in Dehua Kilns were also unearthed.

At Angkor, the famous world cultural heritage site, the Angkor International Investigation Team from Sophia University in Japan found a celadon-glazed urn with four lugs and embossed loong design as well as carved water waves pattern when they were conducting archaeological excavations. That is an urn with loong pattern produced by Cizao Kilns.

Song Dynasty porcelain wares produced in Quanzhou are often seen in salvaged items from the seabed in Thailand. The Bangkok University Museum in Thailand houses and displays celadon-glazed urns and urns with loong pattern produced by Cizao Kilns in the Song-Yuan era. Many porcelain wares, including products of Tong'an Kilns in the Yuan Dynasty, have also been found in the Mekong River and its nearby waters.

斯里兰卡曾出土宋元时期德化窑烧制的莲瓣碗和墩式碗。1959 年，斯里兰卡社会文化部将它们作为国礼赠送给原中国历史博物馆（今中国国家博物馆）永久收藏。在斯里兰卡还出土了安溪窑的喇叭口青瓷碗。

在印度尼西亚国家博物馆中，保存着大量的中国瓷器，很多是从海底捞出来的，其中有不少是泉州的外销产品。该馆陈列品中的酱釉小口瓶、剔花玉壶春瓶、龙瓮、青釉褐彩和绿釉的军持等，都是磁灶窑的产品。

美籍传教士沙善德曾写道：“在古代之陶瓷贸易中，自宋以还，皆以各式‘龙瓮’为主要，所谓‘龙瓮’者，盖瓮上绘有二龙绕于此瓮。此种‘龙瓮’为爪哇、渤泥及菲律宾的猎头部落所珍存，而且代代相传，尊之为神秘之法宝。”这里提到的龙瓮就是磁灶窑的外销产品。

Bowls with lotus petals pattern and stump-like bowls fired in Dehua Kilns during the Song-Yuan period were unearthed in Sri Lanka. In 1959, the Department of Social and Cultural Affairs of Sri Lanka presented them as a national gift to former China History Museum (present-day National Museum of China) for permanent collection. Trumpet-mouthed celadon bowls from Anxi Kilns were also found in Sri Lanka.

The National Museum of Indonesia houses a large number of Chinese porcelain wares, many of which were salvaged from the seabed. There are a lot of Quanzhou's export products among them. The brown-glazed small-mouthed bottles, *yu hu chun* bottles with engraved floral pattern, urns with loong pattern, celadon-glazed kendis painted with brown splashes, and green-glazed kendis in the showcase, are all products of Cizao Kilns.

Malcolm F. Farley, an American missionary, wrote that in ancient ceramic trade, different types of urns with loong pattern had been the main commodities since the Song Dynasty. Two loongs were painted on the urn, and that was why it was called "urn with loong pattern." This type of urn was treasured by the hunting tribes of Java, Borneo, and the Philippines, passed down from generation to generation, and considered the mysterious treasure in their culture. The above-mentioned urns were export products of Cizao Kilns.

爱国华侨、有“研究中国古外销陶瓷第一人”之称的韩槐准著有《南洋遗留的中国古外销陶瓷》一书，书中提到在印度尼西亚搜集的宋代青白瓷罐就是安溪窑产品。该书还介绍了印度尼西亚国家博物馆陈列的一部分青白釉军持和青白瓷瓶，它们是宋代碗坪仑窑烧造的产品。此外，1957 年在印度尼西亚的苏拉威西岛南部出土了宋代德化窑白瓷盒，东爪哇出土的一件宋代折腰缠枝纹军持也是德化窑系屈斗宫窑的产品。

Han Huaizhun, a patriotic overseas Chinese known as "the first person to study ancient Chinese export ceramics," wrote the book *Ancient Chinese Export Ceramics Found in Nanyang* (literally meaning "southern ocean," a term used in Ming and Qing dynasties denoting Southeast Asian lands), which mentions that the bluish-white porcelain jars from the Song Dynasty collected in Indonesia were products of Anxi Kilns. The book also talks about some bluish-white glazed kendis and bluish-white porcelain bottles on display in the National Museum of Indonesia, which were products of Wanpinglun Kilns in the Song Dynasty. Additionally, a white porcelain box from Dehua Kilns of the Song Dynasty was unearthed from southern Sulawesi in Indonesia in 1957, and a kendi with angled belly and interlocking vegetal scrolls pattern from the Song Dynasty found in East Java was also a product of Qudougong Kiln in Dehua.

在西奈半岛的考古工作中，发掘了不少德化窑青白瓷器。埃及首都开罗南郊的福斯塔特遗址，出土了12,000多件中国古代陶瓷标本，一个由日本学者组建的调查团曾经对这些陶瓷标本进行整理，在他们发表的资料中，提到了磁灶窑的黄绿釉器。坦桑尼亚的多处遗址中都发现了中国陶瓷，其中不乏泉州地区产品，例如，坦桑尼亚的基尔瓦基斯瓦尼古代遗址群发现了中国陶瓷，经研究，其中一些瓷器很有可能就是德化窑系的青白瓷、磁灶窑系的绿釉瓷和同安窑系的青瓷。在肯尼亚出土的宋代青瓷玉壶春瓶，与安溪、晋江的产品极其相似。

Many pieces of bluish-white porcelain from Dehua Kilns were unearthed in Sinai Peninsula excavation work. More than 12,000 samples of ancient Chinese ceramics were found at the Fustat ruins in the southern suburbs of Cairo, the capital of Egypt. A survey team composed of Japanese scholars once went through those ceramic pieces and mentioned yellow-and-green glazed ceramics from Cizao Kilns in their published work. Chinese ceramics were found in many ancient ruins in Tanzania, some of which were produced in Quanzhou. For example, some pieces of ceramics found in Ruins of Kilwa Kisiwani might be bluish-white porcelain products from Dehua Kilns, green-glazed porcelain products from Cizao Kilns, and celadon from Tong'an Kilns. A Song Dynasty *yu hu chun* bottle unearthed in Kenya is pretty similar to products from Anxi and Jinjiang.

宋元泉州的外销陶瓷在东亚、东南亚、南亚、西亚、非洲许多国家和地区的古代遗迹中均有大量发现，可以说，“泉州制造”对这些国家和地区人民的生活方式和价值观念产生了深刻的影响。美国汉学家薛爱华在《撒马尔罕的金桃：唐代舶来品研究》一书中写道：“舶来品的真实活力存在于生动活泼的想象的领域之内，正是由于赋予了外来物品以丰富的想象，我们才真正得到了享用舶来品的无穷乐趣。”其实，海外诸国引进泉州制造的陶瓷器等舶来品也是这样。例如，从低端到高端一应俱全的生活日用器皿推动了当地饮食器具甚至饮食方式的变革，文明程度得以提升；龙瓮传入东南亚，改变了当地的殡葬方式，人们的精神信仰和价值观念也有了新的蜕变；急须、珠光青瓷等茶器对日本茶道影响深远；军持对伊斯兰教在东南亚的传播起到了重要作用……

悠远的外销陶瓷贸易史，不仅写下“泉州制造”对世界的影响，也记录了以海外市场为导向的“定烧”模式下包容外来文化的过程，一些国家还曾仿制宋元泉州生产的外销陶瓷，这是一种文化的相互融合，折射了中外文化美美与共的交流互鉴之光，留给今天的是泉州海上丝绸之路文化沉甸甸的历史见证。

2017 年 9 月 23 日，菲律宾华裔陶瓷专家庄良有接受中新社记者专访时介绍福建德化瓷。（中新图片 供图）

On September 23, 2017, Zhuang Liangyou, a Chinese Filipino ceramic expert, introduced Dehua porcelain while meeting with reporters from China News Service. (Courtesy of CNSphoto.com)

Export ceramics produced in Song-Yuan Quanzhou were discovered in large quantities in ancient ruins of many countries and regions in East Asia, Southeast Asia, South Asia, West Asia, and Africa. We can say that ceramics made in Quanzhou had had a profound impact on the lifestyle and values of the people in these countries and regions. Edward H. Schafer, an American sinologist, wrote in his *The Golden Peaches of Samarkand: A Study of Tang Exotics*, "... exotic goods ... Their real life is in the bright world of the imagination, where we take our true holidays." That, to some extent, explains why foreign countries imported products made in Quanzhou. For example, a wide range of daily utensils, from low-end to high-end, promoted the transformation of local dining utensils and even dining habits, facilitating the advance of civilization. The introduction of urns with loong pattern to Southeast Asia changed local funeral customs, and people's spiritual beliefs and values also underwent new changes. Tea utensils such as *ji xu* and celadon with pearly luster had a profound influence on Japanese tea ceremony. Kendis played an important role in the spread of Islam in Southeast Asia.

The long history of export trade in ceramics not only records the influence of Quanzhou products on the world, but also documents the process of growing open to foreign cultures under the customized production model oriented toward overseas markets. Some countries had even imitated the style of export ceramics produced in Song-Yuan Quanzhou. That is a form of cultural communication featuring mutual exchange, appreciation, and learning between Chinese and foreign cultures, leaving behind striking historical testimony to Quanzhou's Maritime Silk Road culture.

扬帆出洋与满载而归

Sailing Overseas and Returning Fully Loaded

“南海 I 号”沉船：世界上迄今发现的年代最早、船体最大、保存最完整的远洋贸易沉船

The “Nanhai No. 1” Shipwreck: The Earliest, Largest in Size, and Best Preserved Oceangoing Trade Ship in the World Ever Discovered

“华光礁 I 号”沉船：中国远洋海域发现的第一艘古代沉船

The “Huaguang Reef No. 1” Shipwreck: The First Ancient Sunken Ship Found in Chinese Deep Sea

泉州湾宋代海船：中国唯一已出水的海外返航古船

Song Dynasty Oceangoing Ship in Quanzhou Bay: The Only Ancient Ship Returning from Overseas in China Ever Discovered

从泉州港扬帆出洋的“南海Ⅰ号”“华光礁Ⅰ号”远洋商船，和满载香料回航的泉州湾宋代海船，时隔七八百年后重见天日，惊艳世界，它们不仅是祖先探索大海的履历，更是我们发现海丝泉州历史文化基因的钥匙，是长达400年波澜壮阔的海外贸易史的重要见证者。

The oceangoing merchant ships such as "Nanhai No. 1" and "Huaguang Reef No. 1" which set sail from Quanzhou Port, and the Song Dynasty Oceangoing Ship in Quanzhou Bay loaded with spices returning to Quanzhou Bay, have re-emerged after seven or eight centuries and impressed the world. They are not only records of our ancestors exploring the sea, but also the key to discovering the historical and cultural memes of Quanzhou as an important point on the Maritime Silk Road. They are important witnesses to the magnificent 400-year history of overseas trade.

"南海Ⅰ号"沉船试发掘现场。（中新图片 供图）
The trial excavation site of "Nanhai No. 1" Shipwreck. (Courtesy of CNSphoto.com)

“南海Ⅰ号”沉船：世界上迄今发现的年代最早、船体最大、保存最完整的远洋贸易沉船

发现与发掘。“南海Ⅰ号”沉船是向外运送瓷器时在近海不幸罹难沉没的一艘南宋商船，沉没地点位于广东省附近海域，它是目前世界上发现的海上沉船中年代最早、船体最大、保存最完整的远洋贸易商船。1987年，中英联合打捞队意外在阳江市东平港以南的海域发现了这条深埋在水下二十多米的古沉船，经过前期海上调查发掘工作，2007年12月28日，成功将其整体打捞进入特建的广东海上丝绸之路博物馆“水晶宫”。截至2019年，船舱内和散落于船体外的文物基本提取登记，文物总量达到18万件以上，船载货物主要是陶瓷和金属产品两大类，陶瓷器数量最多，因此有人将“南海Ⅰ号”称为“海上敦煌”。

“南海Ⅰ号”考古队工作人员对沉船的出水文物进行脱盐处理。（中新图片 供图）
A member of the “Nanhai No. 1” Shipwreck archaeological team is performing desalination on cultural relics from the shipwreck. (Courtesy of CNSphoto.com)

The "Nanhai No. 1" Shipwreck: The Earliest, Largest in Size, and Best Preserved Oceangoing Trade Ship in the World Ever Discovered

About the discovery and excavation. The "Nanhai No.1" Shipwreck is a Southern Song Dynasty merchant ship that sank tragically while transporting porcelain in the waters off the coast of China. The shipwreck site is near Guangdong Province. It is the earliest, largest, and best preserved oceangoing trading vessel ever discovered in the world. In 1987, a joint salvage team consisting of Chinese and British experts accidentally discovered this ancient sunken ship buried deep underwater at a depth of more than 20 meters in the sea area south of Dongping Port in Yangjiang City. After preliminary investigation and excavation work at sea, on December 28, 2007, the ship was successfully salvaged as a whole and placed in the specially built "Crystal Palace" of Maritime Silk Road Museum of Guangdong. As of 2019, almost all of the cultural relics inside the cabin and scattered outside the hull were collected and registered, with a total of more than 180,000 pieces. The cargo carried by the ship is mainly divided into two categories: ceramics and metal products, with ceramic artifacts in the majority. Some people therefore call the ship "Underwater Dunhuang."

行船路线。美国学者罗伯特·芬雷说："人类物质文化首度步向全球化，是在中国的主导下展开。在绝大部分的人类历史时光之中，中国的经济都为全世界最先进最发达。"

在历史上，中国的底色不仅有象征厚重农业文明的黄色，还有象征发达海洋贸易的蓝色。八百多年前，泉州这个具备显著的地理优势、先进的造船技术、完善的管理体系和坚实的制度保障等优越条件的良港，一跃成为享誉中外的"东方第一大港"，各路人士纷至沓来，呈现一派"涨海声中万国商"的繁荣景象。

宋代时，开辟了许多新的航运线路，最远可至阿拉伯与东非。根据地理位置和始发港，可以将这些航线分为北向航线和南向航线。"南海Ⅰ号"走的就是南向航线，从泉州港出发，经过上下川岛、阳江海域，过海南岛东北端海域，再过"万里石塘"（南沙群岛的古称）到达东南亚国家。

About its sailing route. American scholar Robert Finlay pointed out that the first step toward globalization of human material culture was led by China, and that throughout most of human history, China's economy was the most advanced in the world.

In history, China not only pursued "yellow" development which featured profound agricultural civilization, but also pursued "blue" development which featured maritime trade. Over 800 years ago, Quanzhou, with its remarkable geographical advantages, advanced shipbuilding technology, sound management system and solid institutional guarantees, leapt to become the renowned "the largest port in the East," attracting people from all over the world and presenting a prosperous scene of "merchants from all nations thronging to Quanzhou amidst the sound of rising tides."

During the Song Dynasty, many new shipping routes were opened up, extending as far as Arabia and East Africa. These routes can be divided into northbound and southbound routes according to geographical locations and ports of departure. The "Nanhai No. 1" once followed the southbound route, departing from Quanzhou Port, passing through Shangchuan Island, Xiachuan Island and Yangjiang waters, crossing the northeastern waters of Hainan Island, and then passing across *Wanli Shitang* (ancient name for Nansha Islands) to reach the countries in Southeast Asia.

"涨海声中万国商"场景再现。（段燕飞 摄）

Scene reconstruction of "merchants from all nations thronging to Quanzhou amidst the sound of rising tides." (Photo by Duan Yanfei)

“南海Ⅰ号”的沉没地点位于南向航道上，沉没时船头向南，南向210°。古代航海主要依靠自然风作为动力，冬季从北往南吹东北季风，而夏季则吹东南季风。船上装载的绝大部分是泉州生产的瓷器、漆器、铁器等。它的始发港是泉州港，正如《梦粱录》记载的那样：“若欲船泛外国买卖，则自泉州便可出洋。”“南海Ⅰ号”沉船曾出水“淳熙元宝”铜钱以及底部有“癸卯”年墨书的德化窑瓷罐（南宋淳熙癸卯年即1183年），也刚好与泉州九日山记载南宋淳熙十年（1183）冬季启航祈风的石刻内容相呼应。

The sinking location of the ship is on the southbound shipping route, and as the ship sank, its bow was facing south, at an angle of 210°. In ancient times, sailing mainly relied on natural winds as a source of power. In winter, the monsoon blows from north to south, while in summer, the monsoon blows from south to north. The vast majority of the cargo on board were ceramics, lacquerware, ironware and other products produced in Quanzhou. It departed from Quanzhou Port, as mentioned in *Records of a Dream of Sorghum*: if you want to sail overseas for trading, you can depart from Quanzhou Port. Copper coins with the "Chun Xi Yuan Bao" mark, and a Dehua porcelain jar with the ink writing "Gui Mao" at its bottom (which corresponds to the year of 1183 in Chunxi period of the Southern Song Dynasty), were found from the wreck. This matches the contents of the stone inscriptions on Jiuri Mountain in Quanzhou which record the ritual ceremony to pray for favorable winds when ships departed in winter in 1183.

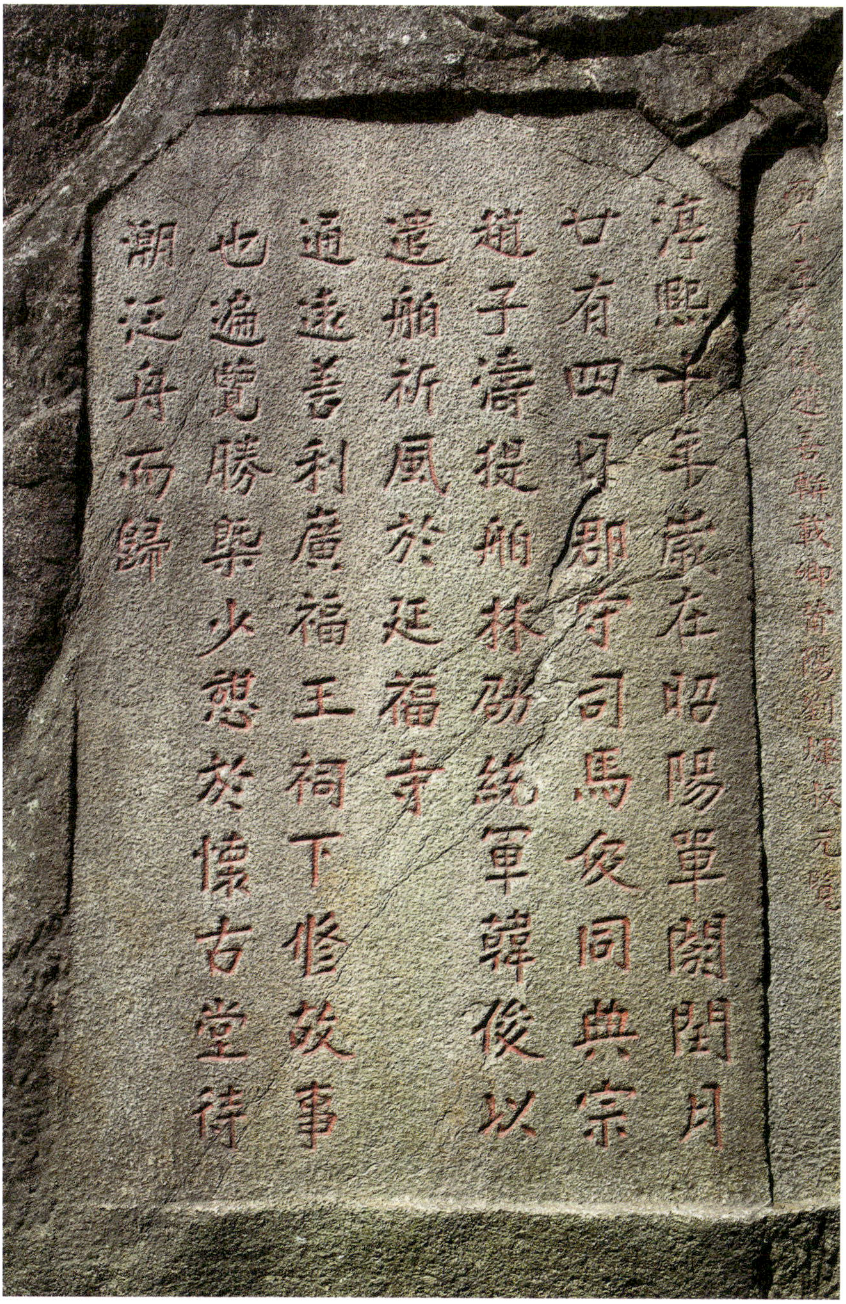

南宋淳熙十年（1183）冬季启航祈风石刻。（成冬冬 摄）

Stone inscriptions recording the ritual ceremony to pray for favorable winds when ships departed in winter in 1183. (Photo by Cheng Dongdong)

出水的“泉州制造”。中国古代陶瓷器制作精美、价格低廉，在海内外广受青睐。沉船出水陶瓷器型主要有碗、盘、碟、壶、盅、瓶、盒、罐等，大多是中国南方地区的窑场生产的，如江西景德镇窑、浙江龙泉窑以及福建德化窑、磁灶窑、义窑等，也有少数其他窑口的产品。釉色包括青白、白、青、绿、酱褐等，其中数量最多的是德化窑生产的白釉瓷，另外还有磁灶窑的酱釉类和低温铅绿釉类瓷器、以建窑建盏（兔毫盏）为代表的黑釉瓷、南安罗东窑瓷器、福清东张窑瓷器、同安汀溪窑珠光青瓷以及极少的陕西耀州窑青瓷。

“南海 I 号”出水瓷器数量众多，器型多样，特别是融合了中外文化元素，既饱含自身传统文化内涵，展现厚重的历史文化传承，又受到域外社会历史文化影响，文化交流的烙印十分清晰。

中国民间常用瓷器制造历史悠久，历代器物造型多有演变，但基本遵循一定的形制演变趋势。这些出水的德化窑、磁灶窑瓷器反映了中国历史长河中逐步形成的传统饮食文化、茶文化、香文化、养鸟文化等，由此也逐步充实了独具时代特征和东方特色的器用文化。仿金属瓷器，如青白釉香炉、碟、盒、执壶，在造型上借鉴仿制了金属器，形成了一种别具一格的器物之美。

展出的“南海 I 号”沉船出水瓷器。（中新图片 供图）
Porcelain wares salvaged from "Nanhai No. 1" Shipwreck on display. (Courtesy of CNSphoto.com)

About the products made in Quanzhou salvaged from the wreck. Ancient Chinese ceramics were exquisitely crafted and affordable, widely popular at home and abroad. The main types of ceramics from the wreck include bowls, plates, dishes, pots, cups, bottles, boxes, jars, most of which were produced in kilns in southern China such as Jingdezhen Kilns in Jiangxi, Longquan Kilns in Zhejiang, and Dehua Kilns, Cizao Kilns, as well as Yiyao Kilns in Fujian. There are also a few products from other kilns. In terms of glaze color, there are bluish-white, white, celadon, green, brown, etc., with the white-glazed porcelain produced in Dehua Kilns in the majority. Besides, there are brown-glazed porcelain and porcelain with green lead-containing glaze fired at low temperatures from Cizao Kilns, the black-glazed porcelain represented by the *jian zhan* (featuring cups with rabbit hair pattern) from Jianyao Kilns, porcelain from Luodong Kilns in Nan'an, porcelain from Dongzhang Kilns in Fuqing, celadon with pearly luster from Tingxi Kilns in Tong'an, and a few celadon products from Yaozhou Kilns in Shaanxi.

A large number of ceramics in various shapes were salvaged from "Nanhai No. 1" Shipwreck, blending Chinese and foreign cultural elements. They not only embodied the traditional culture of their own, presenting the profound significance of historical and cultural heritage, but also absorbed historical and cultural elements from overseas, with clear imprints of cultural communication.

Chinese ceramics for daily use have a long history, and the shapes of these products have continued to change over generations, but they have generally followed a certain trend in shape evolution. These Dehua Kilns and Cizao Kilns ceramics salvaged from the wreck reflect the traditional food culture, tea culture, incense culture, bird-raising culture, and other aspects that have gradually formed over the long course of Chinese history. As a result, the unique utensil culture with contemporary characteristics and eastern flavor was enriched. The metal-like porcelain, such as bluish-white glazed porcelain incense burners, dishes, boxes, and pitchers, imitated the design of metal utensils, creating ceramic beauty with distinctive style.

此外，“南海 I 号”在 2014 年至 2016 年还出水了九百余件墨书陶瓷器，德化窑墨书器有粉盒、瓶、执壶、罐、大盘等，磁灶窑墨书器有盖、瓶、小口罐、碗、盆、执壶等，大多书写在底部露胎处，少部分磁灶窑陶罐书写在内腹部，一些酱釉梅瓶书写在外腹部，楷书、行书较多，字迹大都清晰可辨，部分墨书虽然内容相同，但写法不同，或为不同人书写。

学者对 2014 年至 2016 年出水墨书陶瓷器进行整理后，归纳了姓名类 、“直”字类、器物用途类、“纲”字系列、地名类、花押类、符号类、其他类共 8 类。墨书主要作标记货主或者商号、器物用途之用，其中姓名类数量最多，多为姓氏、姓氏 +“直”、姓氏 +“上”、姓氏 + 数字、姓氏 + 数字 +“记”等，带“记”墨书可能是商号名称。官员和民间海商都是海上贸易的参与者，墨书中出现了陈、戴、谢、林、蔡、黄、庄、杨、萧、王、李、方、郑、许等大量姓氏，足见参与人员之多。

虽然部分墨书内容难以辨识，且在研究过程中避免不了推测，但不可否认的是，墨书为我们提供了一个还原南宋远洋贸易生活场景的有效途径，启发我们进一步探秘宋代中国的海上贸易活动。

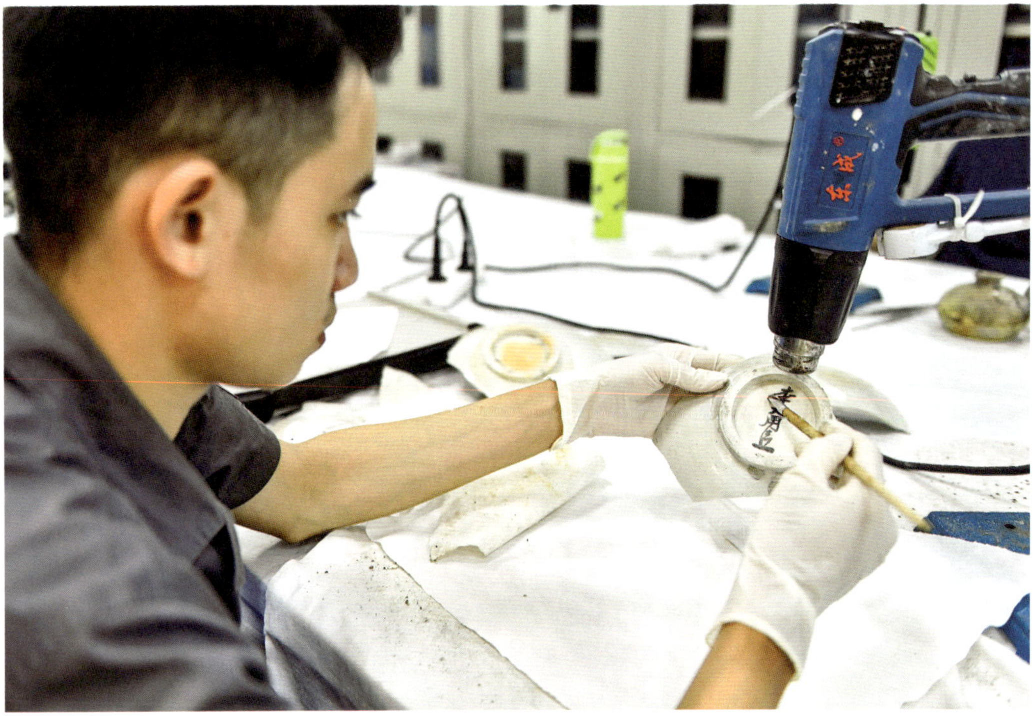

“南海 I 号”考古队工作人员对沉船出水文物的墨书进行封护。（中新图片 供图）
A member of the "Nanhai No. 1" Shipwreck archaeological team is applying protective coating to the ink writing on the salvaged cultural relics. (Courtesy of CNSphoto.com)

Furthermore, from 2014 to 2016, over 900 pieces of ceramics with ink writing were salvaged from "Nanhai No. 1" Shipwreck. The wares with ink writing from Dehua Kilns include powder boxes, bottles, pitchers, jars, and large plates, while the wares with ink writing from Cizao Kilns include lids, bottles, small-mouthed jars, bowls, basins, and pitchers. Most of ink writing are on the unglazed bottom part, except for some pottery jars from Cizao Kilns which have their ink writing on the inside, and some brown-glazed plum bottles which have their ink writing on the exterior. The characters are mainly in regular script or running script, with clear and legible handwriting. Although some have the same contents, their handwriting styles differ, possibly indicating that they were written by different people.

Scholars have classified the ceramics with ink writing salvaged from 2014 to 2016 into eight categories: people's names, writing with the character *zhi*, writing indicating vessel use, writing with the character *gang*, places' names, signatures on contracts, symbols, and the others. Ink writing was primarily used to mark the owner of the goods or the commercial brand as well as the vessel use. Most of them are people's names, with forms such as one's surname, one's surname plus the character *zhi*, one's surname plus the character *shang*, one's surname plus numbers, and one's surname plus numbers followed by the character *ji*. The ink writing with the character *ji* is likely to be the name of a commercial brand. Officials and sea merchants participated in maritime trade, and a lot of surnames such as Chen, Dai, Xie, Lin, Cai, Huang, Zhuang, Yang, Xiao, Wang, Li, Fang, Zheng, and Xu can be seen in ink writing, reflecting the huge number of participants.

Although some of the characters are difficult to identify and speculation is unavoidable during the research process, it is undeniable that the ink writing provides an effective means of restoring the scene of maritime trade during the Southern Song Dynasty, which inspires us to further explore China's maritime trade activities during the Song Dynasty.

"南海 I 号"沉船出水的磁灶窑绿釉印花卉纹折沿菱口碟。（栗建安 供图）

A green-glazed dish with impressed floral pattern and water chestnut flower-shaped foliated rim from Cizao Kilns, salvaged from "Nanhai No. 1" Shipwreck. (Courtesy of Li Jian'an)

“南海 I 号”船型。“南海 I 号”属于福船——中国古代四大船型之一。福船指的是福建造的海船，也是郑和下西洋的主力船型。“南海 I 号”保存之好、规模之大在同时期的考古发现中可谓绝无仅有，遗产价值和研究价值不可估量。目前，在泉州后渚、法石、宁波东门口和海南华光礁都发现了宋代海船，后三处的海船已被严重破坏。相较这四艘沉船，“南海 I 号”的船体保存更加完整，上甲板及其以下部分保存相当完好，舷板和隔舱板色泽如新，水线甲板、艉舵孔等结构比较完整，托梁、桅夹、船壳板、肋骨、加强筋和纵隔板等清晰可辨，一些造船工艺，如船板搭接工艺，也可从中窥见。

“南海 I 号”是一艘尖头福船，船身长约 30.4 米，宽约 9.8 米，高约 8 米，共有 15 个水密隔舱，是目前发现的古代航船中舱数最多的，超过了元代马可 · 波罗在游记中描述的 13 舱船体，排水量可以达到 600 吨，载重经过专业人士推测应该是 800 吨，在当时应该是一个 2,000 料到 3,000 料之间的海船，规模中等偏大，一般能搭载 100 到 200 人。

About the ship type of "Nanhai No. 1." "Nanhai No. 1" is a *Fu-Chuan*, one of the four major types of ancient ship in China. *Fu-Chuan* refers to the ships built in Fujian. It was also the main type of vessel used by Zheng He's fleet on their voyages to the western seas. Its well-preserved hull and large size make it unparalleled among archaeological discoveries of the same period. The value of the cultural heritage is immeasurable, and it is very much worthy of in-depth research. Currently, Song Dynasty sea vessels have been discovered in several locations, including Houzhu and Fashi in Quanzhou, Dongmenkou in Ningbo and Huaguang Reef in Hainan. However, three of those shipwrecks have been severely damaged. Compared to the above-mentioned sunken ships, the hull of "Nanhai No. 1" is better preserved, with the upper deck and its lower parts remaining intact. The sides and bulkheads have retained their color and luster, and the waterline deck, stern rudder holes, and other structures remain comparatively intact. The support beam, mast clips, hull planks, ribs, reinforcement ribs, and longitudinal bulkheads are all clearly distinguishable. Several shipbuilding techniques, such as the method of joining hull planks, can also be learned from examining this vessel.

"Nanhai No. 1" is a *Fu-Chuan* with pointed bow, with a length of about 30.4 meters, a width of about 9.8 meters, and a height of about 8 meters. It boasts 15 watertight compartments, with the largest number of compartments among the ancient ships discovered so far, surpassing the 13-compartment ship described by Marco Polo in his travelogue. The displacement can reach 600 tons, and the load capacity is estimated by professionals to be 800 tons. It was considered a medium- to large-sized sea vessel between 2,000 and 3,000 *liao* (a Chinese unit of timber volume), capable of carrying 100 to 200 people.

"华光礁 I 号"沉船：中国远洋海域发现的第一艘古代沉船

发现与发掘。西沙群岛"华光礁 I 号"南宋沉船处于古代海上丝绸之路的要冲，同时也是中国在远洋海域发现的第一艘古代沉船，6 层结构，其重要意义不言而喻。1996 年，渔民在西沙群岛华光礁环礁内缘潜水捕鱼，发现了这艘沉船，此后，这艘沉船曾多次遭到非法盗掘。1998 年 12 月至 1999 年 1 月，原中国历史博物馆和海南省文物部门联合对沉船进行抢救性试掘，共出水陶瓷器、铜镜残片等遗物 850 多件，后来出版《西沙水下考古（1998—1999）》考古报告，初步确认该沉船为中国南宋时期海外贸易的商船。

2007 年 3 月至 5 月，中国国家博物馆和海南省文体厅组建西沙考古工作队开始正式对沉船遗址进行考古发掘，围绕遗址中心布设 50 个 2m×2m 的探方，按探方逐层清理船内遗物，总发掘面积约 370 平方米，并完成了船体全面测绘。2008 年 11 月至 12 月，西沙考古工作队进行第二阶段的发掘，对船体构件进行编号测绘，并分解提取运回海南省博物馆进行脱盐、脱水保护处理。这艘沉船总共出水了近 1 万件陶瓷器和 500 多块船板。

The "Huaguang Reef No. 1" Shipwreck: The First Ancient Sunken Ship Found in Chinese Deep Sea

About the discovery and excavation. The "Huaguang Reef No. 1" Shipwreck of the Southern Song Dynasty in Xisha Islands was found at a vital point of the ancient Maritime Silk Road. It is also the first ancient sunken ship discovered by China in deep sea, with a six-layered structure. Its enormous significance is crystal clear. In 1996, fishermen were diving for fish at the atoll of the Huaguang Reef in the Xisha Islands when they discovered the sunken ship. Since then, the ship had been robbed multiple times. From December 1998 to January 1999, the former China History Museum and the cultural heritage department in Hainan Province jointly conducted a salvage trial excavation of the sunken ship. More than 850 artifacts, including fragments of ceramics and copper mirrors, were recovered. The archaeological report *Underwater Archaeological Study in Xisha Islands (1998—1999)* was later published. The preliminary findings confirmed that the sunken ship was a merchant vessel involved in overseas trade during the Southern Song Dynasty in China.

From March to May 2007, the National Museum of China and the Hainan Provincial Department of Culture and Sports set up the Xisha archaeological team for the official excavation of the sunken ship site in Xisha Islands. They set up 50 excavation units measuring 2m by 2m each centered around the site, and systematically cleaned the relics layer by layer. The total excavation area was approximately 370 square meters, and a comprehensive survey of the ship's structure was also completed. From November to December 2008, the Xisha archaeological team carried out the second phase of excavation, cataloging and surveying the components of the ship, before deconstructing and removing them for desalination as well as dehydration at the Hainan Museum to better protect them. Nearly 10,000 pieces of ceramics and over 500 ship planks were recovered from the sunken ship.

行船路线。秦汉时期已有海外贸易，海上丝绸之路开始形成。唐代，航路已向东延伸至新罗、日本，向南延伸至爪哇、文莱等。宋代在前代的基础上，开辟了很多新的航线，远至阿拉伯与东非。海南岛成为波斯和阿拉伯商船来往于广州、泉州、扬州等通商口岸的避风港和中转站，南海海域商船云集，水陆往来频繁，交通贸易繁荣昌盛。

“华光礁Ⅰ号”沉船出水遗物以陶瓷器和铁制品为主，尤以陶瓷器为大宗，其中大部分是较为粗糙的日用陶瓷。当时开化较晚、经济相对落后的东南亚地区急需华南沿海一带民窑生产的日用陶瓷，尤其是军持、执壶这类外销瓷，还有龙瓮这种带给当地人们精神寄托的圣物。今天，这些器物在东南亚国家的博物馆及私人收藏中大量存在，基本可以确定“华光礁Ⅰ号”是在前往东南亚地区时不幸沉没的。

About its sailing route. During the Qin and Han dynasties (221 B.C.—220 A.D.), overseas trade was already in existence and the Maritime Silk Road began to take shape. By the Tang Dynasty, shipping routes extended eastward to Silla and Japan, and southward to Java, Brunei, and many other destinations. Building upon the foundations laid by previous generations, the Song Dynasty opened up many new sea routes, extending as far as Arabia and East Africa. Hainan Island became a safe harbor and transit point for Persian and Arab merchant ships which traveled to and fro between ports in Guangzhou, Quanzhou, Yangzhou, and elsewhere. In the South China Sea, merchant ships congregated, and frequent maritime and land-based contacts promoted prosperity and development of transportation and trade.

The relics recovered from the "Huaguang Reef No. 1" Shipwreck primarily consist of ceramics and iron items, with ceramics being in the majority. Most of these ceramics were relatively crude and meant for daily use. Countries and regions in Southeast Asia, where civilization and economy were relatively underdeveloped at the time, had a pressing need for those everyday ceramics produced by kilns along the coast of southern China which included exported ceramics like kendis and pitchers, as well as urns with loong pattern that brought spiritual comfort to the local people. Today, these relics can be found in abundance in museums and private collections throughout Southeast Asia, effectively confirming that the ship met its unfortunate end while sailing to Southeast Asia.

出水货物。“华光礁Ⅰ号”的起始港应是泉州港，因为瓷器这种商品都是就近配货，而船上八成的货物都是由德化窑、南安窑、磁灶窑等福建本地民窑烧制而成的。这些陶瓷器种类非常多，主要有碗、盘、碟、盏、瓶、壶、粉盒、罐、钵、军持等；沉船出水青白瓷居多，青瓷次之，酱褐釉瓷最少；器物的装饰手法有刻划、模印、堆贴、雕塑等，有的几种技法组合于一器；主要的纹饰有荷花、牡丹、菊花、宝相花、缠枝花、折枝花、卷草、珍禽、瑞兽、仙人等中国传统特色纹样以及吉祥文字，如“吉”“大吉”等。此外，在一些器物的底、足内还发现了墨书题记或是模印铭文等。货物大部分是民间的生活日用瓷。

“华光礁Ⅰ号”出水白釉贴塑碗。（中新图片 供图）
A white-glazed bowl with embossed decoration salvaged from "Huaguang Reef No. 1" Shipwreck. (Courtesy of CNSphoto.com)

About the recovered goods. The departure point of the "Huaguang Reef No. 1" was likely to be Quanzhou Port, as goods like porcelain were usually collected from nearby locations, and 80% of the cargo on board was made in folk kilns such as Dehua Kilns, Nan'an Kilns, and Cizao Kilns in Fujian. There is a wide variety of ceramics, mainly including bowls, plates, dishes, cups, bottles, pots, powder boxes, jars, and kendis. The majority of the salvaged ceramics from the wreck are bluish-white porcelain, followed by celadon, and brown-glazed ceramics are the fewest. The decoration techniques applied include carving and incising, molding, embossing, sculpting, and combination of these techniques. The primary decorative patterns are lotuses, peonies, chrysanthemums, auspicious composite flowers, interlocking vegetal scrolls, disconnected sprays of flowers, scroll vines, rare birds, auspicious beasts, deities, and other designs which embody traditional Chinese culture, and auspicious words such as "good luck" and "great fortune." In addition, ink writing and impressed texts have been found on the bottom of some utensils. Most of the goods were daily essentials for common people.

沉没原因。“华光礁I号”是南宋时期的一艘商船，船上共有11个残留的水密隔舱。这样一艘大船为何会沉没在西沙群岛海底？从“华光礁I号”沉船的考古发掘报告中可知，该船从泉州港出发，船载大量的外销瓷，在西沙群岛沉没，说明当时它行驶在向西的海上丝绸之路航线上，计划前往东南亚甚至更远的地方。在华光礁的礁盘上只有木质船体的下部结构残存在水下，并没有发现任何上层甲板之物，文物分布集中，考古人员由此断定，船只在靠近礁盘盘体处航行，操控失误，船只被巨浪托起抬入礁盘内浅水珊瑚丛中搁浅，船体破碎。

About the cause of sinking. "Huaguang Reef No. 1" is a merchant ship from the Southern Song Dynasty, and there are 11 watertight compartments remaining on board. Why did such a large ship sink to the bottom of the sea in Xisha Islands? According to the archaeological excavation report of "Huaguang Reef No. 1" Shipwreck, the ship departed from Quanzhou Port, carrying a large amount of porcelain for export, and sank in Xisha Islands, indicating that it was heading west along the Maritime Silk Road and planning to go to Southeast Asia or even farther. Only the lower structure of the ship's wooden hull was found on the reef body of Huaguang Reef, and no upper deck objects were discovered. Cultural relics clustered within this area. So archaeologists came to the conclusion: it was sailing near the reef body, but the operation failed, and it was lifted by huge waves and stranded in the shallow water coral thicket on the reef body, and was finally broken down.

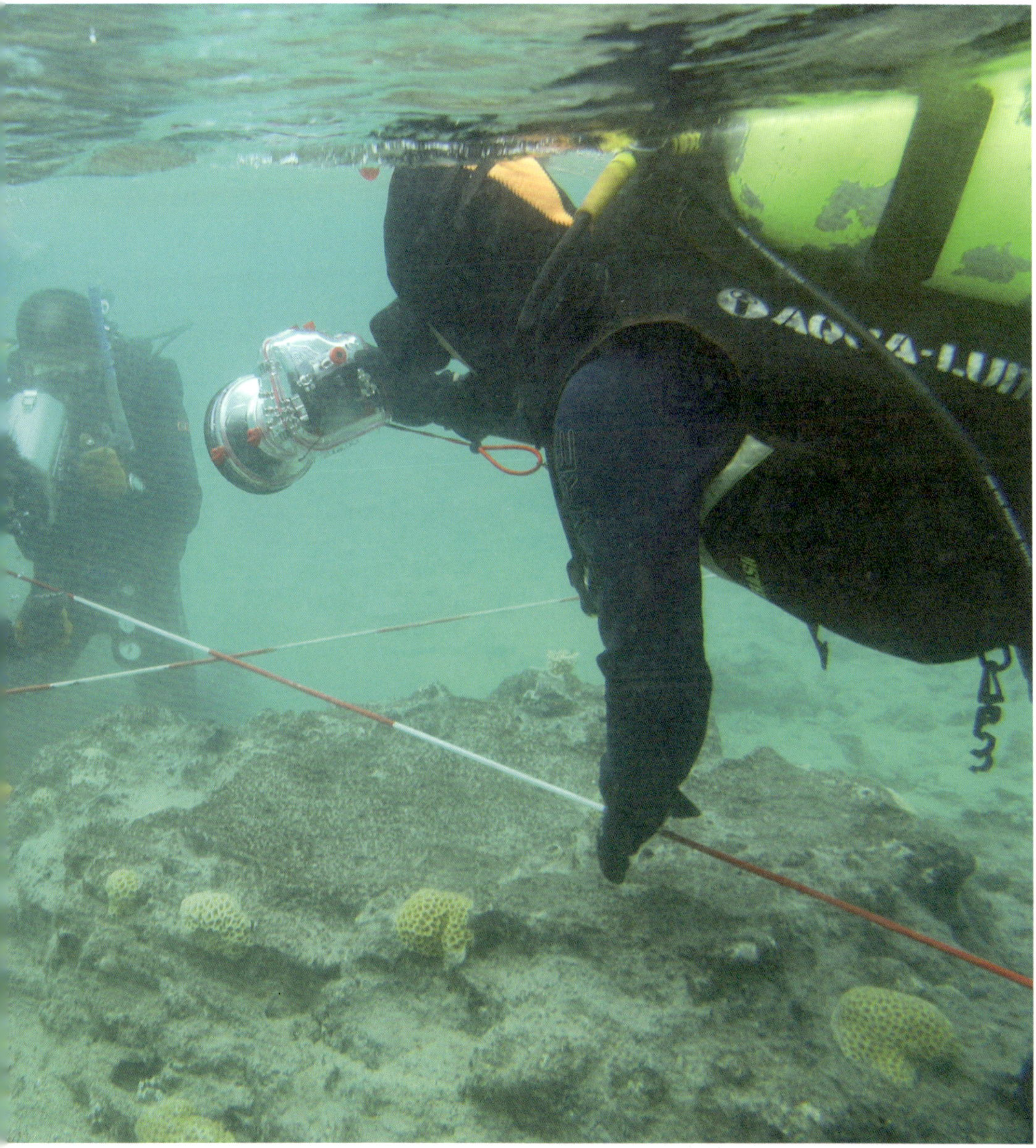

“华光礁I号”沉船遗址考古发掘基线布设。（中新图片 供图）
Setting up the baseline for archaeological excavation of “Huaguang Reef No. 1” Shipwreck. (Courtesy of CNSphoto.com)

“华光礁 I 号”船型。“华光礁 I 号”是一艘典型的福船。“华光礁 I 号”沉船被发现时，船体已经被破坏了一部分，残存船体覆盖面积约 180 平方米，船体残长 20 米，宽约 6 米，舷深 3 到 4 米，发现 11 个残留的水密隔舱，除船体上层建筑外，底层船体保存基本良好，推测该船排水量超过 60 吨。这种船体在国内实属罕见：一是其船板层数多，大部分有五层，局部有六层；二是其船板体量大，大部分主要船板长度在 5 米以上，最长的达 14.4 米，宽度也在 30 厘米以上，最宽的达 48 厘米。底层船体出水的龙骨残长 16.7 米，龙骨是船身体量最大、最长的构件，就像船的脊柱贯穿整个船身。船身还有“保寿孔”，上面打了 7 个小孔，分别放置 7 枚铜钱，下面则是一个大圆孔，放置一枚铜镜，有个吉利的名字——七星伴月，这一装饰特色保留至今，是泉州一带制造远洋木船的独有传统，用于祈求平安渡过被泉州人称为“七星洋”的西沙群岛。西沙群岛一带海域，古时被称为“七洲”，中国古代航海谚语有云“上怕七洲，下怕昆仑”。

“华光礁 I 号”船体的保寿孔。（视觉中国 供图）
“Baoshou holes” on the hull of “Huaguang Reef No. 1” Shipwreck. (Courtesy of VCG.COM)

About the ship type of "Huaguang Reef No. 1." "Huaguang Reef No. 1" is a typical *Fu-Chuan*. When the sunken ship was discovered, part of the vessel had already been destroyed. The wreckage covers an area of approximately 180 square meters, with a length of 20 meters, a width of about 6 meters, and a depth of 3 to 4 meters. Eleven extant watertight compartments were found, and except for the upper structure of the vessel, the hull was well-preserved. It is estimated that its displacement was more than 60 tons. This type of vessel is rare in China, partly because of many layers of planks, with most areas having five layers and some areas having six layers, and partly because the planks are large in size, with most of the main planks being more than 5 meters in length, and the longest 14.4 meters, and being more than 30 centimeters in width, with the widest 48 centimeters. The keel of the vessel recovered from underwater is 16.7 meters long, and it is the largest and longest component of the vessel, like a backbone that runs through the entire hull. The vessel also features "Baoshou (literally meaning 'achieving longevity') holes" with seven smaller holes on top, each holding a copper coin, and a large circular hole below, holding a copper mirror, which is a unique decoration characteristic of oceangoing wooden vessels manufactured in Quanzhou, intended to pray for safety when passing Xisha Islands which were addressed by Quanzhou people as "Seven-Star Ocean." The decorative art, bearing the auspicious name of "Seven Stars Accompanying the Moon," is still kept. The waters surrounding Xisha Islands were once called the "Seven Islands," and an old saying about sea travel in ancient China goes like this, "(One is) afraid of Seven Islands on the outward journey, and afraid of Kunlun on the return journey."

泉州湾宋代海船：中国唯一已出水的海外返航古船

发现与发掘。1973 年 8 月，晋江地区文物管理委员会主任张立协同厦门大学教授庄为玑、福建省博物馆许清泉、晋江地区文化组林文明及泉州文管会和泉州海外交通史博物馆考古人员十余人到泉州湾后渚港考察海外交通史迹时发现了泉州湾宋代海船，9 月报请国家文物局指示，11 月成立泉州湾古船发掘领导小组，1974 年 6 月开始进行发掘工作，历时两个多月，发掘出的沉船残长 24.2 米，残宽 9.15 米，有 13 个水密隔舱，载重量约 200 吨，船体上部结构损坏无存，船首残存部分结构，船身中部底板、舷侧板和水密隔舱壁、桅座、船龙骨等保存较好。

Song Dynasty Oceangoing Ship in Quanzhou Bay: The Only Ancient Ship Returning from Overseas in China Ever Discovered

About the discovery and excavation. In August 1973, Zhang Li, the director of the Cultural Relics Management Committee of Jinjiang District, together with Professor Zhuang Weiji from Xiamen University, Xu Qingquan from Fujian Museum, Lin Wenming from the Cultural Group of Jinjiang District, and archaeologists from Quanzhou Cultural Relics Management Committee and Quanzhou Maritime Museum, were undertaking research on the historical sites of overseas transportation in Quanzhou Bay, when they discovered a Song Dynasty ship at Houzhu Port in Quanzhou Bay. In September, they submitted a report to the National Cultural Heritage Administration for instructions, and in November, the Quanzhou Bay Ancient Ship Excavation Leading Group was established. The excavation work began in June 1974, lasting for more than two months. The salvaged sunken ship measures 24.2 meters in length and 9.15 meters in width, with 13 watertight compartments and a load capacity of about 200 tons. The upper structure of the ship was completely destroyed, but the remaining parts of the bow, the bottom board of the middle section of the hull, sides, watertight compartment bulkheads, mast seats, and keel were well-preserved.

1974 年泉州湾后渚港宋代海船发掘现场。（泉州海外交通史博物馆 供图）
Excavation site of the Song Dynasty Oceangoing Ship in Houzhu Port, Quanzhou Bay, in 1974. (Courtesy of Quanzhou Maritime Museum)

行船路线。泉州湾宋代海船是我国出土的唯一一艘由海外返航的古代远洋海船。泉州湾宋代海船发掘出的货贝产自马尔代夫，来自印度洋；龙涎香和乳香只产于印度洋；降香根据科学分析非常可能是印度原产；胡椒既盛产于爪哇，也盛产于印度西海岸；船体附着物（海生生物，贝壳类居多）绝大多数栖息于印度洋一带。因此，这艘海船从印度洋返航的可能性非常高。宋代熟悉广州贸易的周去非和熟悉泉州贸易的赵汝适两位地理学家，已经明确记录了宋代中国的海船（泉舶和广舶）通航印度洋和阿拉伯世界的路线、日程和季节，提供了可靠的文献旁证。此外，元代也有中国商人在印度东南部海岸活动的有关记录。当然，这艘船也必然到过三佛齐等东南亚地区。

About its sailing route. The Song Dynasty Oceangoing Ship in Quanzhou Bay is the only ancient oceangoing ship in China that returned from overseas ever discovered. The shell money found in the ship was from the Maldives in the Indian Ocean; ambergris and frankincense were only yielded in the Indian Ocean. According to scientific analysis, dalbergia is highly likely to be native to India. Pepper is abundant in Java as well as on the west coast of India. Most of the attachments (marine organisms, mostly shellfish) found on the ship's hull are native to the Indian Ocean. Therefore, it is highly probable that the ship returned from the Indian Ocean. Two geographers of the Song Dynasty, Zhou Qufei who was familiar with Guangzhou trade and Zhao Rukuo who was familiar with Quanzhou trade, clearly recorded the routes, schedules, and seasons of the Song Dynasty Chinese oceangoing ships (*quan bo* and *guang bo*) traveling to the Indian Ocean and the Arab world, providing reliable documentary evidence. In addition, there are records of Chinese merchants engaging in activities on the southeast coast of India in the Yuan Dynasty. Of course, this ship must have also visited places such as Srivijaya in Southeast Asia.

出水货物。泉州湾宋代海船出水的遗物非常丰富，除了各种工具外，还有香料、药物、木货牌签、各种金属器、陶器和瓷器、铜钱和铁钱、各种编织物、装饰品、皮革制品、果核、贝壳、动物骨骼、文化用品及其他，共计14类69项，均为国家一级文物。其中，香料药物占第一位，有4,700多斤，有降真香、檀香、乳香、龙涎香、沉香、槟榔、胡椒……这些进口商品是当时被广泛应用于日常生活和医药的热门货。

出水的每件遗物都独具特色，除了香料药物等，还有一些引人注目的木货牌签，牌签上用毛笔字标注了人名、地名、商号或其他记号，再将其用绳子与货物捆在一起。它们类似于现代托运货物时打印出的标签，从中能感受到当时的社会风貌，以及不同阶层人们的追求与享受。

About the salvaged goods. The relics on the Song Dynasty Oceangoing Ship in Quanzhou Bay were extremely rich. In addition to various tools, there were spices, medicinal herbs, wooden tags, various metal objects, pottery and porcelain, copper and iron coins, various knits, decorations, leather products, fruit kernels, shells, animal bones, cultural artifacts, and others. There were a total of 69 items, all of which were first grade national cultural relics, classified into 14 categories. Among them, spices and medicinal herbs were in the majority, weighing over 4,700 *jin*. There were rosewood heart wood, sandalwood, frankincense, ambergris, agarwood, betel nuts, pepper, and other spices. These imported goods were widely used in daily life and medicine at that time.

Each of the relics retrieved from the sunken ship had unique characteristics. In addition to spices and medicinal herbs, there were also intriguing wooden tags. The tags were marked with names, locations, business names, or other symbols in brush strokes, and then tied to the goods with ropes. They were similar to modern tags printed when checking in luggage, allowing us to feel the social atmosphere and the pursuit and enjoyment of members of different classes at that time.

例如，“南家”用于标记居住在泉州的宋皇族后裔的货品；“狗间记号”“西河酱瓜”无疑是商家记号，“西河”是林姓的族号，可知这个酱瓜店的老板是林先生；“安郡”“河郡”“兆郡”“昶郡”等十几块带“郡”的牌签，可能是住在泉州的宗室贵族们的封号；有的牌签上有“曾干水记”“林干水记”“张干水记”字样，关于这些书“幹”（即“干”）字木牌，有学者认为标记的是替官员和大地主经营私人产业的“干人”所运的货物，也有学者认为标记的是宋朝负责协助处理官府行政事务的干办官所运的货物；除了中国人名之外，还有“山中”和“哑哩”这些外国人的名字，可见当时作为东方第一大港的泉州商贸繁荣，吸引了大量的外国人在这里做生意；那些有“尤工”“杨工”“三九工”以及“张什”“王美”“小陈”字样的牌签，应该与船上的水手或打杂工有关，书“工”字木牌可能是水手携带私人货物的说明。

For example, the mark of "Family of Southern Clan" shows that the goods were owned by members of imperial family living in Quanzhou; the "Dog Room Mark" and "Xihe Pickles" were undoubtedly business marks, and "Xihe" was the clan name of the Lin Family, which indicates that the boss of this pickle shop was Mr. Lin; there are a dozen tags with the word "County," such as "An County," "He County," "Zhao County," "Chang County," etc., and they may indicate the titles of the nobles of the imperial clan who lived in Quanzhou; some tags bear the mark of "Zeng Gan Shui Ji," "Lin Gan Shui Ji," and "Zhang Gan Shui Ji," which some scholars believe to mark the goods transported by *gan ren* who helped officials and large landlords to operate their businesses, and some scholars believe to mark the goods carried by *gan ban* who assisted in administrative affairs during the Song Dynasty, judging by the character "Gan." In addition to Chinese names, there are also foreign names such as "Shan Zhong" and "Ya Li," indicating that the prosperous trade in Quanzhou had attracted a large number of foreigners doing business here in the largest port in the East. The tags with the characters "You Gong," "Yang Gong," "San Jiu Gong," "Zhang Shi," "Wang Mei," and "Xiao Chen" were likely related to the sailors or errand workers, and the wooden tags bearing the character "Gong" were probably for marking the personal belongings carried by seamen.

泉州湾宋代海船出水物：货贝。（成冬冬 摄）

Shell money salvaged from the Song Dynasty Oceangoing Ship in Quanzhou Bay. (Photo by Cheng Dongdong)

泉州湾宋代海船出水物：木货牌签。（成冬冬 摄）

Wooden tags salvaged from the Song Dynasty Oceangoing Ship in Quanzhou Bay. (Photo by Cheng Dongdong)

沉没原因。沉船位于离居民点很近的海滩，船体基本完好且水平埋于海滩，连主龙骨也没有受挫痕迹或是漏洞，故而排除搁浅或者触礁的可能；船舱内器物破碎、散乱，船桅、甲板以上的结构均无留存，结合沉船的位置，推测泉州湾宋代海船不是单纯由于遇上台风而沉没的。海船在海上遇上台风，往往先砍倒船桅让船随风漂荡，争取幸免于沉没。如在港内，只需靠近安全地带避风或加强锚稳定船身，从后渚港地理环境来看，一般台风可避。出水时未见船桅，加上船中器物破碎、散乱，可见泉州湾宋代海船可能是在遭受人为的破坏（兵祸）后又遭受风浪冲击而沉没的。

南宋末年，元兵南下，攻占临安，宋端宗赵昰逃亡至福州，元派唆都元帅紧追入闽。当时的海外交通大港泉州港，成为宋元争夺的重要地方，双方的代表人物分别是蒲寿庚和张世杰，海船是他们争夺的主要物资。据《晋江县志》记载："景炎元年，宋端宗即位于福州，寻入海航于泉州港，命蒲寿庚将海舟以从，寿庚闭城拒命。"《宋史》中提到，张世杰在南宋景炎元年（1276）率宋军由福州南下，经过泉州港时"舟不足，乃掠其舟（蒲船）并没其赀"，然后退走潮州。于是本来已与元朝暗中联系的蒲寿庚，就索性降元了。景炎二年（1277）夏秋间，张世杰从广东返军围泉州，蒲寿庚一面闭城拒守，一面派人向元军统帅唆都求援。后来唆都派兵援泉，张世杰乃解围而去。张世杰开始围攻泉州是在农历七月，已是海舶趁南风从海外归抵泉州之后；而围城三月这段时间，台风袭击泉州。据此可以推断，泉州湾宋代海船返航抵达后渚港，可能是在起卸了部分货物之后，遇上宋军围城，兵荒马乱，船上人员被俘或逃散，船上贵重物资被抢，船桅及上部船板被破坏，最终在台风来临时沉没了。

About the cause of sinking. The sunken ship was located on a beach very close to a residential area. The ship's hull remained intact and was buried horizontally in the beach, with no signs of damage to the main keel or punctures. Therefore, the possibility of grounding or hitting a reef was ruled out. The objects inside the ship's compartments were broken and scattered, and the mast and structures above the ship's deck were not preserved. Taking the location of the shipwreck into consideration, the chances are that encountering a typhoon was not the only reason why the ship sank. Generally, when ships encounter typhoons at sea, they first cut down the masts and let the ships drift with the wind to avoid sinking. If the ship is in the harbor, just approach a safe zone to avoid the wind or strengthen the anchor to stabilize the ship's body. Considering the geographical environment of Houzhu Port, ships moored here can usually survive typhoons. The absence of the ship's mast during excavation, combined with the fact that the objects inside the ship's compartments were broken and scattered, suggests that the ship might have sunk due to the impact of waves after suffering human-made damage (possibly warfare).

In the late Southern Song Dynasty, the Yuan army marched south and captured Lin'an. Zhao Shi, Emperor Duanzong of Song, fled to Fuzhou, and the Yuan court sent General Suodu to pursue him into Fujian. Quanzhou Port, a major port for overseas trade at that time, became an area of strategic importance, where representatives from both sides, Pu Shougeng and Zhang Shijie, contended for control of ships. According to *Local Chronicles of Jinjiang County*, in 1276, Emperor Duanzong of Song ascended the throne in Fuzhou. He commanded Pu Shougeng to provide ships for sea journey from Quanzhou Port, but Pu refused to obey. As written in *History of Song*, in 1276, Zhang Shijie led the Song army south from Fuzhou and, when passing through Quanzhou Port, lacked ships, so they took Pu's ships and goods before retreating to Chaozhou. Pu Shougeng, who had been secretly in contact with the Yuan court, surrendered to the Yuan court. In the summer and autumn of 1277, Zhang Shijie returned from Guangdong to besiege Quanzhou. While Pu Shougeng was guarding the city, he also sent someone to ask for help from the Yuan general Suodu. Later, Suodu sent troops to rescue, and Zhang Shijie withdrew. Zhang Shijie began to besiege Quanzhou in the seventh lunar month, after the ships, taking advantage of the south wind, arrived in Quanzhou from overseas; during the three months of the siege, a typhoon struck Quanzhou. From this, it can be deduced that the ship, after returning to Houzhu Port and unloading some cargo, encountered disorder when the Song army surrounded the city. Some of the people on board were captured, and others scattered. The valuable assets on board were looted. The ship's mast and upper deck were damaged, and eventually the ship sank when a typhoon came.

收藏在泉州湾古船陈列馆里的泉州湾宋代海船。（陈起拓 摄）
The Song Dynasty Oceangoing Ship in Quanzhou Bay housed in Quanzhou Bay Ancient Ship Exhibition Hall. (Photo by Chen Qituo)

泉州湾宋代海船船型。泉州湾宋代海船是一艘在返航即将靠岸时不幸在泉州湾罹难的中型远洋福船，能够承载的货物相当于一支拥有700头骆驼的大型商队所能运输的总量。作为20世纪70年代我国最重要的考古发现之一，泉州湾宋代海船也是至今国内已发掘的年代较早、体量较大、保存相对完整的古代沉船，它的发现对研究我国海外交通史、造船史、对外关系史等具有重要的学术价值。

这艘远洋木帆船复原尺寸可达34米长、11米宽。专家结合船型结构特点、船舱出土遗物及沉积环境等，推断这是南宋末年的远洋商船。水密隔舱极大增强了海船的抗沉性和船体的坚固性，且便于货物的装卸，这种先进设计可上溯到唐代，比欧洲早了近千年。

泉州湾宋代海船的绞关木。（泉州海外交通史博物馆 供图）

A wooden capstan of the Song Dynasty Oceangoing Ship in Quanzhou Bay. (Courtesy of Quanzhou Maritime Museum)

About the ship type of the Song Dynasty Oceangoing Ship in Quanzhou Bay. The Song Dynasty Oceangoing Ship in Quanzhou Bay was a medium-sized *Fu-Chuan* that unfortunately met its demise while approaching the shore of Quanzhou Bay on its return journey. Its cargo capacity was equivalent to that of a large caravan with 700 camels. As one of the most significant archaeological discoveries in China in the 1970s, the Song Dynasty Oceangoing Ship in Quanzhou Bay is a relatively early, large, and well-preserved ancient shipwreck that has been excavated. The discovery of the ship is of great academic value to the study of China's overseas transportation history, shipbuilding history, and foreign relations history, etc.

The restored wooden oceangoing ship with sails can reach 34 meters in length and 11 meters in width. Experts have taken into consideration the structural characteristics of the ship type, the unearthed artifacts, and the sedimentary environment to speculate that this was an oceangoing merchant ship in the late Southern Song Dynasty. Watertight bulkheads greatly reduced the possibility of sinking and enhanced the toughness of the ships and made loading and unloading of goods easier. This advanced design can be traced back to the Tang Dynasty, nearly a thousand years earlier than that in Europe.

从《诸蕃志》到《岛夷志略》

From Records of Foreign Countries *to* A Brief Account of Island Inhabitants

赵汝适与《诸蕃志》

Zhao Rukuo and *Records of Foreign Countries*

汪大渊与《岛夷志略》

Wang Dayuan and *A Brief Account of Island Inhabitants*

泉州湾宋代海船出水部分物品。其中，香料数量十分可观。（泉州海外交通史博物馆 供图）

Some items salvaged from the Song Dynasty Oceangoing Ship in Quanzhou Bay. Among them, the quantity of spices is considerable. (Courtesy of Quanzhou Maritime Museum)

赵汝适与《诸蕃志》

《诸蕃志》是南宋福建路市舶司提举赵汝适所著的一部海外地理与文化专著，成书于南宋宝庆元年（1225）。初任市舶司提举时，“暇日阅诸蕃图……迺询诸贾胡，俾列其国名，道其风土，与夫道里之联属，山泽之蓄产，译以华言”。他向这些从不同国家和地区来泉州经商的海外商人了解海外诸国方位、山川、途程、物产等情况，将资料翻译成中文并汇编成册，名叫《诸蕃志》。该书内容丰富，其中虽有讹误之处，仍不失为研究宋代海上交通和对外关系的重要文献，对研究海外国家风土物产、南宋泉州海外贸易史均有一定价值。所记述的海外情况与海外交通贸易，比欧洲《马可·波罗游记》早 70 多年。

Zhao Rukuo and **Records of Foreign Countries**

Records of Foreign Countries is a monograph on overseas geography and culture written by Zhao Rukuo, who served as Superintendent of Fujian Maritime Trade Office in the Southern Song Dynasty. It was completed in 1225. Shortly after he took office in Maritime Trade Office, he read through the maps of various countries in his spare time and asked various foreign merchants to list the names of the countries they were from, describe the geography, explain how far they were from here, and introduce the resources. And Zhao translated the materials he collected into Chinese. He learned about the location, topography, distance from Quanzhou, and products of various countries from overseas merchants who came to Quanzhou for business, translated the information into Chinese, and compiled it into a book named *Records of Foreign Countries*. The book is rich in content. Although there are some errors, it is still an important work for studying maritime transportation and foreign relations in the Song Dynasty. It is also of certain value to studying the customs and products of foreign countries, as well as the history of maritime trade in Quanzhou during the Southern Song Dynasty. The description of overseas situations and overseas transportation and trade is more than 70 years earlier than *The Travels of Marco Polo* in Europe.

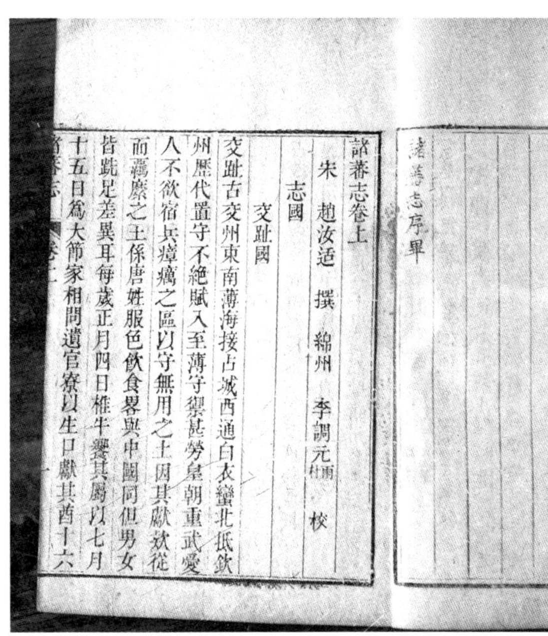
諸蕃志序畢

諸蕃志卷上
宋 趙汝适 撰 綿州 李調元 雨村 校
志國
交趾國
交趾古交州東南薄海接占城西通白衣蠻北抵欽
州歷代置守不絕賦入至薄守禦甚勞皇朝重武愛
人不欲宿兵瘴癘之區以守無用之土因其獻款從
而羈縻之王係唐姓服色飲食畧與中國同但男女
皆跣足差異耳每歲正月四日椎牛饗其屬以七月
十五日爲大節家相問遺官僚以生口獻其酋十六

宋赵汝适《诸蕃志》。（成冬冬 摄）
Records of Foreign Countries by Zhao Rukuo in the Song Dynasty. (Photo by Cheng Dongdong)

赵汝适其人。赵汝适，字伯可，宋宗室，生于南宋乾道六年（1170）。绍熙元年（1190）补将仕郎，翌年授迪功郎、临安府余杭县主簿；庆元二年（1196）授修职郎；之后转潭州湘潭县、绍兴府、婺州武义县、临安府等多地任职，屡有升迁；嘉定十七年（1224）八月，理宗赵昀登位，恩转朝散大夫，九月升提举福建路市舶；宝庆元年（1225）七月兼权知泉州，同年十一月兼知南外宗正事，身兼三职，任期三年，在任期间积极发展海外贸易，《诸蕃志》就是他在身兼三职时著成的；后转江西饶州等地任职，出于健康原因，绍定四年（1231）恩转朝议大夫，主管官告院，七月申请退休，当月卒，享年 62 岁。

About Zhao Rukuo. Zhao Rukuo, also known as Zhao Boke, was a member of the imperial clan of the Song Dynasty. He was born in 1170. In 1190, he gained the title of *jiang shi lang*. The following year, he was appointed as *di gong lang*, a ninth rank officer, and Secretary in Yuhang County of Lin'an Prefecture. In 1196, he was appointed as *xiu zhi lang*, an eighth rank officer. He was later transferred to various posts in Xiangtan County of Tanzhou, Shaoxing Prefecture, Wuyi County of Wuzhou, Lin'an Prefecture, and other places, promoted several times. In August in the lunar calendar of 1224, Zhao Yun, Emperor Lizong of Song, ascended the throne, and Zhao Rukuo was appointed as a civil official of the fifth rank. In September in the lunar calendar of the same year, he was promoted to Superintendent of Fujian Maritime Trade Office. In July in the lunar calendar of 1225, he also served as the acting governor of Quanzhou and in November in the lunar calendar, the director of the Southern Clan Office, holding three positions and serving a three-year term. During his tenure, he actively developed overseas trade and wrote *Records of Foreign Countries*. Later, he was transferred to Raozhou and other places in Jiangxi. Due to health reasons, he was appointed as an official in charge of *Guangaoyuan*, a department responsible for issuing certificates of appointment and rewards, in 1231 and retired from his post in July in the lunar calendar of the same year. He passed away in the same month at the age of 62.

主要内容。《诸蕃志》共分两卷，上卷《志国》，下卷《志物》。

《志国》记载了东至日本，西至东非索马里、西北非摩洛哥及地中海东岸诸国的风土物产及自中国沿海至海外各国的航线里程及所达航期，其中的斯加里野国篇记述的是西西里岛的地理和岛上的活火山。这是中文古典典籍中最早记述意大利西西里岛和埃特纳火山的著作。《诸蕃志》对非洲的记载，比以前的一些地理著作更为详细。它记载了非洲的层拔国（一说即今桑给巴尔）、弼琶啰国（今索马里沿海的柏培拉）、中理国（今索马里东北海岸）、木兰皮国（位于西非）、勿斯里国（今埃及）、昆仑层期国（今马达加斯加及其附近的非洲沿岸）的有关情况。

About its main content. It is divided into two volumes: "Records of the Countries" and "Records of the Things."

"Records of the Countries" records the geography and products of various countries from Japan in the east to Somalia, Morocco, and Mediterranean countries in the west. It also describes the navigation routes and journey time from China's coastal areas to other countries. The Sicily section describes the geography of Sicily and the active volcano on the island. It is the earliest Chinese classical literature that records the island of Sicily and Mount Etna in Italy. Its records of Africa is more detailed than some previous geographical works. It describes the situations of Cengba (some believe it refers to present-day Zanzibar), Bipaluo (now Berbera along the coast of Somalia), Zhongli (on present-day northeastern coast of Somalia), Almoravide (in West Africa), Wusili (present-day Egypt), and Kunluncengqi (in present-day Madagascar and its surrounding area along the coast of Africa).

《志物》记载了各种动植物、矿石，其中以香料为主，计有：脑子（即龙脑）、乳香、没药、血碣、金颜香、笃耨香、苏合香油、安息香、沉香、檀香、丁香、肉豆蔻、降真香、麝香木等。植物中记载吉贝最详备，并对草棉、海岛棉、攀枝花三种棉作了区分。书中对海生动物砗磲的形态有准确描述。对矿物中的猫儿睛、琉璃亦有较详尽的记载。此外，特别重视对各个国家和地区珍稀动植物的记载，例如，介绍弼琶啰国时提到“又产物名骆驼鹤，身顶长六七尺，有翼能飞，但不甚高。兽名徂蜡，状如骆驼，而大如牛，色黄，前脚高五尺，后低三尺，头高向上，皮厚一寸”。这里说的就是鸵鸟和长颈鹿。

"Records of the Things" records different kinds of animals, plants, and minerals, among which spices are the main categories, including camphol, frankincense, myrrh, katir, sweet benzoin, pistacia terebinthus, storax, styrax benzoin, aloeswood, sandalwood, clove, nutmeg, acronychia pedunculata, and muskwood, etc. Among the plants, the record of ceiba pentandra is the most detailed, and distinctions are made between gossypium herbaceum, gossypium barbadense, and bombax. There is an accurate description of the form of *che qu* (Tridacna gigas), a kind of marine animal. There is also a more detailed record of minerals, such as chrysoberyl and glass. In addition, it also pays special attention to the rare animals and plants of various countries and regions. For example, the author mentioned in "Bipaluo" an animal named *luo tuo he* which was six or seven *chi* (a Chinese unit of length. One *chi* equals about 0.33 meters) tall. It had wings but couldn't fly very high. Also cited was the animal named *cu la* which looked like a camel but as large as a cow, yellow in color, with front legs five *chi* high and back legs three *chi* high, head high up, and the skin one *cun* (a Chinese unit of length. One *cun* equals about 0.03 meters) thick. He was describing no other than ostrich and giraffe.

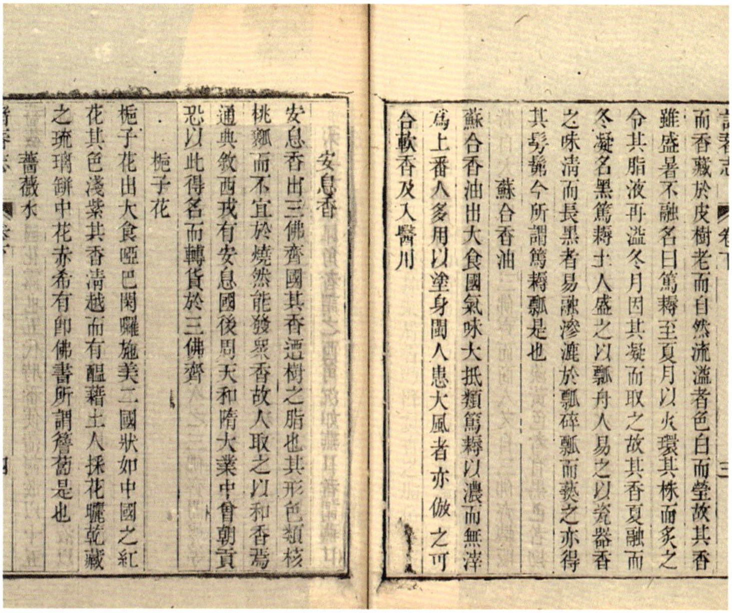
而香藏於皮樹老而自然流溢者色白而瑩故其香
雖盛暑不融名曰篤耨至夏月以火環其株而炙之
令其脂液再溢冬月因其凝而取之故其香夏融而
冬凝名黑篤耨土人盛之以瓢舟人易之以瓷器香
之味清而長黑者易融滲漉於瓢碎瓢而爇之亦得
其髣髴今所謂篤耨瓢是也

蘇合香油

蘇合香油出大食國氣味大抵類篤耨以濃而無滓
爲上番人多用以塗身閩人患大風者亦倣之可
合軟香及入醫用

安息香

安息香出三佛齊國其香迺樹之脂也其形色類核
桃瓤而不宜於燒然能發衆香故人取之以和香焉
通典敘西戎有安息國後周天和隋大業中曾朝貢
恐以此得名而轉貨於三佛齊

梔子花

梔子花出大食啞巴閑囉施美二國狀如中國之紅
花其色淺紫其香清越而有醞藉土人採花曬乾藏
之琉璃缾中花赤希有即佛書所謂薝蔔是也

薔薇水

《诸蕃志》中关于苏合香油和安息香的记载。（林瀚 供图）

A record of storax and styrax benzoin in *Records of Foreign Countries*. (Courtesy of Lin Han)

泉州湾宋代海船出水的安息香。（成冬冬 摄）

Styrax benzoin salvaged from the Song Dynasty Oceangoing Ship in Quanzhou Bay. (Photo by Cheng Dongdong)

《诸蕃志》与泉州。《诸蕃志》对泉州海外交通记载很详细，凡记载我国与东南亚诸国、印度、阿拉伯以及北非各国的航线距离、日程、方位，多以泉州为基准。例如，三佛齐“在泉之正南，冬月顺风月余方至凌牙门”，阇婆国“于泉州为丙巳方，率以冬月发船，盖藉北风之便，顺风昼夜行月余可到”，渤泥国“在泉之东南”，这是书中以泉州为原点来描述各地方位；真腊国“自泉州舟行顺风月余日可到”，占城国“自泉州至本国顺风舟行二十余程”，故临国“泉舶四十余日到蓝里住冬，至次年再发，一月始达”，这是书中以泉州为起点来计算日程；注辇国“水行至泉州约四十一万一千四百余里”，这是书中以泉州为起点来计算距离。

***Records of Foreign Countries* and Quanzhou.** *Records of Foreign Countries*, including detailed accounts of overseas transportation of Quanzhou, records the distance, journey time, and orientation of sailing routes between China and Southeast Asian countries, India, Arabian countries, as well as North African countries, with Quanzhou as the reference point. For example, Srivijaya was located directly to the south of Quanzhou, and it took more than a month to get to Lingga by sailing downwind during winter; Java was located to the southeast of Quanzhou, and ships could reach it in about a month during winter, taking advantage of the north wind; Borneo was to the southeast of Quanzhou. The location of the above-mentioned places was described with Quanzhou as the point of reference. Chenla could be reached by boat from Quanzhou in just over a month by sailing downwind; Champa could be reached from Quanzhou in about twenty days by sailing downwind; as for Kulam (in present-day Kollam in India), it took more than forty days for ships from Quanzhou to reach Lamuri where they stayed for the winter and then set off again the following year, arriving in a month. The journey time was calculated with Quanzhou as the starting point. Chola (an ancient country in southern India) was approximately 411,400 *li* away from Quanzhou by water. The distance was measured with Quanzhou as the starting point.

书中也有关于外国人在泉州生活的记录。南毗国的罗巴、智力干父子“今居泉之城南”。北宋雍熙年间，自称天竺国人的僧人啰护哪航海而至，番商“竞持金缯珍宝以施”，此外，还在泉州城南修建了佛寺宝林院。外商在泉州还建有丛冢。“大食国”条云：“有番商曰施那帏，大食人也。蹯寓泉南，轻财乐施，有西土气习，作丛冢于城外之东南隅，以掩胡贾之遗骸。”泉州与日本也有交通联系。日本“多产杉木罗木，长至十四五丈，径四尺余，土人解为枋板，以巨舰搬运至吾泉贸易，泉人罕至其国”。香料的进口对泉州民俗产生了较大影响。苏合香油，出产自大食国，可以治大风病。“番人多用以涂身。闽人患大风者亦仿之。”降真香“能辟邪气。泉人岁除家无贫富皆爇之如燔柴”，这说明除夕烧降真香辟邪在泉州已成为普遍现象。

The book also contains records of foreigners living in Quanzhou. A father and son from Namburi came to Quanzhou and settled in the southern part of the city. During the Yongxi period (984—987) of the Northern Song Dynasty, Rahula, a monk who claimed to be from Tianzhu, sailed to Quanzhou, and foreign merchants raced each other to offer gold fabrics and precious treasures to him. In addition, Baolin Temple, a Buddhist temple, was built in the south of the city. Foreign merchants also built tombs in Quanzhou. According to records in “Dayi,” Silavi, a foreign merchant from Dayi, settled down in the south of Quanzhou. He loved to spend money generously. He followed the customs of the western regions and built tombs outside the city in the southeast corner to bury the remains of the foreign merchants. Quanzhou also had transportation connections with Japan. Japan was known for abundant cedar and cypress trees resources. The trees grew to a height of fourteen to fifteen *zhang* and had a diameter of more than four *chi*. The local people used them as beams and boards, and transported them to Quanzhou on huge ships for trade. Quanzhou people rarely visited the country. The import of spices had a significant influence on the folk customs of Quanzhou. Storax, produced in Dayi, could cure leprosy. “Foreigners often slather their bodies with storax, and people in Fujian who suffer from leprosy also imitate the practice.” Acronychia pedunculata was believed to be able to dispel evil spirits, and Quanzhou people burnt it like burning firewood during the Chinese New Year’s Eve, whether they were rich or poor. It had become a common practice in Quanzhou.

汪大渊与《岛夷志略》

《岛夷志略》是一部记述海外诸国见闻的著作，由元代航海家汪大渊所著，一卷，共分一百条，对二百多个国家和地区的疆域、土产、风土人情作了详细的记载。相比《诸蕃志》多得于市舶之口传，汪大渊《岛夷志略》皆亲历而手记之，内容翔实，记述准确，是研究元代海外贸易可靠的史料，也是研究古代亚非等地区历史地理的重要著作。明代马欢著《瀛涯胜览》，受汪大渊的影响很深，费信的《星槎胜览》、巩珍的《西洋番国志》也大量借鉴了《岛夷志略》。

Wang Dayuan and A Brief Account of Island Inhabitants

A Brief Account of Island Inhabitants, written by Wang Dayuan, a traveler of the Yuan Dynasty, is a book that records observations and experiences overseas. It comprises one volume with 100 essays detailing the territories, products, and customs of more than 200 countries and regions. Compared with *Records of Foreign Countries*, *A Brief Account of Island Inhabitants* by Wang Dayuan is based on personal experience and handwritten notes. It is rich in content and accurate in description, making it a reliable historical source for studying overseas trade during the Yuan Dynasty. It is also an important work for researching the history and geography of ancient Asia and Africa. During the Ming Dynasty, Ma Huan wrote *The Overall Survey of the Oceans Shores*, which was greatly influenced by Wang Dayuan. Fei Xin's *The Overall Survey of the Star Raft* and Gong Zhen's *Records of Countries in Western Seas* also drew heavily from *A Brief Account of Island Inhabitants*.

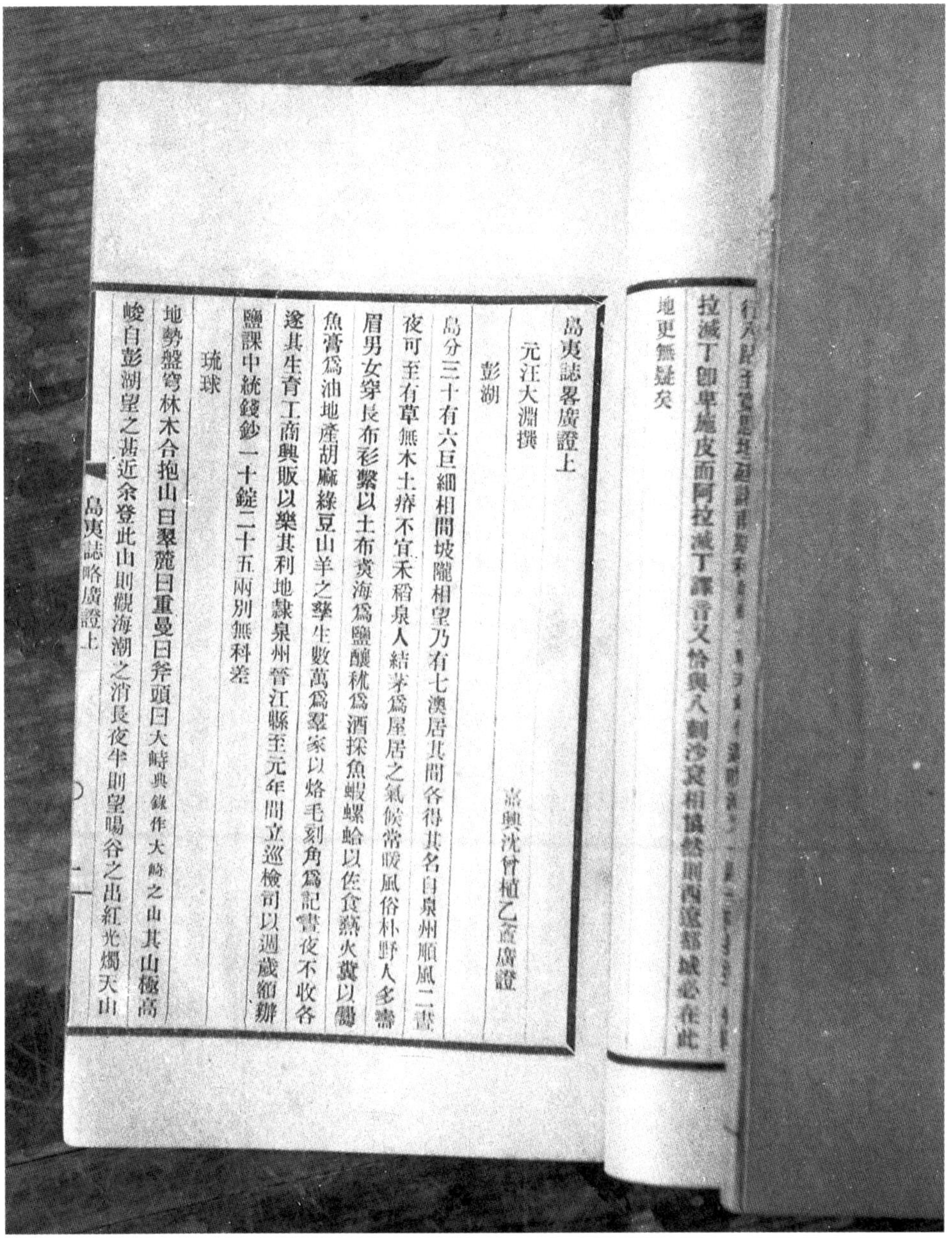

拉滅丁卽卑施皮而阿拉滅丁譯音又恰與入剌沙豆相協然則西洋都城當在此
地更無疑矣

島夷誌畧廣證上
元汪大淵撰　嘉興沈曾植乙盦廣證
彭湖
島分三十有六巨細相間坡隴相望乃有七澳居其間各得其名自泉州順風二晝夜可至有草無木土瘠不宜禾稻泉人結茅爲屋居之氣候常暖風俗朴野人多壽眉男女穿長布衫繫以土布煮海爲鹽釀秫爲酒採魚蝦螺蛤以佐食爇牛糞以爨魚膏爲油地產胡麻綠豆山羊之孳生數萬爲羣家以烙毛刻角爲記晝夜不收各遂其生育工商興販以樂其利地隸泉州晉江縣至元年間立巡檢司以週歲額辦鹽課中統錢鈔一十錠二十五兩別無科差
琉球
地勢盤穹林木合抱山曰翠麓曰重曼曰斧頭曰大峙典錄作大崎之山其山極高峻自彭湖望之甚近余登此山則觀海潮之消長夜半則望暘谷之出紅光燭天山

島夷誌略廣證上

元汪大渊《岛夷志略》。（成冬冬 摄）
A Brief Account of Island Inhabitants by Wang Dayuan in the Yuan Dynasty. (Photo by Cheng Dongdong)

汪大渊：东方的马可·波罗。汪大渊，字焕章，江西南昌人，从小聪明好学。元至顺元年（1330），年仅20岁的汪大渊搭乘泉州远洋商船从泉州港出海了，这次航行从泉州经占城、马六甲、爪哇、苏门答腊、缅甸、印度、波斯、阿拉伯、埃及，再横渡地中海到非洲西北部的摩洛哥，再回到埃及，出红海到索马里，折向南直到莫桑比克，再横渡印度洋回到斯里兰卡、苏门答腊、爪哇，再到澳大利亚，从澳大利亚到加里曼丹岛，又经菲律宾群岛，元统二年（1334）夏秋间返回泉州，历时五年，此次航海活动主要是在印度洋区域。至元三年（1337）冬，汪大渊第二次从泉州出航，游历东南亚群岛，阿拉伯海、红海、地中海、莫桑比克海峡及澳大利亚各地，至元五年（1339）夏秋间返回泉州，此次游历范围比第一次小。

Wang Dayuan: Marco Polo of the East. Wang Dayuan, also known as Wang Huanzhang, was born in Nanchang, Jiangxi. He was clever and studious from a young age. In 1330, at the age of only 20, Wang Dayuan embarked on a long journey from Quanzhou port on a merchant ship. This voyage took him from Quanzhou to Champa, Malacca, Java, Sumatra, Myanmar, India, Persia, Arabia, Egypt, and then across the Mediterranean Sea to Morocco in northwestern Africa. He then returned to Egypt, sailed through the Red Sea to Somalia, headed south to Mozambique, and crossed the Indian Ocean back to Sri Lanka, Sumatra, Java, Australia, and Kalimantan. After passing through the Philippines, he returned to Quanzhou between the summer and autumn of 1334. It was a journey that lasted for five years and mainly focused on the Indian Ocean places. In the winter of 1337, Wang Dayuan set sail from Quanzhou for the second time, traveling to islands in Southeast Asia, the Arabian Sea, the Red Sea, the Mediterranean Sea, the Mozambique Channel, and various parts of Australia. He returned to Quanzhou between the summer and autumn of 1339. Compared with his first journey, he traveled less extensively in his second journey.

汪大渊随商船游历多地，每到一处皆记其山川、习俗、物产以及贸易等情况。元至正九年（1349），恰逢泉州路达鲁花赤偰玉立命吴鉴修《清源续志》，因泉州是设置市舶司的城市，系海外各国人、物聚集之地，对各国风土人情应有相应的档案资料，于是邀请汪大渊著《岛夷志》，并附于《清源续志》之后。第二年，汪大渊带着他写的《岛夷志》回到老家江西南昌，单独刊印，流传甚广。《岛夷志》已佚未行世，《岛夷志略》即《岛夷志》之节略，即简行本。

《岛夷志略》与泉州。汪大渊两次出海均从泉州附舶，撰成《岛夷志》附于《清源续志》之后，这与元代泉州海外交通空前发达不无关系，那时，泉州已成为世界最大的贸易港之一。正如汪大渊《岛夷志后序》所云："顾以清源舶司所在，诸蕃辐辏之所，宜记录不鄙。谓余方知外事，属《岛夷志》附于郡志之后，非徒以广士大夫之异闻，盖以表国朝威德如是之大且远也。"

During his journey to various places by taking merchant ships, Wang Dayuan recorded the geography, customs, products, and trade in each place he visited. In 1349, Wu Jian was ordered by Xie Yuli, Quanzhou Darughachi (the governor of Quanzhou), to compile *Sequels to Qingyuan Chronicles,* an official record of Qingyuan (an ancient name for Quanzhou). As Quanzhou was where the Maritime Trade Office was set up and people as well as products from various countries gathered here, it was important to have archival information about foreign customs and traditions. Wang Dayuan was asked to write *An Account of Island Inhabitants* and have it attached to *Sequels to Qingyuan Chronicles*. The following year, Wang Dayuan returned to Nanchang, his hometown, and printed his *An Account of Island Inhabitants* as a book, which became widely known. Unfortunately, the original *An Account of Island Inhabitants* has been lost. A condensed version known as *A Brief Account of Island Inhabitants* still exists.

***A Brief Account of Island Inhabitants* and Quanzhou.** Wang Dayuan twice sailed to sea from Quanzhou, and wrote *An Account of Island Inhabitants*, later included in *Sequels to Qingyuan Chronicles*. That was closely related to the unprecedentedly developed overseas transportation in Quanzhou during the Yuan Dynasty, when it had become one of the largest trade ports in the world. As written by Wang Dayuan in the postscript of *An Account of Island Inhabitants*, he recorded what he had learned about foreign countries and regions not only to share with scholars and officials, but also to highlight the great strength and virtue of the Yuan court, as Qingyuan (Quanzhou) was where Maritime Trade Office was set up, and the city had attracted a large number of foreign merchants, which was well worth recording.

《诸蕃志》和《岛夷志略》体现了从商业利益出发探索海外地理文化，这样的观念比西方早数个世纪。在西方发现东方之前，中国已经有了基于商业贸易的世界眼光。《诸蕃志》作者赵汝适为中国的读者描绘了他在交流中听闻的外部世界，比马可·波罗向世界介绍中国早了70多年；有“东方的马可·波罗”之誉的汪大渊20岁时的第一次远航，比克里斯托弗·哥伦布首航美洲早了162年，以亲历写成《岛夷志略》，把一个更真实的世界呈现在书中。他们构建了立足东方来观察海外世界的文本体系，为宋元时期从事海外贸易的官员、海商进一步拓宽海外贸易视野奠定了知识基础，为宋元泉州手工业布局提供了有益参考，“买世界”和“卖世界”的盛景让这座城市愈发活力洋溢。

Records of Foreign Countries and *A Brief Account of Island Inhabitants* reflect the idea of exploring geography and culture of foreign countries through engaging in trade, which emerged centuries earlier than similar ideas came up in the West. Long before the West discovered the East, China had developed a global vision based on commercial activities. Zhao Rukuo, the author of *Records of Foreign Countries*, depicted for Chinese readers the external world he heard about in his exchanges, more than 70 years earlier than Marco Polo's introducing China to the rest of the world. Wang Dayuan, known as "Marco Polo of the East," embarked on his first long voyage at the age of 20, 162 years earlier than Christopher Columbus's first voyage across the Atlantic Ocean. He wrote *A Brief Account of Island Inhabitants* based on his personal experiences, presenting a more authentic world in the book. They constructed a textual system to observe the overseas world from the perspective of the East, laying a knowledge foundation for officials and merchants who engaged in overseas trade during the Song and Yuan dynasties, and providing valuable guidelines for the layout of the handcraft industry in Quanzhou at the time. The flourishing scenes of "buying from the world" and "selling to the world" had made this city even more vibrant.

参考文献

[1] 福建博物院，晋江博物馆．磁灶窑址：福建晋江磁灶窑址考古调查发掘报告 [M]. 北京：科学出版社，2011.

[2] 北京大学考古文博学院，泉州市文化广电和旅游局，安溪县人民政府，等．安溪下草埔遗址 2019 ～ 2020 年度考古发掘报告 [M]. 北京：文物出版社，2021.

[3] 国家文物局水下文化遗产保护中心，广东省文物考古研究所，中国文化遗产研究院，等．南海 I 号沉船考古报告之二——2014 ～ 2015 年发掘 [M]. 北京：科学出版社，2018.

[4] 福建省泉州海外交通史博物馆．泉州湾宋代海船发掘与研究（修订版）[M].2 版．北京：海洋出版社，2017.

[5] 孟原召．闽南地区宋至清代制瓷手工业遗存研究 [M]. 北京：文物出版社，2017.

[6] 王连茂．刺桐杂识 [M]. 中国海外交通史研究会，福建省泉州海外交通史博物馆，编．北京：海洋出版社，2018.

[7] 王铭铭．刺桐城：滨海中国的地方与世界 [M]. 北京：生活・读书・新知三联书店，2018.

[8] 李玉昆．泉州海外交通史略 [M]. 泉州历史文化中心，编．厦门：厦门大学出版社，1995.

[9] 李玉昆．耕海集 [M]. 中国海外交通史研究会，福建省泉州海外交通史博物馆，编．北京：海洋出版社，2019.

[10] 叶文程．中国古外销瓷研究论文集 [G]. 北京：紫禁城出版社，1988.

[11] 叶文程，林忠干．福建陶瓷 [M]. 福州：福建人民出版社，1993.

[12] 陈鹏鹏．陈鹏鹏文史类稿 [M]. 泉州历史文化中心，编．泉州：闽南文化出版社，2018.

[13] 黄天柱．泉州稽古集 [M]. 北京：中国文联出版社，2003.

[14] 吴金鹏，陈思．磁灶窑址 [M]// 泉州市文物局，泉州市文物考古研究所．泉州文物 · 国保篇．北京：九州出版社，2021.

[15] 孙健，李滨，徐海滨．揭秘华光礁一号沉船 [J]. 华夏地理，2007(10):158—169.

[16] 王浩．西沙群岛水下考古之行——“华光礁 I 号”南宋沉船发掘纪实 [J]. 武汉文博，2008(01):34—37.

[17] 沈睿文，易曙峰．安溪青阳下草埔冶铁遗址的几点初步认识 [J]. 自然与文化遗产研究，2021,6(03):48—58.

[18] 栗建安．世界遗产视野下的泉州古窑址考古与研究 [J]. 自然与文化遗产研究，2021,6(03):40—47.

[19] 袁冰凌．略论宋元泉州手工业生产布局的形成 [J]. 福建文博，1991(1/2):141—147.

[20] 羊泽林 . 从西沙华光礁一号沉船上的青釉褐彩器看福建釉下彩瓷的生产及外销 [C]// 中国古陶瓷学会 . 中国古陶瓷研究（第十四辑）. 北京 : 紫禁城出版社 ,2008.
[21] 吴金鹏 . 宋元时期晋江磁灶窑经营理念和商业模式初探 [C]// 中国古陶瓷学会 . 中国古陶瓷研究（第十四辑）. 北京 : 紫禁城出版社 ,2008.
[22] 吴金鹏 , 黄华东 . 海洋文明语境下谈晋江磁灶窑对海外的影响 [C]// 福建省闽南文化研究会 . “世遗土楼 · 海丝文化”南靖高峰论坛论文汇编 . 漳州：[出版者不详]，2020.
[23] 陈思 . 宋元时期磁灶窑海外贸易 [J]. 海内与海外 ,2021(11):50—53.
[24] 中国航海学会 , 泉州市人民政府 . 泉州港与海上丝绸之路 [M]. 北京 : 中国社会科学出版社 ,2002.
[25] 德化陶瓷研究论文集编委会 . 德化陶瓷研究论文集 [G]. 泉州：[出版者不详]，2002.
[26] 颜雅婷 . 磁灶窑址：宋元泉州留给世界的釉色记忆 [N]. 泉州晚报 ,2021-05-27.
[27] 颜雅婷 . 德化窑址：“窑”跨古今 瓷通四海 [N]. 泉州晚报 ,2021-05-28.
[28] 陈林森 . 这一藏在深山的“铁担当”行销“海丝”千年……[N]. 泉州晚报 ,2021-06-03.
[29] 海米菌 . 元代斥巨资来泉州文身有多荣耀 | 云游刺桐 [EB/OL].(2022-03-28)[2023-02-01]. https://mp.weixin.qq.com/s/yNtrUI5s1VcyQwsnxsVvUA.
[30] 肖婉撰文 , 吴金鹏审核 .【宅家听讲“宝”】磁灶窑外销特色产品：龙纹军持 [EB/OL].(2021-10-02)[2023-04-01].https://mp.weixin.qq.com/s/tCY2rxE-B6dTscMPwAeDBA.
[31] 陈思撰文 , 吴金鹏审核 .【宅家听讲“宝”】磁灶窑外销特色产品：急须 [EB/OL].(2021-10-03)[2023-04-01].https://mp.weixin.qq.com/s/m_GEiu1GhNdB16MWpAuJdw.
[32] 陈思撰文 , 吴金鹏审核 .【宅家听讲“宝”】磁灶窑外销特色产品：黄釉铁绘花纹盆 [EB/OL].(2021-10-04)[2023-04-01].https://mp.weixin.qq.com/s/SWOhJAjJIybLYjpegHSsOw.
[33] 陈思撰文 , 吴金鹏审核 .【宅家听讲“宝”】磁灶窑外销特色产品：小口瓶 [EB/OL].(2021-10-05)[2023-04-01].https://mp.weixin.qq.com/s/MWtkVJ6sX21Lcm_zBN-tKA.
[34] 陈思撰文 , 吴金鹏审核 .【宅家听讲“宝”】磁灶窑外销特色产品：龙瓮 [EB/OL].(2021-10-06)[2023-04-01].https://mp.weixin.qq.com/s/YJzpWeiXZSxB7LVP0jbuUA.
[35] 陈思撰文 , 吴金鹏审核 .【宅家听讲“宝”】磁灶窑外销特色产品：绿釉花口碟 [EB/OL].(2021-10-07)[2023-04-01].https://mp.weixin.qq.com/s/ryJBQHZvdoSZQN8SmZX4ZQ.

图书在版编目（CIP）数据

丝路扬帆：宋元泉州的商品制造：汉英对照 / 中共泉州市委宣传部编. --福州：福建人民出版社，2024.6（2025.3重印）
（世遗之城：泉州）
ISBN 978-7-211-09043-3

Ⅰ.①丝… Ⅱ.①中… Ⅲ.①制造工业—工业史—泉州—宋元时期—汉、英 Ⅳ.①F426.4

中国国家版本馆 CIP 数据核字（2023）第 079067 号

丝路扬帆——宋元泉州的商品制造
SILU YANGFAN——SONGYUAN QUANZHOU DE SHANGPIN ZHIZAO

特约撰稿：吴金鹏
翻　　译：苏炎奎
责任编辑：李雯婷
美术编辑：陈培亮
责任校对：陈　璟
装帧设计：雅昌（上海）设计中心
出版发行：福建人民出版社　　电　　话：0591-87533169(发行部)
网　　址：http://www.fjpph.com　　电子邮箱：fjpph7211@126.com
地　　址：福州市东水路 76 号　　邮政编码：350001
经　　销：福建新华发行（集团）有限责任公司
印　　刷：雅昌文化（集团）有限公司
地　　址：深圳市南山区深云路 19 号
电　　话：0755-86083235
开　　本：787 毫米×1092 毫米　1/16
印　　张：14
字　　数：355 千字
版　　次：2024 年 6 月第 1 版
印　　次：2025 年 3 月第 2 次印刷
书　　号：ISBN 978-7-211-09043-3
定　　价：63.00 元